D1766770

PERSEUS

The son of Zeus, Perseus belongs in the first rank of Greek heroes. Indeed to some he was a greater hero even than Heracles. With the help of Hermes and Athena he slew the Gorgon Medusa, conquered a mighty sea monster and won the hand of the beautiful princess Andromeda. This volume tells of his enduring myth, its rendering in art and literature, and its reception through the Roman period and up to the modern day.

This is the first scholarly book in English devoted to Perseus' myth in its entirety for over a century. With information drawn from a diverse range of sources as well as varied illustrations, the volume illuminates the importance of the Perseus myth throughout the ages.

Daniel Ogden is Professor of Ancient History at the University of Exeter.

Gods and Heroes of the Ancient World

Series editor Susan Deacy
Roehampton University

Routledge is pleased to present an exciting new series, Gods and Heroes of the Ancient World. These figures from antiquity are embedded in our culture, many functioning as the source of creative inspiration for poets, novelists, artists, composers and filmmakers. Concerned with their multifaceted aspects within the world of ancient paganism and how and why these figures continue to fascinate, the books provide a route into understanding Greek and Roman polytheism in the twenty-first century.

These concise and comprehensive guides provide a thorough understanding of each figure, offering the latest in critical research from the leading scholars in the field in an accessible and approachable form, making them ideal for undergraduates in Classics and related disciplines.

Each volume includes illustrations, time charts, family trees and maps where appropriate.

Also available:

Zeus
Keith Dowden

Prometheus
Carol Dougherty

Medea
Emma Griffiths

Dionysos
Richard Seaford

Oedipus
Lowell Edmunds

Susan Deacy is Lecturer in Greek History and literature at Roehampton University. Her main research interests are Greek religion, and gender and sexuality. Publications include the co-edited volumes *Rape in Antiquity* (1997), and *Athena in the Classical World* (2001), and the monograph *A Traitor to Her Sex? Athena the Trickster* (forthcoming).

 # PERSEUS

Daniel Ogden

Routledge
Taylor & Francis Group

LONDON AND NEW YORK

First published 2008
by Routledge
2 Park Square, Milton Park, Abingdon, Oxon OX14 4RN

Simultaneously published in the USA and Canada
by Routledge
270 Madison Ave, New York, NY 10016

*Routledge is an imprint of the Taylor & Francis Group,
an informa business*

Typeset in Utopia by
RefineCatch Limited, Bungay, Suffolk
Printed and bound in Great Britain by
Antony Rowe Ltd, Chippenham, Wiltshire

British Library Cataloguing in Publication Data
A catalogue record for this book is available from the British Library

Library of Congress Cataloging in Publication Data
Ogden, Daniel.
    Perseus / Daniel Ogden.
        p. cm.
    Includes bibliographical references and index.
    1. Perseus (Greek mythology) I. Title.
    BL820.P5O33 2008
    292.2′13 – dc22
    2007031552

ISBN10: 0–415–42724–X (hbk)
ISBN10: 0–415–42725–8 (pbk)
ISBN10: 0–203–93213–7 (ebk)

ISBN13: 978–0–415–42724–1 (hbk)
ISBN13: 978–0–415–42725–8 (pbk)
ISBN13: 978–0–203–93213–1 (ebk)

わが最愛の妻
江里子に

Some say that Perseus did more than Heracles but did not receive the glory for it, because he killed Dionysus and threw him into the Lernaean lake.

(Scholiast to Homer *Iliad* 14.319)

The story of Perseus opens up a thousand vistas to the student.

(Hartland 1894–6: iii, 184)

CONTENTS

SERIES FOREWORD

It is proper for a person who is beginning any serious discourse and task to begin first with the gods.

(Demosthenes, Epistula 1.1)

WHY GODS AND HEROES?

The gods and heroes of classical antiquity are part of our culture. Many function as sources of creative inspiration for poets, novelists, artists, composers, filmmakers and designers. Greek tragedy's enduring appeal has ensured an ongoing familiarity with its prot-agonists' experiences and sufferings, while the choice of Minerva as the logo of one the newest British universities, the University of Lincoln, demonstrates the ancient gods' continued emblematic potential. Even the world of management has used them as repre-sentatives of different styles: Zeus and the 'club' culture for example, and Apollo and the 'role' culture: see C. Handy, *The Gods of Management: Who they are, how they work and why they fail*, London, 1978.

This series is concerned with how and why these figures continue to fascinate and intrigue. But it has another aim too, namely to explore their strangeness. The familiarity of the gods and heroes risks obscuring a vital difference between modern meanings and ancient functions and purpose. With certain exceptions, people today do not worship them, yet to the Greeks and Romans they were real beings in a system comprising literally hundreds of divine powers. These range from the major gods, each of whom was worshipped in many guises via their epithets or 'surnames', to the heroes – deceased individuals associated with local communities – to other figures such as daimons and nymphs. The landscape was dotted with sanctuaries, while natural features such as mountains, trees and rivers were thought to be inhabited by religious beings. Studying ancient paganism involves finding strategies to comprehend a world where everything was, in the often quoted words of Thales, 'full of gods'.

In order to get to grips with this world, it is necessary to set aside our preconceptions of the divine, shaped as they are in large part by Christianised notions of a transcendent, omnipotent God who is morally good. The Greeks and Romans worshipped numerous beings, both male and female, who looked, behaved and suffered like humans, but who, as immortals, were not bound by the human condition. Far from being omnipotent, each had limited powers: even the sovereign, Zeus/Jupiter, shared control of the universe with his brothers Poseidon/Neptune (the sea) and Hades/Pluto (the underworld). Lacking a creed or anything like an organised church, ancient paganism was open to continual reinterpretation, with the result that we should not expect to find figures with a uniform essence. It is common to begin accounts of the pantheon with a list of the major gods and their function(s) (Hephaistos/Vulcan: craft, Aphrodite/Venus: love, and Artemis/Diana: the hunt and so on), but few are this straightforward. Aphrodite, for example, is much more than the goddess of love, vital though that function is. Her epithets include *hetaira* ('courtesan') and *porne* ('prostitute'), but also attest roles as varied as patron of the citizen body (*pandemos*: 'of all the people') and protectress of seafaring (*Euploia, Pontia, Limenia*).

Recognising this diversity, the series consists not of biographies of each god or hero (though such have been attempted in the past), but of investigations into their multifaceted aspects within the complex world of ancient paganism. Its approach has been shaped partly in response to two distinctive patterns in previous research. Until the middle of the twentieth century, scholarship largely took the form of studies of individual gods and heroes. Many works presented a detailed appraisal of such issues as each figure's origins, myth and cult; these include L.R. Farnell's examination of major deities in his *Cults of the Greek States* (five volumes, Oxford, 1896–1909) and A.B. Cook's huge three-volume *Zeus* (Cambridge, 1914–40). Others applied theoretical developments to the study of gods and heroes, notably (and in the closest existing works to a uniform series), K. Kerényi in his investigations of gods as Jungian archetypes, including *Prometheus: Archetypal image of human existence* (English tr. London 1963) and *Dionysos: Archetypal image of the indestructible life* (English tr. London 1976).

In contrast, under the influence of French structuralism, the later part of the century saw a deliberate shift away from research into particular gods and heroes towards an investigation of the system of which they were part. Fuelled by a conviction that the study of isolated gods could not do justice to the dynamics of ancient religion, the pantheon came to be represented as a logical and coherent network in which the various powers were systematically opposed to one another. In a classic study by J.-P. Vernant for example, the Greek concept of space was shown to be consecrated through the opposition between Hestia (goddess of the hearth – fixed space) and Hermes (messenger and traveller god – moveable space: Vernant, *Myth and Thought Among the Greeks*, London, 1983, 127–75). The gods as individual entities were far from neglected however, as may be exemplified by the works by Vernant, and his colleague M. Detienne, on particular deities including Artemis, Dionysos and Apollo: see, most recently, Detienne's *Apollon, le couteau en main: une approche expérimentale du polythéisme grec* (Paris, 1998).

In a sense, this series is seeking a middle ground. While approaching its subjects as unique (if diverse) individuals, it pays attention to their significance as powers within the collectivity of religious beings. *Gods and Heroes of the Ancient World* sheds new light on many of the most important religious beings of classical antiquity; it also provides a route into understanding Greek and Roman polytheism in the twenty-first century.

The series is intended to interest the general reader as well as being geared to the needs of students in a wide range of fields from

Greek and Roman religion and mythology, classical literature and anthropology, to Renaissance literature and cultural studies. Each book presents an authoritative, accessible and refreshing account of its subject via three main sections. The introduction brings out what it is about the god or hero that merits particular attention. This is followed by a central section which introduces key themes and ideas, including (to varying degrees) origins, myth, cult, and representations in literature and art. Recognising that the heritage of myth is a crucial factor in its continued appeal, the reception of each figure since antiquity forms the subject of the third part of the book. The volumes include illustrations of each god/hero and where appropriate time charts, family trees and maps. An annotated bibliography synthesises past research and indicates useful follow-up reading.

For convenience, the masculine terms 'gods' and 'heroes' have been selected for the series title, although (and with an apology for the male-dominated language), the choice partly reflects ancient usage in that the Greek *theos* ('god') is used of goddesses too. For convenience and consistency, Greek spellings are used for ancient names, except for famous Latinized exceptions, and BC/AD has been selected rather than BCE/CE.

I am indebted to Catherine Bousfield, the editorial assistant until 2004, who (literally) dreamt up the series and whose thoroughness and motivation brought it close to its launch. The hard work and efficiency of her successor, Matthew Gibbons, has overseen its progress to publication, and the former classics publisher of Routledge, Richard Stoneman, has provided support and expertise throughout. The anonymous readers for each proposal gave frank and helpful advice, while the authors' commitment to advancing scholarship while producing accessible accounts of their designated subjects has made it a pleasure to work with them.

Susan Deacy, Roehampton University, June 2005

ACKNOWLEDGEMENTS

Thanks to Susan Deacy, Matthew Gibbons and Richard Stoneman for their support with this volume. Thanks also to Professor W.F. Hansen, of whose work I have long been an admirer, for his helpful comments, and to audiences in Exeter, Wellington and Christchurch. I owe a key reference to Ms Hazel Harvey.

LIST OF ILLUSTRATIONS
AND CREDITS

ABBREVIATIONS

ad loc.   *ad locum*, in the same place

ap.   *apud*, quoted in

AT   A. Aarne and S. Thompson, *The Types of the Folktale*, Helsinki, 1928

DA   C. Daremberg and E. Saglio (eds.), *Dictionnaire des antiquités Grecques et Romaines*, Paris, 1877–1919

EAA   *Enciclopedia dell'arte antica*

FHG   C. Müller (ed.), *Fragmenta historicorum graecorum*, Paris, 1878–85

FGH   F. Jacoby, *Die Fragmente der griechischen Historiker*, Leiden, 1923–

fr.   fragment

IG   *Inscriptiones Graecae*

K–A   R. Kassel and C. Austin (eds.) 1983–. *Poetae Comici Graeci*. Berlin

LIMC   H.C. Ackerman and J.-R. Gisler (eds.), *Lexicon Iconographicum Mythologiae Classicae*, Zurich, 1981–99

ML   R. Meiggs and D.M. Lewis (eds.), *A Selection of Greek Historical Inscriptions to the End of the Fifth Century BC*, 2nd edn, Oxford, 1989

MW   R. Mekelbach and M.L. West 1967. *Fragmenta Hesiodea*. Oxford.

PMG   *Poetae Melici Graeci*

P.Oxy   *Oxyrhynchus Papyri*. Oxford, 1898–

QUCC	*Quaderni urbinati di cultura classica*
RA	*Revue archéologique*
RE	A. Pauly, G. Wissowa and W. Kroll (eds.) 1893–. *Real-Encyclopädie der classischen Altertumswissenschaft.* Stuttgart
Suppl. Hell.	H. Lloyd-Jones and P.J. Parsons (eds.) *Supplementum Hellenisticum.* Berlin
s.v.	*sub voce*, under the heading
TrGF	B. Snell *et al.*, *Tragicorum Graecorum Fragmenta*, Göttingen, 1971–2004

ANCIENT AUTHORS AND FRAGMENTS CITED BY NAMES OF EDITORS

Accius	Ribbeck 1897, Warmington 1935–40
Alcaeus	Campbell 1982–93, Voigt 1971
Apollophanes	Kassel and Austin 1983–
Clement of Alexandria	Potter 1715
Cratinus	Kassel and Austin 1983–
Cypria	West 2003
Ennius	Ribbeck 1897, Warmington 1935–40
Eubulus	Kassel and Austin 1983–
Euphorion	Powell 1925
Hesiod	Merkelbach and West 1967
Ion of Chios	West 1989–92, Campbell 1982–93
Libanius	Förster 1903–27
Livius Andronicus	Ribbeck 1897, Warmington 1935–40
Malalas	Dindorf 1831
Naevius	Ribbeck 1897
Orphica	Kern 1922
Pherecydes	Fowler 2000
Pindar	Snell and Maehler 1987–9
Polyidus	Campbell 1982–93; also Page 1962 (*PMG*)
Sannyrio	Kassel and Austin 1983–
Scholia Aratus *Phaenomena*	Martin 1974
Scholia Germanicus *Aratea*	Breysig 1867
Serenus	Büchner 1982

Simonides	Campbell 1982–93; also Page 1962 (*PMG*)
Sophocles	Pearson 1917; also Snell *et al.* 1971–2004 (*TrGF*)
Stesichorus	Page 1962 (*PMG*), Campbell 1982–93
Vatican Mythographers	Bode 1894, Zorzetti and Berlioz 1995

WHY PERSEUS?

1

INTRODUCING PERSEUS

Whether or not Perseus was indeed a greater hero than his great-grandson Heracles, he has remained at the forefront of the western imagination since emerging into it in *ca*. 700 BC. His story was celebrated in poetry, prose, drama and art throughout antiquity, and in ever wider swathes of the ancient world as power passed from the Greek east to the Latin west. Even in dark medieval days Perseus' tradition remained a living one in the fine star-pictures that illustrated astronomical and astrological codices. With the Renaissance, Perseus came to flourish again in all media, painting not least, reaching a crescendo of popularity in the Victorian age.

Perseus' myth cycle is dominated by the slayings of two iconic monsters. The first is the mysterious and terrible Medusa, usually conceived of as a beautiful woman with serpentine hair, whose glance turns men to stone. Perseus' mission to take the head of Medusa offers us an early and striking version of the theme of the heroic quest, in which the hero moves by stages towards his goal, acquiring magical equipment along the way to help him, much as our own James Bond does today. The second is the sea-monster from which Perseus delivers the western tradition's archetypal damsel in distress, princess Andromeda. This adventure will feel familiar to anyone who knows the legend of St George's delivery of Princess Sabra from the dragon. These tales both belong to a widespread folktale type, which partly explains their continuing capacity to engage us, but it may also be the case that the legend of St George was directly shaped by the myth of Perseus.

The mythical traditions of the major Greek heroes tend to be complex and contradictory, but Perseus' myth cycle is a relatively simple and coherent one. For all that it took on accretions over time and mutated with every contribution to it from author or artist, its core remained remarkably defined and stable. One has only to read through the brief ancient summary of Perseus' adventures laid out below to become acquainted with the hero as he was recognised throughout antiquity. In this respect, Perseus offers a convenient access point to the wider study of Greek heroes and myth cycles.

Whatever further significances Perseus' myth cycle may have carried, it was first and foremost a good, compelling adventure story, and the best introduction to the hero is accordingly the story itself. The myth cycle can be said to have reached its canonical form in the writings of Pherecydes of Athens, *ca.* 456 BC. His lost account of it is summarised in the ancient commentaries on Apollonius of Rhodes' Jason epic, the *Argonautica*, but unfortunately the commentaries do not include his treatment of the Andromeda episode. However, it is evident that the account of Perseus given in the Apollodoran *Bibliotheca* (*ca.* 100 AD) is largely based on Pherecydes', and so we may use this text to plug the gap:[1]

> Acrisius married Eurydice, the daughter of Lacedaemon. Danae was born from them. Acrisius consulted the oracle about a male child and the god in Pytho replied that he would not have one, but that one would be born to his daughter, and that this child was destined to kill him. He went back to Argos and constructed a bronze chamber in the courtyard of his house beneath the ground. And into it he put Danae with her nurse. He kept her under guard in there so that no child might be born to her. Zeus fell in love with the girl and flowed down from the roof in the likeness of gold. And she received it in her lap. Zeus revealed himself and had sex with the girl. Perseus was born from them, and Danae reared him together with her nurse, keeping him secret from Acrisius. When Perseus was three or four, Acrisius heard his voice as he played. He summoned Danae and her nurse through his servants, killed the nurse, and took Danae with her son to the altar of his Courtyard Zeus. Standing alone with her, he asked her from whom she had conceived the child. She said, 'From Zeus'. He did not believe her, but he put her into a chest with her child. He shut it and put it in the sea. Being carried along, they arrived at the island of Seriphos. Dictys the son of

Peristhenes hawled them out of the sea as he was fishing with a net. Thereupon Danae supplicated him to open the chest. He opened it and, learning who they were, took them to his house and reared them as if they were his own relatives.

(Pherecydes *FGH* 3 *fr.* 26 = *fr.* 10, Fowler)

Perseus and his mother lived in Seriphos with Dictys. When Perseus had become a youth, Polydectes, the maternal brother of Dictys, who happened to be king of Seriphos, saw Danae and fell in love with her, but was at a loss as to how to sleep with her. So he prepared a feast and invited many to it, including Perseus. Perseus asked what was the price of attendance. Polydectes said, 'A horse.' Perseus said, 'The head of the Gorgon.' On the sixth day after the feast, when the other banqueters brought their horses, so did Perseus. But Polydectes would not accept it, and demanded instead the head of the Gorgon in accord-ance with Perseus' promise. He said that if Perseus did not bring it, he would take his mother. Perseus was vexed and went off, lamenting his fate, to the remotest corner of the island. Hermes appeared before him and interrogated him, and learned the reason for his lamentation. He told him to cheer up and led the way for him. First he took him to the Graeae, the daughters of Phorcys, named Pemphredo, Enyo and Deino. Athena told him the way. He stole from them their eye and tooth as they were handing it among themselves. When they realised, they shouted out and besought him to give them back to them. For the three of them had been using one tooth and one eye by turns. Perseus said that he had them and that he would give them back if they directed him to the Nymphs that had the Cap of Hades, the winged sandals and the pouch (*kibisis*). So they showed him, and Perseus gave them their things back. He went off to the Nymphs with Hermes, and asked them for the equipment. He put on the winged sandals, slung the pouch around himself, and put the Cap of Hades on his head. Then he travelled in flight to the region of Ocean and the Gorgons, with Hermes and Athena accompanying him. He found the Gorgons asleep. These gods instructed him to cut off the head whilst turning away, and in a mirror they showed him Medusa, who alone of the Gorgons was mortal. He approached, cut off her head with his sickle (*harpē*) and, putting it in his pouch, fled. The other Gorgons, realising what had happened, pursued him. However, they could not see him, because of his Cap of Hades.

(Pherecydes *FGH* 3 *fr.* 26 = *fr.* 11, first part, Fowler)

When Perseus had arrived in Ethiopia, over which Cepheus was king, he found his daughter Andromeda set out as food for a sea-monster (*kētos*). For Cassiepeia, the wife of Cepheus, had competed with the Nereids in beauty and had boasted that she was better than all of them. As a result of this the Nereids became angry and Poseidon, coming to share their anger, sent a flood-tide against the land, and the sea-monster too. Ammon gave a prophecy of deliverance from the misfortune, if Andromeda, the daughter of Cassiepeia, were given to the monster to eat. Cepheus did this under compulsion from the Ethiopians, and bound his daughter to a rock. Perseus, seeing her and falling in love with her, promised to kill the monster for Cepheus, if he would give him the girl to wife, once he had saved her. Oaths were sworn to this effect, and Perseus faced the monster, killed it and released Andromeda. But Phineus plotted against him. He was Cepheus' brother, and had formerly had Andromeda betrothed to him. Perseus discovered the plot, showed him and his fellow conspirators the head of the Gorgon and turned him to stone in an instant.

(Apollodorus *Bibliotheca* 2.4.3.)

When Perseus arrived at Seriphos he came before Polydectes and bade him gather the people, so that he might show them the Gorgon's head, in the knowledge that when they saw it they would be turned to stone. Polydectes assembled the people and bade him show the head. He turned away, took it out of his pouch, and showed it. The people saw it and were turned to stone. Athena took the head from Perseus and mounted it upon her goatskin (aegis). He gave the pouch back to Hermes, and his sandals and cap to the Nymphs.

(Pherecydes *FGH* 3 *fr.* 26 = *fr.* 11, second part, Fowler)

After the petrifaction of Polydectes and his companions, Perseus left Dictys in Seriphos to rule over the remaining Seriphians, but Perseus himself sailed to Argos with the Cyclopes, Danae and Andromeda. He failed to find Acrisius in Argos upon his arrival, for he had withdrawn to the Pelasgians in Larissa for fear. After failing to apprehend him, Perseus left Danae with her mother Eurydice, and so too Andromeda and the Cyclopes. But he himself went to Larissa. Upon arrival he recognised Acrisius and persuaded him to follow him back to Argos. When they were on the point of departure, he came across a competition for young men in Larissa. Perseus stripped off for the competition, took the discus, and threw it. The pentathlon did not yet exist, but people competed separately in each of the competitions. The discus swerved into Acrisius' foot and wounded him. Acrisius fell sick as a result of this and died there in Larissa. Perseus and

the Larissans buried him before the city, and the locals made a hero shrine for
him there. Perseus returned to Argos.

(Pherecydes *FGH* 3 *fr.* 26 = *fr.* 12, Fowler)

The basic narrative can be resolved into three principal episodes
nested within each other after the fashion of Russian dolls. The
outer shell is provided by the family saga which moves from Argos to
Seriphos to Larissa. Within this is set the episode of the Gorgon-
slaying and Perseus' consequent flight from Medusa's sisters. And
within this is set the Andromeda episode. It will be convenient to
devote a chapter to the analysis of each of these major sections of
the myth, and this accounts for the following three chapters.[2]

Chapter 2 discusses Perseus' Greek adventures and his family
saga. What is the significance of baby Perseus' experiences in the
seaborne chest? Greek and international comparanda show this to
embody a folktale motif that marks an individual out for future
greatness and power. Perseus' early life presents us with two further
puzzles. First, what is the motivation of Acrisius in his behaviour
towards Danae and Perseus? We can understand something of it if
we view it in the contexts of his feud with his twin brother Proetus,
and of Greek thinking about ordeals of virginity. Secondly, how
are we to interpret the mechanics of the puzzling trick by which
Polydectes compels Perseus to embark upon the Gorgon mission?
The notion that Perseus is a precocious youth eager to prove his
manhood may be part of the answer. The later part of Perseus' life in
Greece, only dealt with in obscure fashion by the ancient sources
and not covered by the texts above, raises further issues. What is the
significance of the curious war Perseus fights with Dionysus, and in
which he even, according to some accounts, succeeds in killing the
god? Paradoxically, the function of this myth seems to have been to
explain the cult of a very much living Dionysus in the heart of Argos.
A final puzzle is the manner of Perseus' death. Was he killed by
his cousin Megapenthes? Did he accidentally kill himself with the
Gorgon's head? Or was he taken up directly into the stars ('catasterised') to form the constellation named after him?

Chapter 3 is devoted to Perseus' mission against the Gorgon.
What were the nature and origin of Gorgons? Were they and their

detached heads, so popular in art, an outgrowth of the Perseus–Medusa myth? Or was the Perseus–Medusa myth, with its central decapitation vignette, a back-formation from an already established artistic practice of making detached Gorgon-heads? What are the functions of the various pieces of magical equipment Perseus deployed in his Gorgon mission? His Hermes-like winged sandals enable him not merely to escape the pursuit of Medusa's sisters, but also to reach the never-never land in which the Gorgons dwell in the first place. The *kibisis* is a pouch able to withstand and contain the terrible power of the Gorgon's head. The Cap of Hades confers invisibility on Perseus, vital not only for escaping Medusa's sisters, but for approaching her in such a way that she can not fix her gaze upon him. Perseus' *harpē* or sickle-sword is a weapon particularly associated with the slaying of snake-formed monsters. His mirror-shield allows him to approach Medusa without looking on her. Another issue is where the Gorgons lived. Initially they could be located at any extremity of the compass, but they came to be fixed in the extreme west of North Africa, known to the Greeks as 'Libya'. This allowed for the development of two ancillary episodes specific to the Libyan location: the creation of the dreadful snakes of Libya from the drops of the Gorgon's blood, and Perseus' petrifaction of Atlas. How did Medusa's petrifaction work? Was it initiated when she looked at the victim, or when the victim looked at her? In fact ancient authors assume both mechanisms. Medusa's immortal Gorgon sisters Stheno and Euryale seem to have had the same power, and Euryale may also have had another weapon in her terrible voice. A final puzzle is the curious repetition of motifs within the Medusa episode, and indeed between the Medusa episode and the Andromeda episode, of which the most obvious is the proliferation of supernatural female triads. Such repeated motifs may be able to tell us something of the archaeology of the myth.

In chapter 4 we turn to the Andromeda episode. Can the tale be said to have derived from the Near East? Probably not, although it may well have borrowed Near Eastern iconography. The question of the location of this adventure is still more complex than that of the Medusa story. It seems to have originated in Arcadia, close to Perseus' Argive home, before wandering to Persia, to Ethiopias adjacent to the Atlantic or to the Red Sea, and thence to Joppa (Jaffa), and finally to India. Even when Ethiopian, Andromeda never seems to have acquired a black skin, and it may well be that her paradoxical whiteness was a significant factor in some lost versions of her story. What was the nature of the sea-monster or *kētos* sent to devour Andromeda? The monster was often curiously under-described by authors and artists alike, who preferred to concentrate rather on the melodramatic and indeed erotic potential of Andromeda's plight. Perseus is credited with killing it by a variety of means: the idea that he used the Gorgon-head against it may always have been there, but he is also commonly said to have killed it with his sickle, and versions are known too in which he pelted it with rocks, or allowed it to swallow him so that he could hack out its liver from the inside. What are we to make of the close relationship the Andromeda tale exhibits with other Greek 'dragon-slaying' myths, particularly that of Heracles and Hesione, and with a range of international folktale comparanda? Analysis of these may tell us something of the genesis of the Andromeda tale, and suggest that it has a closer relationship with the Medusa tale than first appears.

With chapter 5 we turn away from the mythic narrative to investigate how Perseus was adopted and appropriated by different communities around the ancient world, and how he was deployed by the Greeks to express relationships with other peoples. The myth of Perseus was almost certainly nurtured in the Argolid, where Perseus had been king and founded a number of cities, but other cities too, including those with no natural connection with Perseus' myth, such as Athens and Sparta, aspired to share the glamour he bestowed. From *ca.* 480 BC the Greeks came to see Perseus as the progenitor of the great enemy race, the like-named Persians. Why? Was their motivation defensive, imperialist or merely explanatory? Perseus was an iconic figure for the Argead kings of Macedon. Not only did they derive their family from him and his Argos, but their own foundation myth saluted the imagery of Perseus' birth. Alexander the Great, in particular, identified with Perseus, both for being partly sired by Zeus as Perseus had been, and for aspiring to be lord of Persia. In the wake of the Argeads, Persean imagery was adopted also by the Hellenistic dynasties and in turn by the Roman empire too, last and greatest of the Hellenistic dynasties. Rome integrated Perseus into her own legends, adding prestige to her history and her poetic tradition alike. Perseus' myth was rewritten with a very different agenda by ancient rationalisers, who worked in a tradition parallel to that of the myth proper, but on occasion their writings could have an impact on it.

Somewhat paradoxically, the work of the rationalisers paved the way for the first major development in the reception of the Perseus myth after antiquity, its allegorisation by medieval Latin writers, as we see in chapter 6. Indeed the Perseus myth has been subject to allegorisation ever since, and never more elaborately than in the work of Freud. In the later medieval age the Andromeda episode may, as we have seen, also have helped to form our cherished legend of St George and the Dragon. Since the Renaissance, Perseus has been a major presence in art and literature of all types. His most elaborate artistic treatment is perhaps to be found in Burne-Jones' *Perseus Series*, which weaves together the Classical and medieval strands of his tradition.

It is my assumption that readers turning to this book will first and foremost want to know what the ancient sources, literary and iconographic, tell us about Perseus, and I have accordingly held these strongly in the foreground throughout.

KEY THEMES

2

THE FAMILY SAGA

THE FAMILY SAGA ON STAGE

It was in the tragedies of Classical Athens that Perseus' family saga received its most influential elaboration. Prior to this, it had been known that Zeus had fathered Perseus by Danae since at least *ca.* 700 BC: 'I fell in love with Danae of the fair ankles, the daughter of Acrisius, who bore Perseus, distinguished amongst all warriors', the god declares in the *Iliad* (14.319–20). And Perseus had been enmeshed in the remainder of what was to become his familiar genealogy by at least the mid-sixth century BC ([Hesiod] *Catalogue of women fr.* 129.10–15 and *fr.* 135 MW, Stesichorus *fr.* 227 *PMG*/ Campbell). The comic playwright Menander, writing at the end of the fourth century BC, implies that Zeus' corruption of Danae had by then become a hackneyed theme on the tragic stage: 'Tell me, Niceratus, have you not heard the tragedians telling how Zeus once became gold and flowed through the roof, and had adulterous sex with a confined girl?' (*Samia* 589–91).

Aeschylus devoted a trilogy of tragedies to Perseus and his family. We know that two of these were named *Polydectes* (*TrGF* iii p. 302) and *Phorcides* (i.e. 'Graeae', *frs* 261–2 *TrGF*). But substantial fragments survive only from the accompanying satyr-play, the *Dictyulci Satyri* ('Net-dragging Satyrs', *frs* 46a–47c *TrGF*), which dealt with Dictys' retrieval of Danae and Perseus from the sea in their chest. There have been speculative attempts to date this group of four plays by associating them with flurries of scenes on pots. One theory, which conjectures that the unidentified play focused on Danae and Acrisius, associates the group with the *ca.* 490 flurry of scenes of Acrisius' enclosure of Danae and Perseus in the chest. Another theory associates the group rather with the *ca.* 460 flurry of scenes of Dictys releasing Danae and Perseus from the chest and introducing them to Polydectes, and of scenes of the Graeae. There is a striking variation in the representation of Perseus' age and size on these vases. He can range from being a babe in arms (e.g. *LIMC* Akrisios no. 2 = Fig. 2.2, Danae no. 48), to quite a grown lad (e.g. no. 54). We recall that Pherecydes makes Perseus three or four years old before his discovery (*FGH* 3 *fr.* 26 = *fr.* 10, Fowler).[1]

Sophocles (*floruit* 468–06 BC) wrote an *Acrisius* (*frs* 60–76 *TrGF*), a *Danae* (*frs* 165–70 *TrGF*), and a *Larissaeans* (*frs* 378–83 *TrGF*). Amongst the fragments of the *Acrisius*, we find justifications of the king's behaviour, perhaps at the point at which he first imprisons Danae, and perhaps from his own mouth: 'No one loves life like an

Figure 2.1 The impregnation of Danae.

old man' (*fr.* 66) and: 'For to live my child, is a sweeter gift than anything, for it is not possible for the same people to die twice' (*fr.* 67). Amongst the fragments of the *Danae* we may find Acrisius' voice in the phrase, 'I do not know about the rape. But one thing I do know is that I am done for if this child lives' (*fr.* 165). The *Larissaeans* dealt with Perseus' accidental killing of Acrisius in Larissa. A fragment of this play suggests that it was Acrisius himself that was here laying on the games (*fr.* 378), in contrast to the Teutamides of the Apollodoran account (*Bibliotheca* 2.4.4), and so that he had somehow contrived to make himself king of the city. In another fragment Perseus himself explains what had caused him to misthrow the discus that was to kill his father: 'And as I was throwing the discus the third time Elatos, a Dotian man, caught hold of me' (*fr.* 380).[2]

Euripides' *Danae* (*frs* 316–330a *TrGF*), probably produced

Figure 2.2 Acrisius has the chest prepared for Danae and baby Perseus.

between 455 and 428 (*TrGF* v.1 p. 372), dealt with Danae's impregnation by Zeus and enclosure in the chest (Malalas p. 34 Dindorf). Acrisius evidently lamented his sonless state, and his postponement of the siring of children until old age (*fr.* 316–17). The observation that women are hard to keep under guard presumably refers, somehow, to Danae's incarceration (*fr.* 320). Euripides' *Dictys* of 431 BC (*frs* 330b–48 *TrGF*), perhaps illustrated on vases (*LIMC* Danae no. 7, Polydektes no. 6), seems to have dealt with Polydectes' persecution of Danae and Dictys after Perseus had been sent off against the Gorgon. Perhaps they fled to altars for protection, as in the Apollodoran account (*Bibliotheca* 2.4.2–3; cf. Theon on Pindar *Pythians* 12 at *P.Oxy.* 31.2536.). One fragment appears to preserve Dictys' attempt to console Danae, who believes Perseus to be dead (*fr.* 332).[3]

We can probably access another, unidentifiable but radically different tragic treatment of the saga through the work of the second-century AD mythological compiler Hyginus. He preserves for us a version of the family saga wholly at odds with all other accounts. His action proceeds largely as normal until Danae and Perseus have been enclosed in the chest:

> By the will of Zeus she was brought to the island of Seriphos. When the fisherman Dictys discovered them, breaking open the chest, he found the woman with her baby, and he took them to king Polydectes. Polydectes married her and reared Perseus in the temple of Athena. When Acrisius learned that they were staying with Polydectes, he set out to find them again. When he had arrived there, he begged Polydectes for them. Perseus promised Acrisius that he would never kill him. When Acrisius was held back by a storm, Polydectes died. Whilst they were holding funeral games for him, Perseus threw a discus and the wind carried it off onto the head of Acrisius, and he killed him. And so the gods accomplished what he had not intended. Acrisius was buried, and Perseus set out for Argos and took possession of his grandfather's kingdom.
>
> (Hyginus *Fabulae* 63)

Elsewhere Hyginus specifies that it was Perseus himself who established the funeral games for his foster-father Polydectes (*Fabulae* 273.4). This account obviously represents a complete reconfiguration of the traditional story. Dictys, the Gorgons, Andromeda and the *kētos* adventures have been completely extruded (although Athena stays on as Perseus' protector). Polydectes has been transformed from wicked predator into benign protector (cf. Scholiast Homer *Iliad* 14.319; 'Scholiasts' are commentators on ancient texts, and wrote in the Hellenistic, Imperial and Byzantine periods), and actually marries Danae. Acrisius then of his own accord seeks after Perseus, seemingly because he has had a change of heart. This curious narrative probably derives from a Classical tragedy: it has a distinctively tragic flavour and Acrisius may well have been dragged to Seriphos in part because of the genre's unity-of-place requirement.

The Greek tragedies shaped the tragedies of early Latin literature on similar subjects. In the third century BC both Livius Andronicus (p. 3, Ribbeck³) and Naevius (pp. 7–9, Ribbeck³) wrote *Danae* tragedies, but the fragments can tell us nothing of their action, other than that Naevius' play included the unsurprising detail of a 'ruddy shower of gold' (*fr.* 5).

We can reconstuct little of comic poets' responses to the family-saga part of Perseus' adventures. Amongst the remains of fifth-century BC Old Comedy the single surviving fragment of Sannyrio's *Danae* promisingly gives us Zeus deliberating whether he should get through the hole to gain access to Danae by transforming into a shrew-mouse (*fr.* 8 *K–A*). Of Apollophanes' *Danae* we have only the name (T1 *K–A*). The surviving fragments of Cratinus' *Seriphians* of *ca.* 425 (*frs* 218–32 *K–A*) suggest that it focused on Perseus' return to Seriphos, since Andromeda is referred to as 'a baited trap', presumably for the sea-monster, but perhaps for Perseus (*fr.* 231). Since the demagogue Cleon was ridiculed in the play for his terrible eyebrows and indeed his insanity, he may have appeared in the role of the Gorgon (*fr.* 228). We have just a hint of the action of Eubulus' *Danae*, a Middle Comedy of the earlier fourth century. In its single fragment a woman, no doubt Danae, complains of rough treatment from a man, no doubt Acrisius (*fr.* 22 *K–A*).[4]

THE IMPREGNATION OF DANAE

Pherecydes is the earliest source to describe Zeus' access to Danae in any detail. He implies that Zeus, presumably the Zeus whose altar sat in the courtyard above, transformed himself into golden rain merely for the purpose of getting through the skylight, but then reverted to humanoid form in order to have sex with the girl (Pherecydes *FGH* 3 *fr*. 26 = *fr*. 10, Fowler). It is reasonable enough that Zeus should have shown himself to Danae in humanoid form at some stage, because she needed to know who had impregnated her. But the remainder of the literary sources imply that Zeus retained the form of golden rain to flow directly into Danae's loins, as a sort of golden sperm, as in a passing reference in Sophocles' *Antigone*: 'she took in store the gold-flowing seed of Zeus' (944–50). And this indeed is the way the artists liked to portray the scene, with a shower of golden rain heading straight for Danae's lap (*LIMC* Danae nos. 1–39, the earliest of which dates from *ca.* 490 BC). But for all that he impregnated her in the form of pure seed, Danae was evidently not denied sexual pleasure in the congress. In many images, from the mid-fifth century onwards, she actively welcomes the seed into her lap by holding her dress out of the way to receive it (*LIMC* Danae nos. 7, 8, 9 [= Fig. 2.1], 19, 26, 33), or alternatively uses the fold of her dress to collect it (*LIMC* Danae nos. 5, 10, 12, 31). In some her head is actually thrown back in ecstasy (note especially the mid-fourth-century BC chalcedony intaglio, *LIMC* Danae no. 11).[5]

Latin sources add some interesting touches to Danae's confinement. Horace transforms her subterranean bronzed dungeon into a bronze tower (*Odes* 3.16.1–11, *ca.* 23 BC). This notion was to be a popular one in Latin literature and the later western tradition. Ovid makes the nice point that it was Danae's very confinement that fired Zeus' passion for her (*Amores* 2.19.27–8, *ca.* 25–16 BC). The Vatican Mythographers preserve the intriguing idea that Danae was watched over by girl guards – for obvious reasons – and dogs (First Vatican Mythographer 137 Bode = 2.55 Zorzetti, Second 110 Bode).

THE CHEST AND ITS MYTHOLOGICAL COMPARANDA

The tale of Perseus and Danae fits broadly into a widespread folktale pattern. According to this, a prophecy warns of danger should a king or queen produce a son. Despite attempts to ensure that no such child should be born, it is produced nonetheless and so exposed in a container either by land or, more usually, on water. The child is found and reared by a humble person or even an animal. On coming to manhood the child distinguishes himself and does indeed kill his father, be it by accident or design. With a few qualifications, a great many well-known heroic birth-myths can be fitted into this pattern: from the Greek world itself those of Oedipus, Heracles, Paris, Telephus and the tyrant Cypelus; from the Roman world that of Romulus; from the Near East those of Gilgamesh, Sargon of Akkad, Cyrus, Moses and even Jesus; from India that of the *Mahabharata*'s Karna; and from the Germanic world that of Tristan.[6]

But it is the Greek myth of Auge and her son Telephus that provides a particularly close parallel for Perseus' sea-ordeal. The tale, in one of its most canonical forms, and seemingly the one in which it was already told by Hecataeus at the beginning of the fifth century BC, proceeded as follows. Aleus, king of Tegea in Arcadia, was told by Delphi that a son of his daughter Auge would one day kill his (Aleus') sons, one of whom was Cepheus. To ensure that Auge would not bear a son, Aleus appointed her priestess of Athena, in which role she was bound to remain a virgin. But she was corrupted by Aleus' guestfriend Heracles in the sanctuary itself, either in a single drunken act of rape, or in repeated consensual but clandestine congress, with a pregnancy resulting. She initially hid the baby, Telephus, in the sanctuary, but the desecration of the sanctuary inflicted a sterility upon Tegea which ultimately resulted in the child's discovery. Aleus forced Auge to swear to the identity of the baby's father, but when she did so, truthfully, he did not believe her. He then gave mother and baby over to Nauplius to dump in the sea in a chest, which he duly did. They were carried ashore in Mysia, where they were welcomed by king Teuthras, who married Auge and adopted Telephus. In due course, Telephus did indeed kill Aleus' sons, although we are told nothing of the circumstances in which this occurred.

There are two principal variants. In one, Auge's violation was detected whilst she was still pregnant and it was as Nauplius was taking her off to the sea that she gave birth to her baby suddenly on Mt Parthenios (or Parthenion), 'Mt Virgin'. She hid him in a thicket, later destined to become the site of his sanctuary, where he was nurtured by a doe, thus acquiring the name Telephus (Tēlephos, supposedly from *thēlē*, teat, and *elaphos*, deer). He was then rescued by shepherds and reared by one Corythus. In the other variant tale, Nauplius' conscience got the better of him and he refrained from putting Auge and Telephus in the sea, and rather sold them on, directly or indirectly, to Teuthras. (See Hecataeus *FGH* 1 *frs* 29a, 29b, Aeschylus *Mysians, Telephus*, Sophocles *Mysians*, Euripides *Auge frs* 264a–281 *TrGF* and *Telephus frs* 696–727c *TrGF*, Alcidamas *Odysseus* 14–16, Diodorus 4.33.7–12, Strabo C615, Apollodorus *Bibliotheca* 2.7.4, 3.9.1, Pausanias 8.4.9, 8.47.4, 8.48.7, 8.54.6, 10.28.8, Tzetzes on [Lycophron] *Alexandra* 206. Rather different versions of this saga are found at Hesiod *Catalogue of Women fr.* 165 MW, Hyginus *Fabulae* 99–100, 244 and Aelian *Nature of Animals* 3.47.[7])

Many parallels with the Perseus–Danae narratives are evident: Delphi foretells that a daughter's son will kill kin; her father acts to ensure that she remains a virgin; but she is violated by Zeus or his son; she attempts to conceal the baby; the baby is reared in a temple of Athena; the baby is discovered; the girl swears truthfully to the identity of the baby's father, but is not believed; she is dumped in the sea in a chest with the baby; the pair are brought ashore where they are rescued by a kindly man who looks after them. But there are other links with the Perseus tradition too, in the form of shared personnel. Most noteworthy is the participation of Cepheus, who was evidently at one time identical with the Cepheus who became Perseus' father-in-law (see chapter 5). We learn from Apollodorus that Aleus' sister Sthenoboea was married to Perseus' great uncle Proetus (*Bibliotheca* 3.9.1). And the name of Teuthras curiously recalls that of Teutamides of Larissa, host to Acrisius and Perseus (Apollodorus *Bibliotheca* 2.4.4).[8]

Two further Greek parallels may be noted. A similar tale was also told of Semele and Dionysus by the people of Brasiae:

The people there say, although they agree with no other Greeks in this, that Semele bore the child she conceived from Zeus. She was detected in this by Cadmus and both she herself and Dionysus were cast into a chest. They say that the chest was carried by the waves to their land, and that they gave Semele a splendid burial (for she was no longer alive when they found her), but they reared Dionysus. It was because of this that their city, which had hitherto been called Oreiatae, was renamed Brasiae, that is, because the chest was washed ashore there. For even in our time many apply the term *ekbebrasthai* to things being washed ashore by the waves.

(Pausanias 3.24.3–4)

We may also compare the legend of Phronime, mother of Battus of Cyrene, as recounted by Herodotus (4.154–5). Her wicked step-mother lied to her father Etearchus, king of Oaxus in Crete, to the effect that she had been fornicating, and so he tricked his Theran guestfriend Themison into agreeing under oath to dump her in the sea. Angry at the trick and the injustice, Themison kept to his oath by dumping her in the sea on the end of a rope and then drawing her up again, before passing her on to Polymnestus in Thera, who made her his concubine and in due course fathered Battus by her.[9]

Clearly a deeply traditional story-type finds expression in different contexts. Glotz contended that Greek tales of this sort were indirectly informed by the imagery of an ordeal in which women's virginity was tested by throwing them into water. The notion underpinning such an ordeal is perhaps expressed by a proverb preserved in the texts of Pausanias: 'Only those of the female sex that are still purely virginal dive in the sea' (10.19.2). Presumably we are to understand the coda, 'and live to tell the tale'. Of course, only in the case of Phronime is the girl's virginity still in question. For the other women, being dumped in the sea might seem less of a test than an appropriate punishment. However, in both the Danae and Auge tales (and the Semele tale is compatible) there is a related and live issue to test, namely the veracity of the girls' sworn oath to the effect that they had been impregnated by god or hero. From another perspective, unwanted babies more generally could be thrown into the sea in chests or pots, in myth at any rate. One of the ancient versions of the exposure of baby Oedipus, for example, has the child cast out alone on the sea in a chest (Scholiast Euripides *Phoenissae* 26). And exposure in a chest was something that could be associated with illegitimate babies in particular. Hesychius preserves and explains for us a proverbial phrase ' "Out of a chest": bastard' (s.v. *ek larnakos*).[10]

ACRISIUS' MOTIVATIONS AND THE FEUD WITH THE LINE OF PROETUS

Since no sustained narrative of Acrisius' treatment of Danae survives, we can not get clear insight into the motivations to which he was believed to have been subject. Narrated in summary form, his behaviour is unimpressive to modern eyes, but it is possible to read his actions in the tragic circumstances in which he finds himself with a degree of sympathy. He did, we should recall, act to save his own life, and Perseus himself was able to forgive him. The bronze with which Danae's chamber was clad may, security aside, have offered the consolation of luxury. The Spartan temple of Athena Chalkioikos, 'Of the Bronze House', was decorated with bronze plates (Pausanias 3.17). And Danae was given the service and company of a nurse.

According to one strand of the tradition, Acrisius seems to have been the victim of a plot by his hostile twin brother Proetus, or at any rate to have believed himself to be so. We hear a fair bit about the feud between Acrisius and Proetus and their descendants, but not all of it coheres. Apollodorus tells that the boys had been in dispute even in their mother's womb (à la Jacob and Esau). As they grew to manhood their dispute erupted in civil war, in the course of which shields were first invented (*Bibliotheca* 2.2.1; cf. Pausanias 2.25.7). No doubt the succession to the throne of Argos had been at issue from the first. Pindar's contemporary Bacchylides tells us that the feud was resolved when the people of Argos, weary of civil war between the brothers, prevailed upon Proetus to leave Argos and go off and found Tiryns for himself (11.59–72). Differently, Ovid's Perseus returns to Argos, to find that Proetus has chased out his grandfather, and so he deploys the Gorgon-head to turn him to stone

(*Metamorphoses* 5.236–41). The continuing feud between Perseus and Proetus' son Megapenthes is also reflected in different ways. In the Apollodoran account Megapenthes has inherited the throne of his father's Tiryns and is understandably happy to exchange thrones with Perseus, who feels that he can not himself directly take up the throne of Argos after his accidental killing of Acrisius, perhaps for reasons not merely of shame but also of blood guilt (*Bibliotheca* 2.4.4). But in a list of 'Those who killed their relatives' Hyginus tells that 'Megapenthes the son of Proetus killed Perseus the son of Jove and Danae on account of the death of his father' (*Fabulae* 244). Hyginus may, it has been suggested, have derived the notion that Perseus slew Proetus from Ovid, but this does not explain whence he derived the idea – for which he is the sole authority – that Perseus was then subsequently slain by Megapenthes. An anomalous tragedy is a more likely source.[11]

Pindar held that Danae had been corrupted not by Zeus but by her uncle Proetus, and that it was this that was the origin of the great feud between their two lines (*fr.* 284 Snell-Maehler; cf. Apollodorus *Bibliotheca* 2.4.1). Perhaps the Horatian notion that the story of the impregnating golden shower took its rise from the fact that Danae's guards had been bribed with gold ultimately derived from the same strand (3.16.1–11). When Pherecydes' Acrisius took Danae to one side to name her corrupter under oath at the altar, only to hold her forsworn when she swore that it was Zeus, it was perhaps Proetus' name he expected to hear (*FGH* 3 *fr.* 26 = *fr.* 10, Fowler). If Proetus did find himself deprived of the throne of Argos, we may note, then the impregnation of his brother's only and virgin daughter might well have been a means of ensuring that the throne at least reverted to his own bloodline.[12]

The dumping of Danae and her baby in the sea may, at some level, have been a punitive act, particularly if Acrisius suspected that her corrupter had been Proetus. Alternatively, as we have seen, it may have been to test the truth of her oath. Or again, if Acrisius was convinced that Danae was lying in the oath she took at the altar, then he may have felt compelled to send her into exile by some means in order to protect his state from the anger of the gods against it, should it be harbouring a woman who was not only forsworn by them but had also defamed Zeus. The method of dispatch chosen may have been designed in part to give Danae and Perseus some small chance of a new life in an unknown land, from which the forsworn Danae and the ever-dangerous Perseus could not find their way back to bring doom upon Argos or Acrisius. And there may have been some accounts in which Acrisius repented of his decision. A unique illustration appears on a lekythos of *ca.* 450 BC. It shows Acrisius sitting on a cenotaph for Perseus and Danae, and lamenting (*LIMC* Akrisios no. 10). Cenotaphs were particularly associated with those lost at sea. We have already noted Hyginus' tale, probably derived from a Classical tragedy, of Acrisius following Perseus and Danae to Seriphos, presumably with a view to bringing them home.[13]

PERSEUS' CHILDHOOD

The few texts that bear upon the hero's childhood give us our best chance of seeing him as a sympathetic human figure. The single most endearing text bearing upon him to survive from antiquity is a fragment of Simonides (*ca.* 500 BC), reporting Danae's address to her baby as they are tossed on the ocean in their open chest:

> When the blowing of the wind and the movement of the water laid her flat with fear in the richly-wraught chest, with cheeks not unwet, she cast her dear arm around Perseus and said, 'O child, how I suffer! But you are asleep, and slumber with suckling heart in the joyless bronze-riveted wooden box, set adrift in the unlit night and the dark blue gloom. You take no heed of the thick spray above your hair as the wave goes past, nor of the sound of the wind, as you lie in your purple cloak, with your beautiful face. If this trouble was trouble to you, then you would let my words fall upon your little ear. I bid you child, sleep, and let the sea sleep too, and our immeasurable misfortune. May some change of mind become manifest from you, father Zeus. If any part of my prayer is bold or unjust, excuse me'.
>
> (Simonides *fr.* 543 *PMG*/Campbell [cf. *fr.* 553])[14]

In a similar vein, a charming sketch of Lucian (*ca.* 170 AD) has Thetis weeping for the babe Perseus, whom she has just seen being put into the chest with his mother (*Dialogues in the Sea* 12). Danae was accepting of her own punishment, but pleading for the child's life, whilst baby Perseus laughed to see the sea. Touched by the prettiness of the baby, Thetis and the Nereid Doris resolve to push the chest into the nets of the Seriphian fishermen.

Other texts focus on the playing of the toddler Perseus, either in the Argive dungeon or on Seriphos. As to Argos, for Pherecydes it was the sound of Perseus at play in the dungeon that first alerted Pherecydes' Acrisius to his existence (*FGH* 3 *fr.* 26 = *fr.* 10, Fowler). Later on, Euripides' Danae described to Acrisius how in their prison Perseus would 'jump up and play in my arms and on my breast and win my soul with a mass of kisses, for this is the greatest love-drug for mortals, company, father' (*Danae, fr.* 323 *TrGF*).

As to Seriphos, Aeschlyus' fragmentary satyr-play *Dictyulci Satyri*, 'Net-dragging satyrs', composed either in the 490s or 460s BC, is usually reconstructed along the following lines. Dictys catches the heavy chest in his net. Unable to drag it in without help, he makes a bargain with Silenus: if he and his fellow satyrs help bring it in, he can have a share of the catch. The satyrs duly help, in lazy fashion, and the chest is recovered. They run away in fright at a noise from within. Danae emerges with Perseus and tells her story. Dictys offers to protect her, but Silenus wants his promised share and so intends to carry Danae off and marry her, apparently taking on something of Polydectes' canonical role. Dictys somehow drives Silenus off or strikes an alternative bargain with him (*frs* 46a–47c *TrGF*). In the most substantial fragment Silenus attempts to persuade Danae into marriage by demonstrating an immediate bonding with the infant Perseus (*fr.* 47a). Silenus tells the young Perseus that he will be able to share his mother's bed with him, that he will be able to keep a variety of exciting pets, and that he will have toys to play with. In due course, Silenus will teach him to hunt. Silenus' assertion that the child is 'phallus-loving' (*posthophilēs*) is disquieting, to say the least, for a modern audience, and it surely does carry pederastic overtones of the sort with which an ancient Greek audience would have been more comfortable. But its primary significance in context is probably to assert the child's more general affection for Silenus, who, like the satyrs around him, is most characterised by his permanent and prodigious erethism, represented in the theatre by a massive stage phallus.[15]

Perseus' affinity with the animal world is developed further in two authors of the early third century AD. Aelian indicates that Perseus was held to have taken joy in playing with yet another animal around Seriphos, the so-called 'sea-cicada', a kind of lobster. The Seriphians termed the creature 'the plaything of Perseus' and treated it with the highest reverance (*Nature of Animals* 13.26). We are perhaps to imagine the toddler Perseus playing with the sea-cicadas beside Dictys as he fished, in a carefree moment of his childhood.[16] Oppian, on the other hand, and perhaps compatibly with the *Dictyulci*, makes Perseus the first mortal to have hunted (*Cynegetica* 2.8–13).

POLYDECTES' TRICK

In the canonical version of Perseus' tale, Polydectes conceives his desire for Danae at the point at which her son Perseus is coming to manhood, and therefore acquiring the ability to protect her and assuming guardianship of her. This is why he must be removed from the scene or out-manoeuvred. We are reminded of Telemachus in the *Odyssey*, who is similarly coming to manhood, and so becoming a thorny problem for the suitors who wish to have their way with his mother Penelope in the absence of his father Odysseus.[17]

The mechanism of the trick by which Polydectes removes Perseus from the scene with the Gorgon mission remains obscure. Polydectes prepared a bogus contribution feast supposedly to raise funds to bid for the hand of Hippodamia (whose name signifies 'Horse-taming'), and invited Perseus to it. According to a fragment of Pherecydes as relayed by the Scholiast to Apollonius, 'Perseus asked what was the price of attendance. Polydectes said, "A horse." Perseus said, "The head of the Gorgon." When Perseus duly produced the horse, Polydectes rejected it and demanded the head of the Gorgon instead' (*FGH* 3 *fr.* 26 = *fr.* 11, Fowler). According to Apollodorus, whose account is also based on Pherecydes', when invited to the feast, 'Perseus said that he would not decline even at the price of the

Gorgon's head. So while from the others Polydectes asked for horses, he would not accept horses from Perseus, but commanded him to fetch the Gorgon's head' (*Bibliotheca* 2.4.2). The chief difficulty is that it is Perseus who seemingly spontaneously and without relevant prompting brings up the subject of the Gorgon. A further difficulty is that it is unclear what Perseus was trying to say by doing so. Was he expressing a feeling of generosity towards Polydectes? Was he ironically commenting on Polydectes' greed? Was he foolishly boasting about his own ability to provide? Was he expressing the importance he attached to being invited to the feast, perhaps his first chance to sit with other men? The latter two possibilities lend more dramatic strength to the tale. Thus Polydectes can be understood to have observed the precocious youth's eagerness to be accepted as a man, and to be cunningly exploiting this. Such an interpretation, if accepted, provides a further reason for reading Perseus' Gorgon mission expressly as a myth of maturation (see the following chapter).[18]

The head of the Gorgon was not completely irrelevant to horses. Not only is Medusa herself represented in centaur form in one of the earliest images of her, *ca.* 675–50 BC (*LIMC* Perseus no. 117 = Fig. 3.1), but she was lover of Poseidon, patron of horses, and gave birth to the greatest horse of them all, Pegasus, at her decapitation. If, as we might be tempted to think, Perseus ever volunteered to bring Polydectes Pegasus, the greatest horse of all, as his horse-contribution, there is no trace of it in any extant source. It is hard to imagine what Hippodamia would have wanted with the Gorgon-head.[19]

What did Polydectes do once Perseus had left? According to one strand in the tradition, he did not wait for Perseus to return (presumably he was not expected to return anyway) but raped or forcibly married Danae (Pindar *Pythian* 12.14–16, followed by the second-century BC Cyzicene epigram at *Greek Anthology* 3.11). According to another, Perseus returned in time to find his mother and Dictys as suppliants at an altar, presumably before Polydectes had been able to have his wicked way with Danae (Euripides *Dictys*, Apollodorus *Bibliotheca* 2.4.2–3). Accordingly, Perseus' revenge was severe. For all that he left Dictys as king of Seriphos, presumably with a few friendly Seriphians to be king of, the tradition tends to present him as petrifying the island's entire population (Pindar *Pythians* 10.46–8, 12.6–26, Strabo C487), and indeed the island itself (Eustathius on Dionysius Periegetes 525).

THE WAR AGAINST DIONYSUS

It was after returning from his adventures and taking up the king-ship of Argos that Perseus had his strangest adventure, possibly, according to one source, in the thirty-second year of his reign (Apol-lodorus of Athens *FGH* 244 *fr.* 27, of the second century BC). Dionysus attacked Perseus and the Argives with a maenad army, either at Argos or at Delphi, and Perseus defeated it. According to some versions, Dionysus eventually came to friendly terms with Perseus, and the fruit of this was to be seen in the temple of Cretan Dionysus that the city hosted in historical times. But according to other versions Perseus even contrived to kill either one or both of Dionysus himself and his bride Ariadne in the attack. Ariadne's body ended up in a tomb in Dionysus' temple, but Dionysus himself ended up either in a tomb in Delphi or being thrown into the Lernaean lake in the Argolid. Yet in either case, the god evidently managed somehow to live on, and somehow to acquire worship from the Argives.[20] The tradition was an old one. Already on three Attic vases of *ca.* 500 BC we find Perseus, sword drawn and *kibisis* hanging from shoulder, flanked by maenads (*LIMC* Perseus nos. 29, 30, 231). A series of red-figure South Italian vases from the earlier fourth century show a humanoid Perseus exhibiting the Gorgon-head to groups of satyrs, Dionysus' other favoured companions, who cover their eyes (*LIMC* Perseus nos. 32–5). However, unlike the maenad vases, these can not be linked to the Dionysus episode securely, as they may simply illustrate satyr-plays on the wider Perseus theme (for which see chapter 3).

The earliest literary reference to the tradition is to be found in a fragment of the fourth-century (or earlier) poet Dinarchus of Delos preserved by a number of Christian authors. He told that Perseus killed Dionysus and buried him in a tomb next to the golden statue of Apollo at Delphi (*FGH* 399 *fr.* 1). A scholiast to Aratus, which also focuses on Delphi, may write in the wake of Dinarchus. It tells how Dionysus presided over an army of women and men, and so acquired the epithet 'half-woman' (*mixothēlys*). He trained Ariadne so that she could lead the female division. They attacked Perseus at Delphi, but he killed them both. The soldiers set up a monument to them in the temple there (Scholiast Aratus *Phaenomena* p. 108 Martin, Salamanticensis 233).[21]

The Scholiast to Homer tells that after killing Dionysus, Perseus disposed of the body by a different means, throwing it into the Lernean lake (on *Iliad* 14.319; cf. Eustathius on 14.320). This tradition seems to underpin a rite mentioned by the Argive historian Socrates, who wrote at some point prior to the first century BC: 'The Argives surname Dionysus "Ox-born" (*Bougenēs*). They summon him from the water with trumpets whilst throwing a lamb into the depths for the Gate-keeper. They disguise the trumpets as thyrsi, as Socrates has told us in his *On the sacred*' (Socrates of Argos *FGH* 310 *fr.* 5 = Plutarch *Moralia* 364f). All too late, over three centuries afterwards, Pausanias piously observed that it would not be holy for him reveal to all the annual rites for Dionysus carried out at the lake, which he calls Alcyonian. He does tell us, however, that the lake was a thing of fear: it was apparently bottomless and not even Nero had been able to fathom its depth; and all swimmers in the lake were pulled under. Evidently the notion that Perseus had thrown Dionysus into the lake served as an aetiology for this rite.

We can put the rite in a wider context. Plutarch tells of the *Agriōnia* festival in his Boeotian Chaeronea, in which the women search for Dionysus as if he has run away, and then give up and say that he has fled to the Muses and hidden with them (*Moralia* 717a; cf. 299f for the *Agriōnia* at Boeotian Orchomenos). Hesychius preserves two notices for us about a similarly named festival at Argos, the *Agriania* or the *Agrania*, which we may infer to have similarly included an attempt to recover a (somehow) lost Dionysus, and which accordingly is likely to have been the context of the rite at the Lernaean lake (*s.vv.*). Hesychius compatibly offers the definition 'a festival of the dead amongst the Argives' for the *Agriania* entry.[22]

Perseus' killing of Dionysus is certainly a curious myth, but what is most curious about it is not the fact that a god should die, but that a mere mortal, for all that he is the son of Zeus, should have been able to kill him. Dionysus himself was no stranger to death, nor to ending up in the water. His tomb at Delphi was more commonly associated with his dismemberment, as Dionysus Zagreus, by the Titans in the Orphic tradition (e.g. Philochorus *FGH* 328 *fr.* 7a–b, Callimachus *fr.* 643 Pfeiffer, Euphorion *fr.* 13 Powell, Diodorus 1.96, 3.62.6, 5.75, Plutarch *Moralia* 364f–365a, 996c, Hyginus *Fabulae* 167, Clement of Alexandria *Protrepticus* p. 15 Potter), and it was in this aspect too that Dionysus was 'bull-born' (*taurogenēs, Orphica fr.* 297 Kern). As for the water, we have already noted the strongly Persean tale told at Brasiae according to which Dionysus was thrown into the sea in a chest with his mother Semele. Better known was the tale in which he was driven into the sea to hide with the sea-goddess Thetis by Lycurgus, king of the Edonians, who also pursued his nurses with an ox-goad (Homer *Iliad* 6.130–44, Apollodorus *Bibliotheca* 3.5.1). Dionysus' refuge with Thetis parallels his refuge with the Muses at Chaeronea. It is possible that Dionysus was held to lurk in water, dead or alive, in Attica too, where the Anthesteria was celebrated at the sanctuary of Dionysus 'In the Marshes', *en Limnais* (Phanodemus *FGH* 325 *fr.* 12, etc.).[23]

According to other accounts, Dionysus' attack was rather more successful. The later third-century BC poet Euphorion told that Dionysus had destroyed Perseus' city, commanding ranks of women (*fr.* 18 Powell; cf. *Suppl. Hell. fr.* 418). Writing in the reign of Hadrian (117–38 AD) Cephalion told that Perseus fled before Dionysus with a hundred ships to Assyria, when the land was ruled by Belimos (*FGH* 93 *fr.* 1). Pausanias told that although Dionysus made war on Perseus, he resolved his enmity and was then greatly honoured by the Argives with the special precinct in which his Cretan bride Ariadne was in due course buried (evidently she did not die in the battle). Her ceramic coffin was discovered during rebuilding work, and at that point the sanctuary was rededicated to the *Cretan* Dionysus in her honour (2.23.7–8, building on Lyceas *FGH* 312 *fr.* 4). Pausanias also observed the burials of the casualties of Dionysus' maenad army within the city they had evidently penetrated, most of them in a mass grave before the sanctuary of Hera Antheia (2.20.4, 2.22.1). The women, Pausanias tells us, had come from the Aegean islands, and for that reason were known as 'Haliae' or 'from the sea', but Dionysus' affinities with the sea and with the sea-goddess Thetis may suggest that the Haliae were, in origin, women from the sea itself.

We have to wait to the very end of antiquity and the *Dionysiaca* of the fifth-century AD Nonnus of Panopolis in Egypt for a full-blown literary account of the war. Dionysus is Nonnus' hero, and can hardly be killed, but the poet sacrifices Ariadne, and curiously narrates her death twice over, in different terms. The first time Perseus accidentally kills Ariadne with a spear whilst aiming for Dionysus (25.98–112). The second time he petrifies her with the Gorgon-head (47.664–712). Hermes proceeds to persuade Dionysus to set up the petrified body of Ariadne as a statue for worship, in a salute to the familiar literary theme of the Gorgon's role in the creation of statuary (cf. chapter 3).

Nonnus appreciates the nice balance between Perseus and Dionysus as adversaries: both are sons of Zeus by mortal women; Dionysus was born in the fire of Zeus' thunderbolts, whereas Perseus was sired by Zeus in the form of golden rain; Dionysus turned a Tyrrhenian ship to stone, whereas Perseus turned the sea-monster to stone; Dionysus saved Ariadne, whereas Perseus saved Andromeda (47.498–519). He also makes nice a contrast between Perseus' snake-haired Gorgon-head and the snakes with which Dionysus' maenad army tie up their hair (47.540, 552). He might have added to this their parallel seaborne adventures as babes.[24]

But this was not Dionysus' first assault on Argos: he had attempted to impose his rites on the city before, during the reign of Proetus. When Proetus' daughters refused to receive the rites, the god drove them mad: they killed Proetus, ran to the mountains and ate their own babies (Hesiod *Catalogue of Women frs* 131–3 MW, Apollodorus *Biblotheca* 1.9.12, 2.2.2, 3.5.2, etc.). These events too may have been celebrated in Dionysus' Argive festival. Hesychius defines *Agrania* as 'a festival in Argos for one of the daughters of Proetus'. An obvious parallelism obtains between Dionysus' pair of attacks on Argos and his attack upon the Thebes of Pentheus, best known from Euripides' *Bacchae*, in which Pentheus is torn apart by his own raving mother Agave. Nonnus saw it too (*Dionysiaca* 47.613–53). The structural similarity and homophony between the names of Perseus and Pentheus may also give us pause for thought. We may compare, too, the god's eventual conquest of King Lycurgus and his Edonians. Kings Pentheus and Lycurgus are killed, whereas Perseus either kills Dionysus or puts up a show of strength against him, but the final outcomes are the same, with the god receiving the worship he seeks. For Burkert, such tales, despite their different courses, explain the arrival of the ever-adventitious Dionysus and the worship he receives, and encapsulate the tension between human rationality and divine madness that his cult enshrined.[25]

THE DEATH OF PERSEUS

The death of Perseus is one of the most obscure parts of his myth. This is paradoxical, because circumstances of death were normally key to a Greek hero's identity and status (the term 'hero' signifying in the first instance a dead man in receipt of worship). Two accounts of Perseus' death survive, but neither was canonical. As we have seen, Hyginus preserves the bare information, probably derived from an anomalous tragedy, that he was killed by his cousin-once-removed Megapenthes in revenge for the killing of his father Proetus (*Fabulae* 244). Rather more interesting is the account of Perseus' death given by the fifth-sixth-century AD Christian chronographer John Malalas:

> After some time King Cepheus, the father of Andromeda, came against him from Ethiopia, and made war upon him. Cepheus was unable to see because of old age. Perseus, hearing that he was making war on him, became very angry and went out against him brandishing the head, and he showed it to him. Because he was unable to see, Cepheus rode against him on his horse. Perseus did not realise that he could not see, and reasoned that the head of the Gorgon he held was no longer working. So he turned it towards himself and looked at it. He was blinded and frozen like a corpse and killed.
>
> John Malalas pp. 38–9 Dindorf (cf. George Cedrenus 1.41)

It is difficult to gauge the tone of this story. Is it tragic? Or are we rather to laugh and visualise the action along the lines of an Oliver

Hardy peering down a hose-pipe to see why the water isn't coming out? Is it a Christian joke at the expense of one of the principal pagan heroes? But such a tale may also have originated in a pagan joke. A favourite theme of the Perseus tradition from the second-century AD Pseudo-Lycophron onwards was that Perseus created statues with the Gorgon-head (see chapter 3). Did some ancient wit then ask the origin of the statue-type of Perseus himself holding the Gorgon-head aloft (e.g. *LIMC* Perseus nos. 49, 61–3), and find the answer in some such story as this?

OVERVIEW

The experiences of Perseus discussed here seem to have been elaborated principally in a series of lost tragedies. These experiences have been examined against two broad contexts. The first is the context of international and Greek mythological comparanda, particularly the myth of Auge and Telephus. The second is the context of the feud between the lines of Acrisius and Proetus, against which Perseus' adventures initially and ultimately unfold. The Dionysus episode is not well integrated into the remainder of Perseus' biography, although it exhibits thematic links with a tale attached to Proetus. Perseus' Greece-based adventures form the outer shell of his myth, within which the story of Medusa is nested. It is to this that we now turn.

3
MEDUSA AND THE GORGONS

THE ORIGINS OF THE GORGON-HEAD AND OF THE MEDUSA STORY

The earliest evidence for Gorgon-heads and the Medusa story falls into four groups which can not be ranked in any uncontroversial chronological order:

1. The Homeric poems, which mention both Perseus (*Iliad* 14.319–20) and Gorgon-heads, but do not bring the two together, and make no mention of full-bodied Gorgons or Medusa. The *Iliad* gives us a gorgoneion (a full-face Gorgon image) on the shield of Agamemnon: 'and on it had been been placed in a central circle a horrible-faced Gorgon with a terrible look, and around it were Terror and Fear' (11.36–7). It also gives us a Gorgon-head, again apparently an image, on the aegis worn by Athena but said to belong to Zeus (5.741–2). The poem further implies that the Gorgon's eyes were already particularly terrible, in describing Hector's eyes akin to those of a Gorgon (8.348–9). The *Odyssey*, however, seems to have the notion of a terrible disembodied head of an actual Gorgon. When Odysseus finally loses his nerve after calling up the ghosts of the dead, he scuttles off with the observation that 'Pale fear seized me, lest dread Persephone should send the Gorgon-head of a terrible monster from Hades for me' (11.633–5). These poems are the products of long oral tradition, but

according to the current consensus moved towards their final form *ca.* 700–650 BC.[1]

2. Hesiod's *Theogony*, also traditionally dated to the period *ca.* 700–650 BC, in which the Medusa story is fully developed in the form that was to become canonical:

> Ceto bore to Phorcys the beautiful-cheeked Graeae, grey from birth. Both the immortal gods and men who walk on the earth call them Graeae, Pemphredo, fair of dress, and Enyo, yellow of dress. She also bore him the Gorgons who live beyond glorious Ocean at the edge of the world near Night, where the shrill-voiced Hesperides dwell, Sthenno and Euryale and Medusa, who suffered balefully. She was mortal, but the other two were immortal and unaging. But with her alone lay he of the dark hair [i.e. Poseidon] in a soft meadow and amid spring flowers. When Perseus decapitated her, out jumped great Chrysaor and Pegasus the horse. The latter took his name from the fact that he was born beside springs (*pēgai*), but the former from the fact that he held a golden sword in his dear hands.
>
> (Hesiod *Theogony* 270–83)[2]

3. The earliest varieties of gorgoneia in art, found from *ca.* 675 BC (*LIMC* Gorgo nos. 1–79). Early gorgoneia (representations of a gorgon's head) soon evolve into a canonical 'lion mask type', and Corinth may have played a central role in this development. These are full-face images, and they typically have bulging, staring eyes. Their mouths form rictus grins with fangs and tusks projecting up and down, and a lolling tongue protrudes from them. Their hair forms serpentine curls, with actual snakes becoming apparent by the end of the seventh century. And they are often bearded. The direct, frontal stare, seemingly looking out from its own iconographical context and directly challenging the viewer, is a shocking and highly exceptional thing in the context of Greek two-dimensional imagery.[3]

4. The two earliest extant images of Perseus decapitating a Medusa and fleeing from her sisters, *ca.* 675–50 BC. In these images the faces of Medusa and the Gorgons are shown frontally, which in itself strongly identifies them with gorgoneia. In the first, on a Boeotian relief *pithos*, we find Perseus, equipped with wingless

cap, *kibisis* and sword, decapitating Medusa in the form of a female centaur, a fitting lover for Poseidon, patron of horses, and mother to Pegasus (*LIMC* Perseus no. 117 = Fig. 3.1). The fact that Perseus is turning away as he does this tells us that it is already established that to look at her face brings death. In the second, on a Proto-Attic amphora, Perseus flees two striding, wasp-bodied, cauldron-headed Gorgon sisters, leaving behind the strangely rotund decapitated corpse of Medusa, whilst Athena interposes herself to protect him (*LIMC* Perseus no. 151). Perseus' accoutrements as found on the centaur vase first manifest themselves in the extant literary tradition a century or so later, alongside his winged boots, in the Hesiodic *Shield of Heracles*, an ecphrastic poem composed perhaps *ca.* 580–70 BC. Hephaestus has decorated Heracles' shield with a marvellous golden figure of Perseus in flight from the Gorgons that contrives to hover above its surface (216–37). Here we learn that his cap is none other than the Cap of Hades, which brings with it 'the darkness of night'.

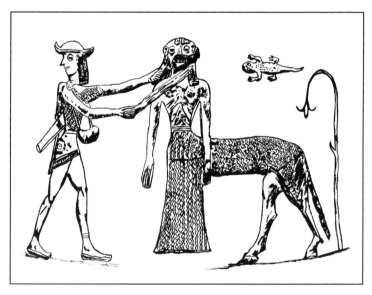

Figure 3.1 Perseus decapitates a centaur-bodied Medusa.

Thereafter, and into the fifth century BC, representations of full-body Gorgons typically give them 'lion-mask' gorgoneion-style faces, and they are often winged.[4]

This pattern of evidence can sustain a number of hypothetical schemes of development. The Medusa tale may have come first and inspired the development of gorgoneia as a spin-off. Gorgoneia may have come first and inspired the development of the Medusa tale as an explanatory back-formation. Or gorgoneia and the Medusa tale may have had separate origins but converged with each other, Medusa's decapitated head becoming identified with bodiless gorgoneia.[5]

If gorgoneia had an origin separate from the Medusa story, then any meaning or mythical context they may have had prior to it is irrecoverable. But we can in any case say something of their function, and function may in fact have been everything. It is clear from the *Iliad* gorgoneion-shield that gives rise to a miasma of Terror or Fear that gorgoneia served as apotropaic shield devices, devices to inflict terror on the enemy. It has been proposed that gorgoneion-shields, with their compelling eyes, may in practical terms have served to distract the closing enemy for a critical split-second. In the archaic age gorgoneia were also deployed in other apotropaic contexts, such as on temple acroteria (pediment plinths) and antefixes (tile-guards), houses, ships, chimneys, ovens and coins, and these gorgoneia, too, are often distinctively round, which may suggest that they are derivative of shield designs.[6]

Beyond this, there are two further complicating issues. The first is whether various groups of terracotta masks, dating from the seventh century BC, have any significant connection with Gorgons or gorgoneia. The most important group derives from Perseus' own Tiryns. These are helmet-like, wearable masks. They do not completely resemble the earliest gorgoneia or full-body Gorgons, but they do share with them bulging round eyes and a wide, open mouth, displaying fangs. They seem partly animalian, but have prominent, strongly humanoid noses. Another group of terracotta masks, these ones not wearable, but made for the purposes of dedication, were given to the Spartan sanctuary of Orthia. These masks, with heavily lined faces, resemble Gorgons or gorgoneia even less. If these masks are related to Gorgons and gorgoneia, then they presumably testify that Gorgons featured in some sort of dramatic or ritual perform-ances in the early archaic period, but of these we can say no more without speculation.[7]

The second complicating issue is whether gorgoneia or the Medusa tale were influenced by Mesopotamian and other Near-Eastern material. Various 'Mistresses of Animals', Lamashtu and Humbaba present cases to answer, at least at the level of icon-ography. On the famous pediment of the temple of Artemis in Corfu of *ca*. 590 BC (*LIMC* Gorgo no. 289) Medusa is depicted with her legs in the distinctive kneeling-running configuration, she has a belt formed from a pair of intertwining snakes (cf. the belts of Stheno and Euryale in the Hesiodic *Shield*, 233–7), and a further pair of snakes project from her neck. She is flanked by her children Pegasus and Chrysaor, the former rearing up, the latter reaching up towards her, and beyond these, on either side, sit magnificent lions. This Medusa bears a striking general resemblance to Near-Eastern 'Mistress of Animals' images and also, more particularly, to Mesopo-tamian images of the child-attacking demoness Lamashtu, who was otherwise brought into Greek culture in her own right as Lamia. Lamashtu can be portrayed as lion-headed, clutching a snake in each hand, with an animal rearing up on either side of her in the Mistress-of-Animals configuration, and riding on an ass (whose function is to carry her away to where she can do no harm). One such image in particular from Carchemish bears a striking resem-blance in its overall arrangement to the Corfu pediment.

In a Perseus scene-type found from *ca*. 550 BC, we find a front-facing, round-headed, grinning-grimacing Medusa, her legs again in the distinctive kneeling-running configuration, flanked by Perseus and Athena, with Perseus decapitating her as he turns his head away (*LIMC* Perseus nos. 113 [= Fig. 3.2], 120–2). This scene-type seem-ingly owes something to Mesopotamian depictions of the very dif-ferent tale of Gilgamesh and Enkidu slaying the wild man Humbaba. In these the hero can turn away to look for a goddess to pass him a weapon. It has been contended that this gesture was misread by Greek viewers to give us Perseus avoiding Medusa's petrifying gaze.

Figure 3.2 Perseus beheads Medusa with her head in the form of an archaic gorgoneion. Hermes attends.

Humbaba's lined and grinning face can also be represented in round terracotta plaques, and these bear a resemblance to the terracotta masks from Sparta mentioned above. If we accept that the connection between the two sets of scenes is more than coincidental, then we are invited to wonder whether the core of the Medusa myth, consisting of her petrifying gaze and her slaughter, originated precisely in the reception and reinterpretation of the oriental vignette.[8]

It is commonly contended that Perseus' name is a speaking one derived from *persas*, the aorist participle of *perthō*, and meaning 'Slayer'. If so, then he might have been invented precisely to be a Gorgon-slayer. But the derivation is highly precarious, and the primary meanings of *perthō* are rather 'sack' and 'plunder'.[9]

THE DEVELOPMENT OF THE QUEST NARRATIVE: AESCHYLUS AND PHERECYDES

By the time Aeschylus wrote his *Phorcides*, the quest narrative surrounding Perseus' decapitation of Medusa was evidently well developed. Perseus had acquired his divine help early. Athena, already associated with a Gorgon-head in the *Iliad*, interposes herself between Perseus and the pursuing Gorgon sisters on one of the earliest images of the hero, the Proto-Attic neck-amphora with the wasp-bodied Gorgons (*LIMC* no. 151, ca. 675–50 BC). She is joined by Hermes in the aftermath of the decapitation on the Gorgon painter *dinos* of ca. 600–590 BC (*LIMC* Gorgo no. 314).[10]

Towards the end of the sixth century BC a pair of vases shows us Perseus visiting a triad of Nymphs and being supplied by them with his winged boots, *petasos*-cap and *kibisis*, with each Nymph bearing one of the gifts (*LIMC* Perseus nos. 87–8). On the second of these they are given the legend 'Neides', i.e. 'Naeads' or 'Water Nymphs'. Pausanias tells that amongst the decorations on the Spartan temple of Athena Chalkioikos, built in ca. 500 BC, was an image of the Nymphs giving Perseus a cap and winged boots only, which may imply that only two Nymphs were shown here (3.17.3).[11]

With Pindar we are able to get a sense of a more rounded quest narrative. He confirms Athena in the role of Perseus' helper, and refers to Perseus either hijacking or throwing away the eye of the Graeae ('he blinded the divine family of Phorcus'). He is also the earliest source to integrate the Gorgon mission into Perseus' family saga by telling us that he used the head against the people of Seriphos (*Pythians* 10.29–48, 12.6–26, of 498 and 490 BC).

Danae and Andromeda were favourite themes for dramatists of all sorts, but the Gorgon episode, surprisingly, seems to have been less favoured. Aeschylus' *Phorcides* (*frs* 261–2 *TrGF*), perhaps written in the 490s or 460s, is the only tragedy we know of to have focused on any aspect of the episode. Perhaps it was neglected by tragedians because it offered little opportunity for tragic conflict. As to other genres of drama, we can point only to a single satyr-play and single comedy. Aristias took second prize in 467 BC with a satyr-play named *Perseus* written by his father Pratinas (Aristias 8 T2 *TrGF*). An Attic lekythos dated to *ca.* 460 shows a satyr running with *kibisis* in one hand and *harpē* in the other (*LIMC* Perseus no. 31). Does this illustrate Aristias' play? In the fourth century Heniochus wrote a Middle Comedy entitled *Gorgons*, but the sole surviving fragment of this play is uninformative (*fr.* 1 *K–A*).[12]

The ancient summaries of the *Phorcides* (*fr.* 262 i–vi *TrGF*) tell that Perseus was sent against Medusa by Polydectes. Hermes supplied Perseus with the Cap of Hades and the winged boots, whilst Hephaestus supplied him with his admantine *harpē*. The Graeae, here just two, served as advanced guards to the Gorgons, to whom they evidently lived adjacently. Perseus watched for the hand-over of the eye between them, snatched it and threw it in the Tritonian lake, and so was able then to approach the Gorgons directly and attack them as they slept. He took off Medusa's head and gave it to Athena for her breast, whilst she put Perseus amongst the stars holding the head. The sole directly quoted phrase to survive from the play, 'Perseus dove into the cave like a wild boar . . .' (*fr.* 261 *TrGF*), seems to have derived from a messenger speech describing Perseus' penetration of the Gorgons' cave to attack Medusa, since we hear elsewhere in the tradition that the Gorgons lived in a cave (Nonnus *Dionysiaca* 25.59, 31.8–25). Hermes would have been very comfortable in the role he plays here, for he provides Perseus with equipment to which he himself has easy access. He flies with a pair of winged boots. He is a frequent visitor to the underworld as the escort of souls, and indeed he had worn the Cap of Hades himself in the battle against the giants (Apollodorus *Bibliotheca* 1.6.). Clearly the Nymphs can have had no role in the drama, since Perseus had no need of them for his equipment.[13]

The Pherecydean version of the Medusa episode returns to the notion that Perseus was armed by the Nymphs rather than by Hermes, but Perseus' visit to the Nymphs is awkwardly thrust between his encounters with the Graeae and their sister Gorgons (*FGH* 3 *fr.* 26 = *fr.* 11, Fowler; see chapter 1 for the text; cf. Apollodorus *Bibliotheca* 2.4.2, Zenobius *Centuriae* 1.41). The purpose of Perseus' meeting with the Graeae is now, in consequence, no longer to disarm the Gorgons' watchdogs, but to find directions to the extraneous Nymphs. Yet Hermes is still very much present as divine helper, and indeed seems to jostle rather awkwardly with Athena in this role, for all that they had been sharing the task for around a century and a half. This is particularly apparent in the directing of Perseus to the Graeae. Pherecydes evidently attempted to combine together a series of established variants in his crowded narrative.

A further indication of this is the fact that the Pherecydean narrative as it stands seems to be preparing Hermes for the role of direct armourer. When Hermes meets Perseus on the island of Seriphos en route to face the Gorgon, and gives him a pep talk, we are reminded of a thematically similar scene in the *Odyssey* (10.277–07). Here the hero Odysseus is en route across the island of Aeaea to accost another dangerous woman with terrible powers, the witch Circe, who transforms men not into stone with her gaze but into animals with a magic potion. Hermes meets him as he goes, gives him the pep talk, and then directly arms him with a special plant, *mōly*, which (it remains unclear) is either to be consumed as an antidote against the potion, or worn as an amulet against Circe's magic more generally.[14]

What of Aeschylus' Hephaestus, who otherwise has no part to play in Perseus' myth cycle? Perhaps Aeschylus accepted from the Nymphs' variant the notion that Perseus should receive three gifts, whilst Hermes had traditionally been giving him just the relevant two. In this case, Hephaestus will have been brought in as a stop-gap to supply a third item. Who worthier to supply Perseus with his famous sickle than the metal-working god himself?

PERSEUS' EQUIPMENT

Perseus acquired his winged boots by *ca.* 600 BC, from which point they are found on vases (*LIMC* Perseus no. 152), and then soon afterwards mentioned in the Hesiodic *Shield* (216–37). In later sources the notion that Perseus got them from Hermes hardened: Lucan (65 AD) is emphatic that Hermes gave Perseus his own boots (9.659–70), and the later second-century AD Artemidorus makes the point even more graphically by asserting that Hermes gave Perseus just one of his boots whilst keeping the other one himself (*Oneirocriticon* 4.63). In making the loan Hermes assimilates Perseus to himself. And indeed in much of his iconography Perseus, as a youthful, beardless hero with winged shoes or winged cap, or both, often strongly resembles Hermes in his, and it can sometimes be difficult to decide whether portrait images are to be assigned to our hero or to his divine patron. Why does Perseus need his winged shoes? Although they enjoy their most dramatic use after the deed when Perseus must fly to safety before the pursuing Gorgons, also on wings, they may also have been needed as the only means of reaching the otherworldly land of the Gorgons in the first place (see below).[15]

The *kibisis*, the bag in which Perseus carries the Gorgon's head once removed, is found already in the *ca.* 675–50 BC centaur-Medusa image (*LIMC* Perseus no. 117 = Fig. 3.1). Mention of it may be found in a papyrus scrap of the *ca.* 600 BC Alcaeus (*fr.* 255 Campbell = Incerti Auctoris *fr.* 30 Voigt), but otherwise it first enters the literary record in the Hesiodic *Shield* (224). Here it is said, in its artistic representation, to be made of silver and fringed with gold. Perseus receives the *kibisis* from the Nymphs in the Pherecydean version of the Gorgon mission, but we are not told whence he obtains it in versions without the Nymphs. In art it most commonly resembles a ladies' shoulder bag (*LIMC* Perseus nos. 29, 48a, 100,

104, 112, 113, 137, 141, 145, 161 [= Fig. 3.3], 170, 171, 192), more occasionally a sort of sash or hammock hanging from Perseus' arm (nos. 31, 159).

The special quality of the *kibisis* was evidently that it was able to serve as a secure toxic container for the head. Not only did the head have to be kept covered, but, in later sources at any rate, it could petrify simply through contact, as in the case of the creation of coral, and it could petrify inanimate material. A magical container was needed, therefore, if it was not itself to turn to stone, and was to hold back the contagion of petrifaction.

Perseus already has the Cap of Hades in the Hesiodic *Shield* (216–37), where it is said to bring 'the darkness of night' as he flees before the Gorgon sisters. Apollodorus later explains, more prosaically, 'With this he himself could see the people he wished, but he could not be seen by others' (*Bibliotheca* 2.4.2). In the Aeschylean version of the myth Perseus receives the cap from Hermes, in the Pherecydean from the Nymphs. Its early associations with darkness

Figure 3.3 Perseus absconds with the head of a fair Medusa in his *kibisis*. Athena attends.

and with Hermes give substance to its underworld origin, but its invisibility function was evidently determined from the first by an obvious pun: *Aïdos kuneē* could be construed equally as 'Cap of Hades' and 'cap of the unseen/invisible', as Hyginus realised (*On astronomy* 2.12). The literary tradition, after the *Shield*, tends to focus on the cap's role in concealing Perseus from the pursuing Gorgon sisters after the deed. But it surely entered Perseus' myth as a device to allow him to approach Medusa without her being able to fix her gaze on him. And as such, it provides us with early evidence for the notion that petrifaction was caused by the Gorgon's gaze, as opposed to by seeing the Gorgon's face. In the iconographic record Perseus sports a dizzying range of headgear, and sometimes none at all. Already on the centaur-Medusa he wears a wingless cap. Subsequently we find him also in a wingless *petasos*, a broad-brimmed hat (from *ca.* 550, e.g. no. 113); with head uncovered (from *ca.* 525, e.g. no. 124); in a winged cap (from ca. 500, e.g. no. 101); in a winged *petasos* (from *ca.* 450, e.g. no. 9); in a winged cap of the elaborate Phrygian style (from *ca.* 400, e.g. no. 69); in a winged griffin helmet (from *ca.* 350, e.g. no. 189); in a wolf-head hat, with or without wings (from *ca.* 350, e.g. no. 95); and in a wingless helmet (from *ca.* 300, e.g. no. 48). Perhaps we are meant to interpret anything Perseus is shown wearing on his head as the Cap of Hades, but the only images that can certainly be taken to represent it are the two in which the Nymphs present him with their gifts (nos. 87–8). In the second of these the Cap of Hades is shown as a wingless *petasos*. For all the prominence of winged headgear in his iconography, Perseus is never explicitly attributed with it in the literary sources. Wings may, perhaps, be an artistic device for conveying the evanescence of the Cap of Hades, but his headgear probably acquired wings initially as a convenient means of conveying the notion that he was wearing winged boots in head-only portraits (of the sort found in, e.g. nos. 16, 9–10, 68). But we do then find full-body portraits in which he nonetheless retains the winged cap, either with (e.g. nos. 91, 171) or without the winged boots (e.g. nos. 7, 8).[16]

In the centaur-Medusa image Perseus uses a sword to decapitate. It is in the art of the late sixth century that we first find him equipped with a *harpē* or sickle (*LIMC* Perseus nos. 114, 124 and 188). The *harpē* first appears in literature in Aeschylus' *Phorcides*, where it is said to be the 'adamantine' gift of Hephaestus. It takes two principal forms in the iconographic tradition. In the earlier images it is a simple short sickle (e.g. *LIMC* Perseus no. 91). In later images, first found in the early fourth century BC, it can become a complex combination of sword and sickle, with both blades sprouting, often somewhat awkwardly and uselessly, from a single stem (e.g. no. 68; cf. the description at Achilles Tatius 3.6–7). The *harpē* is first heard of as an offensive weapon in Cronus' use of one to castrate Uranus (Hesiod *Theogony* 179, etc.), but it soon came to be an instrument associated particularly with the amputation of anguiform monsters: long thin snakes lend themselves to being 'reaped' like a crop. The analogy becomes particularly clear in images of Heracles confronting the Hydra with his *harpē*: its multiple upright snake-necks strongly resemble a crop (*LIMC* Herakles nos. 2003–4, 2012, 2016). Similarly, it was with a *harpē* that Zeus struck down the serpentine Typhon, who had a hundred snake heads, and whose legs consisted of coiling vipers (Apollodorus *Bibliotheca* 1.6.3). And it was with a sickle that Hermes killed the 100-eyed (or 10,000-eyed) Argos, a humanoid monster in the extant tradition, but almost certainly a dragon in origin (Bacchylides 19.15–36, Ovid *Metamorphoses* 1.623–41, 664–88, 714–27, Apollodorus *Bibliotheca* 2.1.2–3). According to Lucan, Hermes used for this the very same sickle he later passed on to Perseus (9.659–70). The imagery of the reaping and harvesting of snakes is explicitly and repeatedly deployed by Nonnus in his references to Perseus' killing of Medusa (*Dionysiaca* 30.277 and 47.608, 'the reaper of Medusa', and, more elaborately, 25.40–4, 31.17–21). Evidently, the sickle remained an appropriate device to use against anguiform monsters even when it was not a question simply of reaping off their snakey bits. Perseus does not give Medusa a haircut, but severs her neck, although we should note that a pair of snakes often grows from Medusa's neck itself in iconography, as on the Corfu pediment (*LIMC* Gorgo no. 289; cf. also Perseus nos. 69, 113). So too Perseus deploys his sickle against the serpentine sea-monster, the *kētos*, but he could hardly have aspired to amputate any (external) part of this massive creature with it (chapter 4).[17]

Perseus' shield was the last item of his canonical equipment to be elaborated by the tradition. In Pherecydes' account Athena and Hermes together hold up a mirror for Perseus as he attacks Medusa, but there is no indication that the mirror is a shield or that it is part of Perseus' own kit. From *ca.* 400 BC we find several pots depicting a moment of calmness after the decapitation in which Perseus uses either a polished shield or a round mirror or a pool of water to enjoy a reflected view of the Gorgon's face (*LIMC* Perseus nos. 66–80). Some of these may suggest that the vignette is to be viewed as an aetiology for Gorgon shield blazons. It is only with Ovid that we find Perseus specifically using his own polished bronze shield to effect the decapitation, though we are not told how he came by it (*Metamorphoses* 4.782–5). Subsequently we learn from Lucan that it was given to him by Athena (9.669–70; cf. Servius on *Aeneid* 6.289). Late Latin sources preserve an interesting twist, of uncertain antiquity. They tell that Athena gave Perseus a shield made of crystal or glass, through which he was able to look, but through which he could not be seen (Vatican Mythographers, First 130 Bode = 2.28 Zorzetti, Second 112 Bode, Scholiast Germanicus *Aratus* 147). The shield is thus partly assimilated to the Cap of Hades. The artists pay little attention to the use of a mirror or shield in the act of decapitation, though mention should be made of a fine second-century AD Roman relief from Hungary in which Athena holds up the shield for Perseus as he beheads a voluptuous Medusa (*LIMC* Perseus no. 132).[18]

WHERE DID THE GORGONS LIVE?

In the *Theogony* the Gorgons live beyond Ocean, the ring of water that surrounded the known world, near Night, i.e. where the sun sets, and where the Hesperides dwell, i.e. in the extreme west. Compatibly, the later sixth-century BC epic *Cypria* located the Gorgons on a rocky island called 'Sarpedon' in Ocean (*fr.* 30.1 West; cf. Pherecydes *FGH* 3 *fr.* 11, Palaephatus *On unbelievable things, FGH* 44 *fr.* 31, *Suda* s.v. *Sarpēdonia aktē*). Had it been turned rocky, like the island of Seriphos, by Medusa's gaze?

Pindar, however, implies that the Gorgons lived adjacently to the Hyperboreans, the mythical people who lived 'Beyond the North', whom Perseus also visited (*Pythians* 10.29–48, of 498 BC; cf. Apollodorus *Bibliotheca* 2.5.11). He explains that their land was not reachable by normal means: 'Neither traveling by ship nor on foot could you find the amazing road to the Hyperborean gathering.' We appreciate the importance of Perseus' winged boots. The pseudo-Aeschylean *Prometheus Bound* locates Graeae and Gorgons alike on the fantastical 'plains of Cisthene' and makes them neighbours of the marvellous Arimaspians (790–809; cf. Cratinus *Seriphians fr.* 309 *K-A*). Herodotus makes the Arimaspians in turn neighbours of the Hyperboreans and tells us that they are one-eyed, which makes them highly suitable neighbours for the Graeae. He also tells us that they were visited, exceptionally, by the flying soul of Aristeas of Proconnesus, which evokes the means Perseus used to arrive in this impossible area (4.13). But the *Prometheus Bound* also contrives to locate Gorgons and Graeae in the far east and the far south too: they live beyond the eastern bound of Ocean, whilst the neighbouring Arimaspians are linked with the 'black' Ethiopians. The neglect of the one point of the compass, the west, in which Hesiod had placed them, is ostentatious, but such directional confusion serves well further to convey the otherworldly location of the Gorgons' home.[19]

But it was specifically Libya, i.e. northwest Africa, that was to become the Gorgons' canonical home (e.g. Herodotus 2.91). Pausanias tells us that the *ca.* 500 BC bronze reliefs on the Spartan temple of Athena Chalkioikos showed Perseus setting out for Libya, although it is hard to imagine how the destination was indicated (3.17.3). However, Libya was certainly the home of the Graeae, and presumably therefore too the Gorgons, in Aeschylus' *Phorcides*, since Perseus threw the eye of the Graeae into Libya's Tritonian lake.[20]

In due course, as the Libyan location of the Gorgons became established, it gave rise to two ancillary tales firmly grounded in the region. The first is the tale of Perseus' petrifaction of Atlas, who then gave his name to the mountain range in modern Morocco. Atlas had been associated with the Hesperides since Hesiod's *Theogony* (517–18). Our earliest trace, probably, of Perseus' encounter with him is the image on a Attic vase of *ca.* 450 BC, in which we seem to have a surprised Atlas watching Perseus decapitate Medusa (*LIMC* Atlas no. 20). If the scene is correctly construed, this is in fact the only ancient image in which Perseus and Atlas are found together. Our earliest literary trace of the encounter is found in the sole fragment to survive of the dithyrambic poet Polyidus, whose floruit was *ca.* 398 BC (Polyidus *fr.* 837 *PMG*/Campbell). He told that Atlas was merely a shepherd petrified by Perseus because he would not accept his identity. The mountain took its name from him, but evidently it was not created in its entirety by the act of petrifaction in this version. We thank Ovid for our most detailed account of the episode (*Metamorphoses* 4.621–62; cf. also Second Vatican Mythographer 114 Bode). Here the giant Atlas is king of the extreme western edge of the world, and Perseus comes to him looking for shelter and rest, declaring himself to be a son of Zeus. Atlas fears that he may be the son of Zeus, Heracles, that is destined to steal his golden apples. These, the apples of the Hesperides, he has enclosed in an orchard guarded by a huge dragon-snake (*drakōn*). When he tries to drive Perseus off with violence, he is shown the Gorgon-head. This time the mountain in its entirety does indeed derive from the suitably vast victim: Atlas' head becomes the peak, his shoulders ridges, his hair woods.[21]

The second is the tale that drops of blood fell from Medusa's head as Perseus flew away with it, and upon falling to the earth below gave rise to the terrible snakes of Libya. The tale is first found in Apollonius (*Argonautica* 4.1513–17), but it is developed with particular relish by Lucan, who prefaces an extended treatment of these snakes with an account of their genesis (9.619–99). We then learn what they can do. When Aulus is bitten by the parching dipsad, he attempts to drink the sea dry, and in despair opens his veins so as to be able to drink his own blood (9.737–60). When Sabellus is bitten by a tiny seps, his body dissolves into the ground (9.762–88). A jaculus shoots straight through Paulus' temples and out the other side (9.822–7). When Murrus drives his spear into a basilisk, its poison shoots straight up the shaft and into his arm, and he has to lop off the arm at the shoulder with his other hand to stop the galloping mortification (9.828–39).

The great heroes of Greek myth are often attributed with a *katabasis*, a descent to the underworld from which they return in triumph: so it is with Heracles, Theseus and Odysseus. Perseus is not explicitly associated with any such a *katabasis*, but some have read the Gorgon mission as one. The case is not strong, but might best be argued in the following terms. The Gorgons' extreme western location near the realm of Night in the *Theogony* (274–5) evokes the location of Odysseus' necromancy-*katabasis* (Homer *Odyssey* 11.12–23). A series of indications, beginning with the *Odyssey*'s reference to Persephone sending up the Gorgon-head, might be taken to associate Medusa loosely with the underworld (see also Euripides *Ion* 989, 1053–4, Apollodorus *Bibliotheca* 2.5.12). Wilk has recently contended that the main features of the 'lion-mask' gorgoneion are typical of a corpse bloated after a few days' putrefaction. In such circumstances the eyes bulge, the tongue protrudes, the lips draw back and the hair separates from the scalp in supposedly snake-like curls. The Gorgon is thus rendered a simple emblem of death, and Perseus' slaughter of Medusa a triumph over death.[22]

Underworlds have been found in other parts of the Perseus cycle too. Some have thought that Seriphos, with its lord Polydectes, 'Receiver of many', should be seen as one. But the name is more plausibly read as 'Receiver of much', and to refer to the contribution feast by which he compels Perseus to the Gorgon mission. It has also been contended that being swallowed by a whale or a sea-monster, as Perseus is in one version of the Andromeda tale, should be considered as akin to an underworld journey, but the case is a desperately tenuous one.[23]

GORGON WEAPONRY

No victims of the living Medusa or the other Gorgons are ever named, but if all variants are taken into account, the tally of victims Perseus petrified with her decapitated head is extensive: Atlas (Polyidus *fr.* 837 *PMG*/Campbell, etc.); Phineus (Ovid *Metamorphoses* 5.1–235, etc.); the *kētos* (Antiphilus at *Greek Anthology* 16.147, etc.); seaweed, to make coral (Ovid *Metamorphoses* 4.735–52, etc.); Polydectes and the Seriphians (Pindar *Pythians* 10.46–8, 12.6–26, etc.) and indeed the island itself (Eustathius on Dionysius Periegetes 525); Acrisius (Lactantius Placidus *Commentary on Statius'* Thebaid 1.25.5, First Vatican Mythographer 137 Bode = 2.55 Zorzetti, Second 110 Bode); Cepheus (Hyginus *Fabulae* 64), Ariadne (Nonnus *Dionysiaca* 47.664–74) . . . and even himself (Malalas p. 39 Dindorf). How does the head do its work of petrifaction? Does the victim have to look at the Gorgon, or does the Gorgon have to look at the victim? The ancient tradition at first was not able to decide, but in due course, it seems, positively chose not to do so. One might seek to resolve this conundrum by hypothesising that petrifaction occurs when eyes of Gorgon and victim meet, when each gazes at the other, but such a hypothesis will hardly satisfy all the literary cases, e.g. that of the creation of coral.[24]

Perseus' success depends upon his somehow being able to break the line gaze between himself and the Gorgon (whichever direction is significant), and the canonical accounts offer us no less than four different explanations as to how he was able to do this. (1.) Perseus beheaded her whilst turning his head away so that he could not look at her (first in the centaur-Medusa image). (2.) Perseus wore a cap of invisibility so that Medusa could not look at him as he tried to kill her (first in the Hesiodic *Shield*). (3.) Perseus attacked Medusa whilst she was asleep, so that she could not look at him (first in Aeschylus' *Phorcides*). (4.) Perseus attacked Medusa using a mirror or reflecting shield, so that he did not look directly at her (first in Pherecydes).[25] Methods (1) and (4) assume that petrifaction occurs when a person looks at the Gorgon. Methods (2) and (3) assume that it occurs when the Gorgon looks at a person. For the remainder of the ancient tradition it was the former analysis that remained, by a shade, the more popular. It becomes pivotal in Malalas' account of Perseus' self-petrifaction, where the head signally fails to petrify Cepheus because of his blindness.

Lucan gives contradictory indications about the mechanism of petrifaction. On the one hand, he is emphatic that it is looking at the Gorgons that petrifies (9.636–41, 652–3). Indeed, it is for this reason that Athena advises Perseus to fly backwards over Africa towards the home of the Gorgons, to avoid accidentally catching sight of them

(9.666–8), and gives him the shiny bronze shield with which to find Medusa (9.669–70). On the other, Lucan asserts that the living Medusa had the power to draw stone over even inanimate things, such as land and sea, which implies that the power lies rather in her gaze (9.646–7). He notes too (following Ovid) that she can petrify animals, even specifying that she can drop birds out of the sky (9.649–53). But this observation may serve poetic wit more than natural history. For he makes the nice point that even Medusa's snakes themselves must avoid looking her in the face or be petrified. And for this reason those above her forehead are 'back-combed' into a hairstyle that would have been strikingly fashionable for the good Roman matrons of Lucan's day: 'They would lash Medusa's neck and she was delighted by this. In the fashion of female coiffure, the snakes hung loose over her back, but rose up straight over her fore-head. Viperous poison flowed when she combed her hair' (9.633–9, 652–3). Lucan takes the conceit that Medusa's snakes have their own separate identity and consciousness further, when he represents them as standing alert and on guard as she herself sleeps (9.671–4).

A more complex handling of the ambiguity is found in Lucian's ecphrastic description of Perseus' battle against the sea-monster in *The Hall*: 'That part of the *kētos* that had seen Medusa is already stone, but the part that remains alive is being hacked at with the sickle (*harpē*)' (22; see chapter 4). Here the fact that the *kētos* is only petrified in part in itself suggests that the effect is caused by the beam of the Gorgon's gaze. On the other hand, Lucian speaks – quite illogically – of the petrified parts of the body themselves 'seeing' the Gorgon.

As a monster with terrible glance, Medusa is appropriately ador-ned with snakes. Terrible serpents, whether large snakes or mythical dragons, were known by the term *drakōn*, which is usually regarded as cognate with *derkomai*, 'look.' The rich snake lore of antiquity includes the knowledge that Ethiopian snakes could flash fire from their eyes like lightning (Diodorus 3.36–7) and that basilisks could kill a man with a glance alone (Pliny *Natural History* 29.66). And indeed snakes could themselves be said to have the look of the Gorgon (Euripides *Heracles* 1266).[26]

How does the actual process of petrifaction run, once initiated?

One might have expected it to begin from the victim's eyes or face, but the Greeks initially seem to have conceptualised the process rather as beginning from the ground. Two mid-fifth-century BC images of the petrifaction of Polydectes show him becoming encased in rough rock from the feet upwards (*LIMC* Polydectes nos. 7–8). The second-century BC Lycophronian *Alexandra* also understands the petrifaction process to begin from the ground, and to consist of an encasing in stone, but it sees the process as a more subtle one that produces not a mere boulder but an actual statue in which the original living detail is preserved (834–46; cf. Tzetzes on 844). The notion that the Gorgon-head should transform men into statues is taken up vigorously by Ovid. His Gorgons' lair is decorated with statues of men and beasts, their former victims (*Metamorphoses* 4.780–91). The conceit of statue-making pervades his elaborate account of the battle between Perseus and Phineus (5.117–235), and Perseus finally jokes that he will turn Phineus into a monument for Cepheus to keep. The account of the transformation suggests that Ovid sees the process as one of a gradual and uniform freezing into stone, and there is no indication that it begins from the ground (5.224–35). At the end of antiquity Nonnus follows a similar line: in battling against Dionysus his Perseus is urged to 'Change the mortal faces of the Bassarids with the eye of the Gorgon into images spontaneously. Decorate your streets with copied stone beauty, making finely wrought statues for Inachian [i.e. Argive] marketplaces' (*Dionysiaca* 47.560–3).[27]

Nonnus alone offers a form of defence against the Gorgon's power. It is a diamond amulet that Dionysus lifts before his face as Perseus brandishes Medusa's head (*Dionysiaca* 47.590–606). As often, Nonnus here points up a parallelism between Dionysus and Perseus (see chapter 2): Dionysus' amulet is born 'in the rain of Zeus', just as Perseus himself had been born in Zeus' golden rain. No wonder, then, that Perseus himself had been able to withstand the living Gorgon.

What of the weaponry of the other Gorgons, the immortal Stheno and Euryale? Their only role in the myth is to pursue Perseus after the deed, and their names equip them well for it. 'Stheno' signifies 'Strength', whilst 'Euryale' signifies 'Wide Jump', a name particularly appropriate to the kneeling-running posture in which the Gorgons were commonly portrayed in the archaic period (e.g. *LIMC* Perseus no. 154). Our sources seldom specify whether they too had the power to petrify, but the Aeschylean *Prometheus Bound* first suggests so in stating of all the Gorgons that 'no man that has seen them will continue to draw breath' (800). Such might also be implied by the fact that Perseus flees Stheno and Euryale wearing his cap of invisibility ([Hesiod] *Shield* 226–7, etc.), but then it is curious that in the pursuit scenes of art Perseus is often depicted as seemingly looking back into the eyes of the pursuing sisters. And, for what it is worth, the pursuing Gorgons, too, have their snakes (e.g. [Hesiod] *Shield* 233; *LIMC* Perseus no. 151).[28]

There are indications that the two sisters, perhaps Euryale in particular, possessed a terrible weapon in their voices, a sort of aural equivalent to Medusa's gaze, and this makes sense in view of the terrible open mouths and lolling tongues of the archaic gorgoneia. In the Hesiodic *Shield* the pursuing Gorgon sisters not only give out wild stares but, for all that a supposedly still and silent image is being described, gnash their teeth and create 'a great ringing, sharp and shrill' as they fly (231–5). Apollodorus' description of the Gorgons as heavily metallic creatures, with golden wings and bronze hands, may explain the latter sound (*Bibliotheca* 2.4.2). Pindar speaks of 'the destructive lamentation' of the pursuing sisters, after hearing which Athena 'made a tune for *auloi* [double oboes] that consisted of all sounds, so that she might imitate with her tools the noisy grief emanating from the swift jaws of Euryale' (*Pythian* 12.6–26; cf. Tzetzes on [Lycophron] *Alexandra* 838). In his undateable *Perseis* epic Ctesias of Ephesus told that Mycenae was founded on the hill upon which the pursuing Gorgons finally came to rest after giving up their pursuit of Perseus as in vain. It was named *Mukēnai* after the bellow (*mukēma*) that the Gorgons gave forth there because of their misery ([Plutarch] *On rivers* 18.6). And Nonnus' Athena challenges Dionysus with the words, 'Did you face the competition that Perseus did? Did you see the stone-transforming eye of Stheno or the invincible bellowing throat of Euryale herself?' (*Dionysiaca* 30.264–7; cf. 25.58, 'Euryale's bellow'). However, the frequently advanced notion that *Gorgōn* originally signified 'howl', on the basis of its supposed connections with Greek *gargaris*, Latin *garrio* and Sanskrit *garğ*, is erroneous, and not even countenanced in the technical linguistic literature.[29]

THE CORRUPTION AND PUNISHMENT OF MEDUSA

For Pindar, writing in 490 BC, Medusa's face was no longer monstrous but beautiful: 'the head of the fair-cheeked Medusa' (*Pythians* 12.6–26). From this point, too, the Gorgons of Perseus scenes in art are often represented essentially as beautiful young women, and no longer shown in ugly full-face. By the fourth century this has become the normal mode of their representation. It is unclear whether detached gorgoneia began to acquire beautiful faces from as early as the mid-fifth century, or only in the early Hellenistic period. All depends on the disputed date of the 'Medusa Rondanini' (*LIMC* Gorgones Romanae no. 25).[30]

It is implicit in the *Theogony* and the bulk of the literary tradition that the Gorgons were born monstrous from the first. However, a back-story, which curiously left Stheno and Euryale out of account, was developed to explain how Medusa alone was transformed into a monster from an initial state of beauty. It is found first in Ovid (*Metamorphoses* 4.794–803, 6.119–20). Medusa had been a normal girl with beautiful hair. Her locks had attracted the attention of Poseidon, who, in the form of a bird, had seduced or raped her in a temple of Athena. The goddess punished the girl for the violation of her temple by turning her hair to snakes. That the patron god of horses should have raped Medusa in the form of a bird sufficiently accounts for the winged horse Pegasus as fruit of the union. This back-story is obviously congruent with the tradition of the 'beautiful Medusa' in art and it is possible that it was merely developed in the Hellenistic period or even by Ovid in response to it. But it seems to borrow the motif of the violation of Athena's temple from the Auge–Telephus myth (discussed in chapter 2).

A later Latin source, Servius' commentary on the *Aeneid*, also associates Medusa's transformation from beautiful woman with her affair with Poseidon and the anger of Athena, but the logic is different. Medusa, buoyed up by the admiration of Poseidon, boasts that her hair is fairer than that of Athena. Outraged by this, the goddess turns her hair into snakes (on 6.289; cf. Second Vatican Mythographer 112 Bode, Tzetzes on [Lycophron] *Alexandra* 838). This variant even more strikingly recalls another established episode in Perseus' story: Cassiepeia's boast that she herself was more beautiful than the Nereids, which brings the Nereids' anger down upon her, with the result that they ask Poseidon, in the opposite role, to punish her. The two punishments share a serpentine aspect.

THE FEMALE GROUPS: GORGONS, GRAEAE, NYMPHS, HESPERIDES AND NEREIDS

Strong thematic similarities obtain between the groups of female powers encountered in turn by Perseus in the course of his Gorgon mission. They all appear, on occasion, in triad form, and they may all be seen as offering a terrible threat, typically of a serpentine nature.

The Graeae, whose name signifies 'old women', first appear in Hesiod's *Theogony*, where they are two. They are not described as monstrous, but as 'beautiful-cheeked' and 'grey from birth', which seemingly implies that they were whole and otherwise youthful girls. We might even imagine them as blonde. In Aeschylus' *Phorcides*, perhaps of the 490s or 460s, where they are two again, they seem to have achieved their canonical form of old women sharing a single tooth and eye. In the Pherecydean account of *ca*. 456 BC they exhibit the same form, but have become three. The mid-fifth-century *Prometheus Bound*, which may or may not have been written by Aeschylus, perhaps melds all these traditions and gives us more in describing the Graeae as 'long-lived girls, three, *swan-shaped*, with a common eye and a single tooth' (794–6). Representations of the Graeae in ancient art are few, no more than six, all on vases made between *ca*. 460 BC and the Hellenistic period. We find no swans here, just disappointingly ordinary women, their blindness vestigially indicated by closed eyes.[31]

The Graeae are certainly a curious type of monster, but they are not unique in Greek myth. We hear also of Lamia (mentioned above), a beautiful Libyan woman loved by Zeus and so punished by Hera. Hera killed Lamia's children, the shock of which transformed Lamia herself into a child killer. Hera also turned her into a beast and deprived her of the ability to sleep. Zeus then mitigated this punishment by giving her the power to remove her eyes and keep them in a cup while she rested. According to Dio Chrysostom, the beast into which she was turned was serpentine. She remained a beautiful woman down to the waist, but became a serpent below, her nether part culminating in a serpent head. The Libyan context, the beautiful mortal woman punished by a goddess for her seduction by Zeus with a serpentine disfiguration, and the removable eyes all have a resonance for the Gorgon–Graeae myth (Heraclitus *De Incredibilibus* 34, Dio Chrysostom *Oration* 5, Scholiast Aristophanes *Peace* 758).[32]

The Graeae possessed speaking names of some interest. The first two (from Hesiod) were Pemphredo, 'Wasp' (cf. *pemphrēdōn*) and Enyo, 'War'. The former puts us in mind of the wasp-like bodies of the Gorgons in one of their earliest depictions (*LIMC* Perseus no. 151). The name of the third was unstable. Apollodorus offers Deino, 'Terror', another highly appropriate name for the sister of a Gorgon (*Bibliotheca* 2.4.2; the corresponding fragment of Pherecydes, *FGH* 3 *fr.* 26 = *fr.* 11, Fowler, offers instead Iaino, 'Healer', probably a corrupt reading). On a fragmentary Hellenistic bowl we find the third Graea named Perso (*LIMC* Graiai no. 4; cf. Heraclitus *De Incredibilibus* 13, where 'Perso' may be an interpolation), then in Hyginus Persis (*Fabulae* preface 9, *On astronomy* 2.12). Less striking than the significance of these names, 'Destruction', appropriately, is their similarity to that of our hero himself, of which more anon.[33]

The three Gorgons and the Graeae, also eventually three, were all alike daughters of Phorcys and Ceto, and therefore full sisters of each other. Both groups of sisters offered threats based upon vision and biting. The Gorgons were not only fringed with biting snakes, but also often displayed a full range of jagged teeth and indeed tusks in their grimacing mouths. Admittedly, it is hard to imagine how the

Gorgons or their snakes ever got close enough to a victim to bite him before petrifaction. The latent threat of the Graeae, we presume, is that they will bite their victim with their tooth, once identified with their watchful eye. We may imagine that such a bite was rather more deadly than that offered by the single crumbling molar of an ordinary old lady, and bear in mind again the affinities of the Graeae with the child-devouring Lamia. Both groups had to be outwitted by Perseus, and in both cases he took something away from them, a head and an eye. It is hardly surprising then that Palaephatus and the rationalising tradition after him should radically (re-)conflate the two groups (Palaephatus *On unbelievable things*, *FGH* 44 *fr.* 31, Servius on Virgil *Aeneid* 6.289; Vatican Mythographers, First 130 Bode = 2.28 Zorzetti, Second 112 Bode, Third 14.1 Bode, Scholiast Germanicus *Aratea* 82, 147 Bresyig).

We remain underinformed about the Nymphs or Naeads episode in the Medusa tale. In extant art they are three, but, as we have seen, they may also, like the Graeae, have been conceptualised as a pair. The vases portray them as beautiful young women and we hear of no monstrous features. Nor are we told that Perseus had somehow to get the better of them to secure their gifts. Even so, we may hypothesise that they possessed a sinister edge. If we look across to the Jason cycle, which has much in common with Perseus', as we shall see, we note that Jason's Argonaut Hylas encounters beautiful Naead-Nymphs whilst drawing water. They fall in love with him, and drag him into their spring to be with them for ever. Theocritus tells that these Nymphs were three in number, and names them as Eunica, Malis and Nycheia (Theocritus *Idylls* 13; cf. Apollonius *Argonautica* 1207–39).

Another group of female powers inhabits the fringe of the Medusa tale: the Hesperides. This group, too, seems to have exhibited some instability in number: Apollonius gives us three and names them as Hespere, Erytheis and Aigle (*Argonautica* 4.1396–1449), but Apollodorus gives us four (*Bibliotheca* 2.5.11). Hesiod already associates the Hesperides with the Gorgons and Graeae in telling us that these two groups live 'beyond glorious Ocean at the edge of the world near Night, where the shrill-voiced Hesperides dwell' (*Theogony* 275). The rationalising Heraclitus goes so far as to identify the Hesperides with the Graeae (*De Incredibilibus* 13, perhaps an interpolation). In the literary sources the Hesperides never directly enter the action of the Medusa story, and the closest connection they have with Perseus is through their brother Atlas, who guarded their apples (Tzetzes on [Lycophron] *Alexandra* 879). However, we seem to find Perseus pictured with the Hesperides, their tree and their apples on a fourth-century red-figure vase (*LIMC* Hesperides no. 62). In art the Hesperides are always humanoid, but their monstrous affinities with the Gorgons and the Graeae become apparent in the dragon-snake, named Ladon, whom they kept to guard their golden apples, and who, like the Gorgons and the Graeae, was a child of Ceto and Phorcys (Hesiod *Theogony* 333–6, Apollonius *Argonautica* 4.1396–8, Ovid *Metamorphoses* 4.647). He can be found winding around the Hesperides' tree on the red-figure vase. That the Hesperides could also be thought of as possessing a more internalised monstrous aspect may be suggested by the fact that Epimenides identified them with the Harpies (*FGH* 457 *fr.* 6b).[34]

If we go further afield in the Perseus cycle, we find other comparanda again. The Nereids or 'Sea Nymphs' that Cassiepeia offended with her boasts constitute another group of female powers. Perseus does not encounter them directly, although he does have to deal with the – serpentine – *kētos* that Poseidon sent against Cepheus' land on their behalf (Apollodorus *Bibliotheca* 2.4.3, etc.; chapter 4). The Nereids are never numbered for us, but Lucian devotes a dialogue to them in which two appear, named Iphianassa and Doris (*Dialogues in the Sea* 14).[35]

These congruences may simply be a natural consequence of the long gestation and elaboration of the Perseus saga: such a process might invite the replication of motifs and assimilation between episodes. But they may in some cases provide clues to the presence of a distinctive folktale lurking in the prehistory of Perseus' saga, as we shall see in the next chapter.

Perseus is curiously linked by name with the female protagonists of his two principal adventures. In Hellenistic poetry at least Perseus himself is said to have borne the by-name *Eurymedōn*, 'Wide Ruler' (Apollonius *Argonautica* 4.1513, Euphorion *fr.* 18 Powell = *Supp. Hell.*

fr. 418). The *med*-element, which signifies 'Ruler', is found also in *Med-ousa* 'Female Ruler' and *Andro-med-a*, 'Man Ruler'. Similarly, his more familiar name strangely coincides with the variant names of the third Graea, Perso or Persis, as we have seen.[36]

ATHENA, PERSEUS, BELLEROPHON AND THE DRAGONS

There is a basic parallelism also between Perseus' two monster fights. Both Gorgons and sea-monster or *kētos* are anguiform or snake-formed creatures, against whom Perseus appropriately uses his sickle (see chapter 4 for more on the serpentine nature of the *kētos*). Already in the *Theogony* the Gorgons are the children of Ceto (i.e. *Kētō*) whose name simply means 'Sea-Monster' and who seems to have been represented as one in art. Indeed Pliny ostensibly makes a full identification between Andromeda's *kētos* and the mother of the Gorgons by applying the proper name 'Ceto' to it (*Natural History* 5.69). The general affinity between *kētē* (this is the plural form) and Gorgons was also sensed by artists at an early stage. Of three sixth-century images we find, in the first, a gorgoneion with a *kētos* on its forehead (*LIMC* Ketos no. 12), in the second, a headless Gorgon whose arms consist of a pair of *kētē* (no. 19) and, in the third, the upper body of a Gorgon mounted on the neck of a *kētos* (*LIMC* Gorgo no. 350).[37]

The first individual with whom the Gorgon-head is associated in Greek myth is not Perseus, but the goddess Athena herself, who already wears it in battle in the *Iliad* (5.741–2). A less widespread tradition contrived to exclude Perseus completely from Athena's acquisition of the head. Euripides' *Ion*, written shortly before 412 BC, seems to speak of Athena having had a one-to-one combat with a single Gorgon monster born directly from the Earth, whose skin she then took to wear on her breast as the aegis (987–96). Later on Hyginus could cite Euhemerus for the notion that the Gorgon was killed directly by Athena (Hyginus *De astronomia* 2.12). At any rate, this parallel tradition serves to explain why Athena should be seen as Perseus' firm companion on his mission against Medusa.

Closely akin to this tale is that in which Athena took on and killed another dragon-like, fire-breathing, earthborn monster actually called 'Aegis', and that too in Libya, although the creature had originated in Phrygia Catacecaumene, where it had 'burned up' the land. We know of it only from Diodorus' recycling (3.70.3–6) of the work of the second-century BC Dionysius Scytobrachion (*FGH* 32 *fr.* 8). We are not given a physical description of this monster, but its name (*Aigis*) implies that it bears some resemblance to a goat (*aix*), and its fire-breathing suggests that it contains a serpentine element, the ancients conceiving of snake-venom as distinctively fiery. As such, the Aegis seems to have borne a strong resemblance to the Lycian Chimaera killed by Bellerophon with Pegasus (Hesiod *Theogony* 319–25). It is described by the *Iliad* as a fire-breathing monster, a lion in front, a dragon-snake in the rear, and in the middle a goat or *chimaira* (6.179–83). In art the Chimaera is almost always represented as a lion with a a goat's head growing up from the centre of its back and with its tail ending in a snake's head (*LIMC* Chimaira, Chimaira [in Etruria] *passim*, Pegasos nos. 152–235).[38]

And Bellerophon brings us full-circle back to the Perseus cycle, both directly and indirectly. First, it was Bellerophon that benefited from Perseus' midwifery of Pegasus. It was he who, with Athena's help, tamed Pegasus and used him in his battle against the Chimaera (Pindar *Olympian* 13.63–6 and 84–90; cf. *Isthmian* 7.44–7). Secondly, Bellerophon's troubles and his own series of labours started when he became embroiled with Perseus' great uncle, Acrisius' brother Proetus, and his wife Anteia or Sthenoboea. When the young Bellerophon was staying with Proetus and Sthenoboea as a guestfriend, Sthenoboea fell in love with him. Her advances spurned, she lied to Proetus that Bellerophon had attempted to force her, whereupon Proetus sent him on to Iobates, king of Lycia, to be killed, since he himself did not want to be guilty of killing a guestfriend. Iobates attempted to accomplish the deed by sending Bellerophon against three terrible foes, including the Chimaera (Homer *Iliad* 6.152–202; Euripides *Sthenoboea* T iia Hypothesis *TrGF*). Of course it is an oddity of this story that Bellerophon should be associated with Proetus and Sthenoboea, co-evals of Acrisius, and yet have access to Pegasus, who was only created by the latter's grandson Perseus.[39]

In the central vignette of Bellerophon's battle against the

Chimaera he attacks the creature from above astride the airborne winged horse Pegasus. This was a popular scene in art, and is found already from the early seventh century (*LIMC* Bellerophon no. 152 etc.). It was popular in literature too: 'And look at this man sitting on a winged horse: he slays the fire-breathing three-bodied force' (Euripides *Ion* 201–4; cf. *Stheneboea fr.* 665a *TrGF*; Hyginus *Fabulae* 57). Tzetzes supplies the most detail: 'Riding on Pegasus he slew the Chimaera by coating his spear with lead and throwing it into her fire-breathing mouth. The lead was melted by this fire and killed her' (on [Lycophron] *Alexandra* 17). This vignette is strongly evocative of the fashion in which Perseus attacks the *kētos* from above, airborne with his winged boots (see chapter 4).

It is hardly surprising that a certain parallelism was detected between Perseus and Bellerophon in antiquity. Pausanias tells us that the deed of Bellerophon against the Chimaera was paired with that of his fellow Argive hero Perseus against the Gorgon in the decorations on Thraysmedes' throne of Asclepius at Epidaurus (2.27.2, *ca.* 375 BC). A pair of anomalous mid-fifth-century BC terracotta plaques from Melos shows Perseus riding a horse whilst lifting Medusa's severed head from her falling body as, in one plaque, a tiny Chrysaor springs out of her neck (*LIMC* Gorgo no. 310a, Perseus no. 166b). Wingless and fully grown though it be, the horse can only be Pegasus, and so Perseus is here strongly identified with Bellerophon. This becomes particularly clear when we compare another Melian plaque from the same period in which a very similar figure, again on a wingless horse, jabs his sword at the Chimaera below, occupying Medusa's position on the other plaque (*LIMC* Pegasos no. 160). Eventually the two heroes became confused to such an extent that the First Vatican Mythographer could devote a chapter of his mythological handbook to 'Bellerophon also known as Perseus' (71 Bode = 1.70 Zorzetti) and tell us that Perseus was sent against 'the Chimaera, the Gorgon and Medusa' (137 Bode = 2.55 Zorzetti).

PERSEUS AND JASON: QUEST NARRATIVES AND MYTHS OF MATURATION

There is a striking affinity between Perseus' quest narrative and that of Jason and his voyage with the Argo to fetch the golden fleece (Pindar *Pythian* 4, Apollonius *Argonautica*, with scholia, Diodorus 4.40–9, Ovid *Metamorphoses* 7.1–349, Valerius Flaccus *Argonautica*, Apollodorus *Bibliotheca* 1.9.16–28, Zenobius *Centuriae* 4.92, Hyginus *Fabulae* 12–23, *Orphic Argonautica*, Tzetzes on [Lycophron] *Alexandra* 175). The opening episode of Jason's story intriguingly maps onto both Acrisius' plight and Polydectes' trick. Pelias is the wicked king of Iolcus and half-brother to Jason's father Aeson, as Polydectes is half-brother to Perseus' adoptive father Dictys. He is warned by an oracle that he will be killed by a man with one shoe, the condition in which he encounters Jason, who has lost a shoe in crossing the river Anaurus. Pelias asks him what he would do if an oracle had foretold that someone was likely to kill him, and Jason replies that he would tell the person to fetch the golden fleece, the mission that Pelias then duly imposes upon him.

And so, like Perseus, Jason too is dispatched to the edge of the world, in his case in an easterly direction, to Colchis, to retrieve an impossible object. Like Perseus, Jason has divine help, from Athena, again, and also from Hera and Aphrodite. Like Perseus, he is aided by magical equipment, in this case his talking ship, the Argo, and the ointment of invincibility provided for him by Medea. Like Perseus' quest, Jason's is one of subordinate stages as he works his way towards his goal. These stages include encounters with a kaleidoscopic correspondence with Perseus'. As Perseus takes directions from the blind Graeae, so Jason takes directions from the blind seer Phineus (Odysseus too in his quest to reach home takes directions from another blind seer, Tiresias: Homer *Odyssey* 11.90–149). Phineus' name forges another sort of link with the Perseus cycle, the significance of which remains obscure.

Like Perseus, Jason and his Argonauts encounter groups of dangerous females. First, there is the community of murderous Lemnian women, who kill their partners after sleeping with them. Secondly, there are the three water-nymphs who snatch away the Argonaut

Hylas. Thirdly, there are the two Harpies, winged like the Gorgons, who snatch away or befoul Phineus' food, and who are then chased off by the Argonautic pair, the winged Boreads, in an inversion of the pursuit of the Perseus by the two surviving Gorgons. In Apollonius' version, further encounters with dangerous females are introduced on the model of the *Odyssey*: the witch Circe, the Sirens, and Scylla and Charybdis.

At the culmination of his quest Jason must do battle with a serpentine monster of his own, the unsleeping dragon-snake that guards the golden fleece, a monster therefore with affinities both to the Gorgons and to the *kētos*, but which in its gold-guarding role most closely resembles Ladon, the dragon-snake kept by the Hesperides to guard their golden apples. A famous vase painted by Douris in *ca*. 480 BC shows Jason being swallowed backwards by a magnificently drawn dragon, which suggests that in one version he may have attacked the creature from within, as the *Alexandra*'s Perseus does Andromeda's sea-monster (*LIMC* Iason no. 32; cf. nos. 33–5). Indeed, like Perseus, Jason must also do battle with multiple dragon-related foes. He must deal also with the Spartoi, an army of men grown from the teeth of the Cadmean dragon-snake, and the terrible bulls that breathe fire in dragon-like fashion. Like Perseus, Jason acquires his bride, Medea, in the course of his adventures. Like Perseus, Jason secures the object he has been sent to retrieve, and returns with it to kill Pelias, with the help of Medea, an outcome reflecting Perseus' killing of both Polydectes and Acrisius. And also like Perseus in the Apollodoran account (*Bibliotheca* 2.4.4), Jason fails to take up the kingship of Iolcus, according to some, going into exile for the killing of Pelias.[40]

The broad comparability between these two quest narratives suggests that, despite the superficially episodic nature of both, they exhibited a fundamental coherence for the ancient Greek mind.

'Single-shoed heroes' or *monokrēpides* like Jason (specifically at Pindar *Pythians* 4.75, Apollonius *Argonautica* 1.11, [Lycophron] *Alexandra* 1310, Apollodorus *Bibliotheca* 1.9.16, Hyginus *Fabulae* 12) were typically boys on the verge of manhood who crossed significant boundaries to accomplish great feats. Jason at once crosses the great physical boundary of the river Anaurus into the territory he intends to reclaim, and at the same time the metaphorical boundary between youth and manhood. Perseus too could be projected as a single-shoed hero. Herodotus tells that when he manifested himself in Egyptian Chemmis he often left behind a single boot (2.91.2–5). Later on, Artemidorus tells us that Hermes gave Perseus just one of his winged boots to wear (*Oneirocriticon* 4.63). Those who wish to see Perseus as a hero of *katabasis* or underworld descent may reflect that those being initiated into the mysteries of the underworld at Eleusis wore a single shoe for the experience.[41]

Indeed, for many, Perseus' Gorgon adventure repesents a trial of initiation or maturation – a trial by which an adolescent proves himself worthy of incorporation into adult society – projected into myth. Its distinctive elements as such are the dispossession of a young prince, his acceptance of a dangerous mission as he reaches the threshold of adulthood, his journey, within this mission, to a marginal area where he acquires deadly weapons and overcomes a terrible foe. Much of this might also apply to the Andromeda episode, with the acquisition of a bride sealing the transition to adulthood. We have noted that one of the most satisfactory interpretations of Polydectes' obscure trick requires that Perseus should precisely be a boy desperate to prove himself a man. In art at any rate, Perseus is almost universally portrayed as a beardless adolescent (*LIMC* Perseus *passim*). Those who hold that Perseus' flight to the Gorgons or his battle with a sea-monster resembles a descent into the underworld may consider his return from them symbolic of his rebirth into a new life as a fully fledged adult.[42]

OVERVIEW

We can not know whether a pre-existing Perseus added a Gorgon-slaying to his accomplishments, or whether Perseus was invented specifically to slay the Gorgon, a mysterious and evolving monster. The Medusa episode as a whole constitutes a tale of a classic quest type, with the various and varying stages by which Perseus makes his way to the Gorgons and accomplishes the deed all receiving their own elaboration. Long gestation in tradition generated a remarkable set of correspondences between the female groups Perseus met in the course of his quest. The adventure may or may not represent, at some level, a paradigmatic trial of initiation or maturation. As the Medusa episode is framed by Perseus' Greece-based adventures, so this episode itself frames that of Perseus' encounter with Andromeda and the sea-monster, and it is to this that we turn next.

4

ANDROMEDA AND THE SEA-MONSTER

THE ORIGINS OF THE ANDROMEDA TALE

The earliest evidence for the story of Andromeda and the *kētos* or sea-monster is a Corinthian black-figure amphora of *ca*. 575–50 BC (*LIMC* Andromeda I no. 1 = Fig. 4.1), subsequent by a good century to the earliest traces of the Medusa episode.

The vase tells a clear story, with the labelled figures of the *kētos*,

Figure 4.1 Perseus pelts the *kētos* with rocks. Andromeda looks on.

Perseus and Andromeda running left to right. The head of the *kētos*, all we see of it, may remind modern eyes of a friendly Alsatian. The rudimentary waves sketched beneath tell us that it attacks from or with the sea. Perseus, his legs astride, launches round rocks (pebbles?) at it with both hands, one to the fore and one behind, from a pile between his feet. He wears his familiar *petasos*-hat and winged boots, and the *kibisis* hangs handbag-like from his outstretched arm. The Gorgon-slaying apparel indicates that the *kētos* episode is already well integrated with the Medusa tradition. Andromeda stands behind Perseus looking on, her arms awkwardly akimbo, and perhaps therefore tied.[1]

The literary record lags behind. The Hesiodic *Catalogue of women* may have been roughly contemporary with the vase, but the surviving fragments only include reference to the bare fact of Perseus' marriage to Andromeda (*fr.* 135 MW). The first recoverable literary account of the episode is probably Pherecydes', on the assumption that his version underlies Apollodorus' (see chapter 1).

As with the Medusa tale, it has been contended that the Andromeda tale derived from the cultures of the Near East. This is hard to prove, however, not least because of the near universality of dragon-slaying myths and their damsel-delivering variants. A specific case has been made that the tale derived quite directly from a Canaanite-Ugaritic cosmic myth. According to this, the sea-god Yam demanded the sacrifice to himself of Astarte, the goddess of love, but the weather-god Baal killed Yam and his sea-monster Lotan, the equivalent of the Biblical Leviathan. But the case is built on a premise that can not easily be accepted, namely that the Andromeda tale was originally located in Phoenician Joppa. The Andromeda tale is in fact associated with Persia and Ethiopia and probably Arcadia, too, long before its arrival in Joppa, as we will see.[2]

One variety of Near-Eastern evidence that does merit attention, however, is a series of Neo-Assyrian cylinder-seals from Nimrud, which show the god Marduk attacking the massive sea-serpent Tiamat. The Corinthian amphora bears a striking resemblance to this scene. Marduk's limbs form a similar configuration to Perseus', although he is thrusting a sword forward towards the snake with the hand in front rather than throwing a stone with the hand behind. A helper stands behind him, as Andromeda stands behind Perseus. Between the two of them a constellation is represented by a series of dots, one of which hovers just above the god's rear hand, almost as if it is a stone he is about to throw. It seems that the constellation has been misinterpreted by the Greek painter or by the tradition within which he works and so has been translated into Perseus' stones. In other representations of the fight between Marduk and Tiamat, we may note, the god uses a sickle against the serpent-monster. Compelling as the correspondences seem to be, what is borrowed here is the image-type, not the tale to which it corresponds. However, the association of a constellation – for all that it is misconstrued on the Corinthian vase – with a potential model for the representation of Andromeda's story is suggestive, when we recall that the catasterisation of Perseus is tightly associated with the Andromeda episode.[3]

THE TRAGIC ANDROMEDA

The *Andromeda*-tragedies of Sophocles and Euripides seem to have influenced the subsequent literary and iconographic traditions profoundly, but unfortunately they survive only in fragments. The narrative underpinning Sophocles' play (*frs* 126–36 Pearson/ *TrGF*) seems to have broadly conformed with the Pherecydean-Apollodoran account, and seems to have ended by looking forward to the future catasterism of the major players ([Eratosthenes] *Catasterisms* 16 and 36). We have no date for the drama, but conventional wisdom holds that it inspired a flurry of Athenian vase images in the decade 450–440 BC. These show black-African servants escorting an Andromeda in oriental dress to her place of sacrifice, or Andromeda already bound between two posts (*LIMC* Andromeda I nos. 2–6). A fragment that speaks of 'the unfortunate woman being hung out' (*fr.* 128a *TrGF*) is compatible with such scenes. If the pots do belong with the play, then they seem to tell us not only its approximate date, *ca.* 450 BC, but also that Andromeda was put out for the monster in the course of the drama, and they seemingly confirm that the setting was Ethiopia.[4]

Euripides' *Andromeda* (*frs* 114–56 *TrGF*) was produced in 412 BC

(Scholiast Aristophanes *Frogs* 53a), and became the subject of an extended parody by Aristophanes the following year in his *Thesmophoriazusae* (1009–1135). This comedy, together with its ancient commentaries, remains our most important source for Euripides' play, but the extraction of the original straight version from its distorting mirror is no easy task.[5]

The play, set again in Ethiopia, evidently opened with Andromeda chained to a rock (*fr.* 122 *TrGF*) as 'fodder for the *kētos*' (*fr.* 115a *TrGF*). She lamented her lot before a female chorus and as she did so asked the Echo in the cave behind her to still her voice (*fr.* 118 *TrGF*), a sequence of which Euripides makes great sport. Perseus arrived on the scene, as he flew back to Argos (not Seriphos, interestingly) with his winged sandals and the head of the Gorgon, and espied her from above (the theatrical crane will have been deployed at this point): 'Ah! What hill do I see with the foam of the sea beating around it? What image of a maiden do I see made from the working of natural stones, the statue of a wise hand?' (*fr.* 125 *TrGF*; cf. *fr.* 124). Andromeda abandoned herself to Perseus in hope of rescue: 'Take me for yourself, stranger, whether you want me to be a servant or a wife or a slave' (*fr.* 129a *TrGF*). Perseus had cause to apostrophise Eros, presumably after falling in love with Andromeda and so determining that he must face the *kētos*: 'Eros, you are the king of gods and people. You should either stop telling people that beautiful things are beautiful, or you should work alongside lovers as they struggle through the toils you have created for them, so that they can be successful' (*fr.* 136 *TrGF*; cf. *fr.* 138). In due course a messenger reported Perseus' victory over the *kētos*, which had come from the Atlantic, and described how the exhausted hero had been revived by local shepherds, who plied him with milk and wine (*frs* 145–6 *TrGF*; cf. Plutarch *Moralia* 22e). Many of these details – Ethiopia, Eros in attendance, the Atlantic *kētos* and the countrymen offering milk and wine – are taken up subsequently in the imaginary painting of Perseus and Andromeda described in the third-century AD *Imagines* of Philostratus (1.29), which may perhaps therefore offer us a synoptic impression of the play's central action.

Our best clue as to how the play ended is offered by the pseudo-Eratosthenic *Catasterisms*:

Constellation of Andromeda. She is placed in the stars on account of Athena, as a reminder of Perseus' labours. Her arms are outstretched, in the position in which she was set forth for the *kētos*. In response to this, after being saved by Perseus, she elected not to remain with her father and mother, but voluntarily went off to Argos with him, with noble thoughts in mind. Euripides tells the story clearly in the drama he wrote about her . . .

([Eratosthenes] *Catasterisms* 1.17 (cf. 1.15))

The Scholiast to Germanicus' *Aratus*, also seemingly drawing ultimately on Euripides, tells that Cepheus and Andromeda were translated to the stars by Athena, whilst Perseus and the sea-monster were translated to the stars by Zeus (pp. 77–8, 137–9, 147, 173 Breysig; cf. Hyginus *On astronomy* 2.11). The future catasterisation of Perseus and Andromeda and the other principals will have been foretold at the close at the play, no doubt by a *deus ex machina*, and no doubt this was Athena herself.

Vases showing Andromeda tied between two posts in the supposedly Sophoclean fashion continued to be produced after Euripides' production, but from the beginning of the fourth century BC they are joined by a series that show Andromeda tied rather to the rock-arch entrance to a cave, and these are thought to reflect the Euripidean Andromeda, the cave being the natural home of Euripides' Echo. The earliest, a red-figure crater of *ca.* 400 BC (*LIMC* Andromeda I no. 8), is held to illustrate Euripides' play more closely than others. On this Andromeda is bound to a rock, surrounded by the figures of Perseus, Cepheus, Aphrodite, Hermes and a woman who may represent either the chorus or Cassiepeia.[6]

This pair of tragedies evidently did much to maintain interest in Andromeda in the age of Alexander and the early Hellenistic period. Nicobule, a rare female writer working at some point prior to Pliny the Elder, told that in his final dinner Alexander himself performed an episode from Euripides' *Andromeda* from memory (*FGH* 127 *fr.* 2). Some remarkable events recorded by Lucian testify to the continuing popularity of Euripides' play in the age of the Successors (*How to Write History* 1). During the reign of Lysimachus (306–281 BC) the tragic actor Archelaus performed his *Andromeda* for the people of Abdera in a midsummer heatwave, as a result of which a feverish

disease fell upon them. After a series of distressing physical symp-
toms, they became crazy for tragedy and would shout out the
Andromeda's monodies, notably 'Eros, you tyrant over gods and
men' (*fr.* 136 *TrGF*). The fever and folly dissipated only with the win-
ter freeze. It was about the same time that Eratosthenes compiled the
original version of his *Catasterisms* or 'Star myths' and drew heavily
and explicitly on both *Andromeda* tragedies to do so, their finales in
particular (*frs* 15–17, 22 and 36). New tragedies, too, were devoted to
Andromeda in the early Hellenistic age by Lycophron (*TrGF* 100 T3)
and Phrynichus 'II', the son of Melanthas (*TrGF* 212 T1).

The early Hellenistic period was also the age in which the Latin
poets began to put Greek themes into their own tongue, and they,
too, were evidently caught up in the contemporary passion for
Andromeda tragedies. We know of three Latin *Andromedas*. In the
third century Livius Andronicus wrote an *Andromeda* the unique
fragment of which appears to refer to Poseidon's flooding (Ribbeck[3]
i p. 3 = Warmington: ii pp. 8–9). Ennius' *Andromeda* belonged to the
later third or earlier second century BC. The fragments (Ribbeck[3] i
pp. 30–2 = Warmington: i pp. 254–61) tell us that Cassiepeia's boast
was once again the cause of Andromeda's distress (*fr.* 3). The sea-
monster 'was clothed in rugged rock, its scales rough with barnacles' (*fr.* 4), perhaps in anticipation of its petrifaction by Perseus.
And the disarticulated limbs of the slain monster were scattered
by the sea, which foamed with its blood (*fr.* 8). Accius wrote his
Andromeda in the second century AD (or early first). The surviving
fragments (Ribbeck[3] i pp. 172–4 = Warmington ii pp. 346–353)
describe Andromeda as imprisoned in a jagged rock, in a condition
of filth, cold and hunger (*fr.* 8). No doubt this cave was also the
precinct fenced around with the bones of the sea-monster's former
victims and rank with the remains of their decaying flesh (*fr.* 10).
Roman audiences always enjoyed their gore.[7]

THE IMPERIAL ANDROMEDA

The most elaborate account of the tale of Perseus' rescue of
Andromeda to survive is to be found in Ovid's *Metamorphoses*

(4.663–5.235), which reached its final form in 8 AD. This is the account that has had the most central and profound impact on the subsequent western tradition. Once again, the boast of Cassiope (the variant form of the name Cassiepeia favoured in Latin) is the source of the trouble, but the Nereids and Poseidon are extruded from the tale. We are only told that Ammon, the great prophetic god of Egyptian Siwah, has ordained that Andromeda be sacrificed to the sea-monster. Perseus overflies Ethiopia after petrifying Atlas, and espies Andromeda pinned out on the rock below. He falls in love with her at once, and makes an agreement with her ready and willing parents that he may marry her if he delivers her. Perseus dispatches the monster by stabbing it repeatedly in its flank. To Ovid again we owe our only extended narrative of the Phineus episode. As Perseus and Andromeda are celebrating their wedding feast with Cepheus, Phineus bursts in with his followers to claim the bride formerly betrothed to him. A bloody battle breaks out with the followers of Cepheus, reminiscent both of Iliadic battle scenes and more particularly of the battle of the Lapiths and the Centaurs at the wedding feast later in the same poem (12.210–536). The immediate impact of the *Metamorphoses* account can be seen in Manilius' poetic explanation of the origin of the constellation of Andromeda, published a few years later (*Astronomica* 5.538–634), about which we will have more to say. The popularity of the Andromeda tale in 79 AD Pompeii is amply attested by the many surviving frescoes in the city showing her story (*LIMC* Andromeda I nos. 33–41, 67–72, 91–3, 100–1, 103–12). We may presume that the entirety of Roman Italy was so decorated.

The popularity of Andromeda in Roman murals goes a long way towards explaining her popularity also in the literature of *ekphrasis*, the evocation of imaginary paintings in words, that came to thrive from the second century AD onwards. In his later second-century AD novel *Leucippe and Cleitophon*, Achilles Tatius gives us an *ekphrasis* of an imaginary diptych painting which balances a panel of Prometheus bound to his rock with one of Andromeda bound to hers (3.6–7). As often, we find Perseus coupled with Heracles, who rescues Prometheus in the corresponding panel. *Ekphrasis*-literature likes to confuse boundaries between artistic representation and supposed real life. Here, we are told, we have a painting of a notionally real woman, who, beautiful and suspended in the cave-mouth, consequently resembles a statue displayed in an alcove. A spiny serpentine *kētos* breaks the waves to lurch towards us, as Perseus, naked save for his Cap of Hades, cloak and winged sandals, descends from the air to the attack. We find a broadly similar *ekphrasis* of an imaginary Andromeda fresco in Lucian's *The Hall* (22), probably written *ca.* 170 AD. In the early third century the elder Philostratus offered another *ekphrasis* of a painting, this time one depicting the happy scene just after Perseus' killing of the *kētos*, which reddens the sea with its blood (*Imagines* 1.29). This vignette, in which the local cowherds (not shepherds here) ply the recovering Perseus with milk and wine, seems to owe much to Euripides, as we have seen. In Heliodorus' mid-fourth-century novel *Ethiopica* we are told of further imaginary paintings of Perseus and Andromeda, no doubt in salute to the tradition of Andromeda *ekphraseis* that had flourished over the previous two centuries (4.8, 10.14; cf. 10.6). These decorate the walls of the Ethiopian royal palace in which the heroine Charicleia is born. We learn that in one of them Perseus is shown releasing a completely naked Andromeda from the rock. The role of this painting in the novel is a pivotal one, and one that constitutes an interesting commentary on the Andromeda tradition.

THE CATASTERISMS

It is conceivable that the constellations of Perseus, Andromeda, Cepheus, Cassiepeia and the *kētos* were developed in conjunction with the remainder of the Andromeda story as we know it. This is first attested iconographically, as we have seen, *ca.* 575–50 BC. It has been precariously contended that the constellation of Perseus must have been identified before *ca.* 550, on the basis that it bisects the zodiac, which was brought into Greece at this time. Otherwise, all we can do is note that the catasterisms may have featured in Aeschylus' *Phorcides* ([Eratosthenes] *Catasterisms* 22) at some point in the earlier fifth century, and that they certainly featured in Sophocles' *Andromeda* of *ca.* 450 BC ([Eratosthenes] *Catasterisms* 16, 36, etc.).[8]

The tradition of making star-pictures in which the characters underlying the constellations are drawn beneath the relevant groupings of stars is usually held to go back to Eudoxus of Cnidus (floruit *ca.* 360 BC). Our earliest iconographic record of this tradition is to be found on the globe of the second-century AD Farnese Atlas in Naples (*LIMC* Perseus no. 195). Eudoxus' star-pictures were taken up avidly by subsequent astronomical and astrological literature, and were evidently much reproduced in it: Aratus' *Phaenomena*; Eratosthenes' original *Catasterisms*, and the 'pseudo-Eratosthenic' version of it that survives; Hipparchus' commentary on Eudoxus and Aratus; the translations of Aratus into Latin by Cicero and Germanicus, with the Latin commentaries on the latter; Manilius' *Astronomica*; Hyginus' *Astronomia*. It is to these texts that we owe much of the information we have about the wider Andromeda myth. The *Catasterisms* describes the constellation of Perseus in the following terms:[9]

He has the following stars:

on each shoulder: one bright one [i.e. two in all]
on the tip of his right hand: one
on his elbow: one
on the tip of his left hand, in which he appears to hold the Gorgon's head: one
on the head of the Gorgon: one
on his torso: one
on his right hip: one bright one
on his right thigh: one bright one
on his knee: one
on his shin: one
on his foot: one dim one
on his left thigh: one
one his knee: one
on his shin: two
around the Gorgon's locks: three

In total, nineteen. The head and the sickle are seen without stars, but they seem to be visible to some in the form of a dense cloud.

([Eratosthenes] *Catasterisms* 22)

The *Catasterisms* tells us that Andromeda is represented in the stars 'with her arms outstretched, in the position in which she was set forth for the *kētos*' (17). However, vase images, without stars superimposed, of Perseus carrying sickle and Gorgon-head and of Andromeda with chained arms splayed were flourishing in ancient art from at least the mid-fifth century, a century before Eudoxus wrote (*LIMC* Perseus no. 31, Andromeda I no. 2, etc.). This may oblige us to accept that Eudoxus himself built on established traditions.

The most creative extant literary deployment of the catasterisation theme is that of the fifth-century AD Nonnus, who imagines the continuing feelings of the figures in their catasterised form (*Dionysiaca* 25.123–42). His observation that an Andromeda living among the stars would hardly be pleased to be confronted for all eternity with a *kētos* restored to life on equivalent terms is a sweetly logical one. Nice, too, is his notion that it must be an indignity for Cassiepeia in her constellation to be dipped into the sea, realm of the vengeful Nereids, as she descends below the horizon. And so too the notion that the implacable eye of the Gorgon might be moved to tears for Andromeda.

But the catasterisations remain mysterious because we hear nothing of the mechanism by which they were achieved, nor, puzzlingly, when they were achieved. As to the 'how', we must assume by default that the human characters were translated directly to the stars from life (only in the case of Perseus himself do we have traces, problematic ones, of death stories: chapter 2). But for the *kētos* translation to the stars evidently meant a sort of return from the dead. And a further complication in the case of the *kētos* is the fact that, according to some accounts, a large part of its body remained at the site of the battle after being transformed into a rock by Perseus' Gorgon-head (thus, e.g., Nonnus *Dionysiaca* 31.10). The 'when' is even more puzzling. The catasterisations neatly round off the episode of Perseus' delivery of Andromeda from the *kētos* by enveloping the five principal actors, but, in the context of the broader Perseus myth and biography, they can hardly be understood to have taken place as the direct and immediate finale of this episode. Even if we hear little more of Cepheus and Cassiepeia on planet earth, Perseus and Andromeda, we know, live on, move on, Persia aside, to Seriphos,

Argos, Larissa and Tiryns, and become parents to dynasties. Are we to assume that each actor was catasterised at the relevant point after a happy dotage? In short, the catasterisations sit awkwardly with the wider Perseus cycle in its canonical version.

EROS AND EROTICISM

The two principal women in Perseus' life, his mother Danae and his bride Andromeda, were both often portrayed in poses suggestive of sexual abandon, albeit without tangible lover. As we have seen, in Greek art Danae typically welcomes Zeus in the form of impregnating golden rain into her lap with her head thrown back in a fashion suggestive of sexual ecstasy (chapter 2).[10]

Andromeda, on the other hand, is the western tradition's archetypal damsel in distress. The vignette in which a powerless, vulnerable girl is tied up, arms splayed, before a powerful, as it were super-masculine, monster is one laden with erotic potential, as movie directors are well aware (think of Fay Wray waiting for King Kong), and this was a potential that ancient artists and writers were also happy to realise to the full. In iconography, as we have seen, Andromeda is typically portrayed with her arms splayed wide (in the catasterised pose), with her hands chained on each side, either to posts (the supposedly Sophoclean configuration) or to the bare rock (the supposedly Euripidean configuration). It is a pose of complete vulnerability, and one in which she seemingly spreads her arms wide to welcome a lover. And it is of course in this pose that she instils desire in Perseus (*LIMC* Andromeda I *passim*).[11]

It is likely that Euripides made much of the erotic charge offered by the chained Andromeda. As we have seen, his Perseus challenges Eros to help him defeat the *kētos*, since he has inspired him with love for Andromeda (*fr.* 136 *TrGF*), and the association between Eros and the *kētos* was taken up by the tradition. Whether or not Eros accepted the challenge in Euripides' play, he did do on a fine Apulian *loutrophoros*-vase of *ca.* 350–40 (*LIMC* Perseus no. 189 = Fig. 4.2). Here Eros rides the *kētos* whilst Perseus grapples with it from the front (eroses or 'putti' are often found riding *kētē* more

Figure 4.2 Perseus battles the *kētos* whilst Eros rides it, before a tied Andromeda.

generally in decorative scenes, as are Nereids). A first-century AD epigram of Antiphilus incorporates a brief *ekphrasis* of a painting in which 'the competiton set by Eros is the *kētos*' (*Greek Anthology* 16.147; cf., again, Philostratus *Imagines* 1.29).[12]

Comic poets seem to have made the most of the vignette's erotic potential. At some point before 423 BC Phrynichus brought a drunken old woman onto the stage to perform a lewd dance before being eaten by a *kētos* (*fr.* 77 *K–A* = Aristophanes *Clouds* 556, with Scholiast). The ancient commentaries tell us that this had been in parody of an *Andromeda* tragedy, presumably Sophocles'. Aristophanes had fun with Euripides' *Andromeda*. His grizzled and distinctly unfeminine Mnesilochus takes on the role of the delicate ingenue Andromeda with the finesse of a pantomime dame. The Scythian policeman, all too literally minded, is keen to suggest ways in which Euripides, in the role of Perseus, might satisfy his apparent desire for the bound heroine:

> *Euripides*: O maiden, I pity you as I see you hanging here.
>
> *Scythian*: She's not a maiden, but a sinful old man, a thief and a criminal.
>
> *Euripides*: You're talking rubbish, Scythian. For she is Andromeda the daughter of Cepheus.
>
> *Scythian*: Look at her fig. It doesn't seem very small, does it?
>
> *Euripides*: Pass her hand to me, so that I may touch the girl, pass it, Scythian. All men have diseases, and I myself have been seized by desire for this girl.
>
> *Scythian*: I don't envy you. But if his arsehole was twisted round here, I would not have any problem with you taking him and buggering him.
>
> *Euripides*: Why do you not allow me to release her, Scythian, and fall onto the bed and bridal couch?
>
> *Scythian*: If you're so desperate to bugger the old man, then drill a hole through the plank and bugger him from behind it.
>
> (Aristophanes *Thesmophoriazusae* 1110–20)

The Scythian thus proposes that Euripides should drill a hole in the back of the plank to which Mnesilochus is tied and bugger him through it. The 'plank' may be an intra-dramatic reference to a post to which Mnesilochus-Andromeda is tied, or an extra-dramatic reference to the wooden scenery depicting the rock-arch cave-entrance before which Mnesilochus is tied. Middle Comedies, Antiphanes *Andromeda* (*fr.* 33 *K–A*) and Phormus' *Cepheus*, perhaps to be identified with his *Perseus* (*Suda* s.v. *Phormos*), may also have exploited Andromeda's plight in similar ways, but we know nothing of them.[13]

In the Latin tradition Manilius gives us an explicitly eroticised description of the girl's plight:

> There could only be one expiation for these crimes, the surrender of Andromeda to the maddened sea, so that the creature could devour her gentle limbs. This was her wedding. Relieving the suffering of the people with her own, the weeping victim was decked out for her sacrifice. She put on the dress that had not been intended for this kind of vow, and the funeral without funeral of the living virgin was hastened on. As soon as they had come to the shore of the hostile sea, her soft arms were spread across the hard rocks. They fastened her feet to the crags and chained her up, and there hung the girl, doomed to die, on her virgin cross. But even as she paid the penalty she preserved the modesty of her demeanour. The tortures themselves became her. As she gently bent her snow-white neck backwards, she seemed to have control of her figure. The folds of her dress slid down her arms, and her loose, flowing hair clung to her shoulders. Halcyons made lament as they flew around you and they mourned your lot with piteous song. They shielded you by overlapping their wings. At the sight of you the sea halted its waves, and for your sake it held back from drenching the rocks. A Nereid lifted her face from the sea water, and, in pity for your lot, wetted even the waves with her tears. The breeze too, warming your hanging limbs with gentle breath, made a tearful sound across the tops of the cliffs. At long last a lucky day brought Perseus, victorious over the monstrous Gorgon, to that shore. When he saw the girl hanging from the rock, Perseus, the one whom his Gorgon-enemy had not been able to stop short with her face, froze, and he could scarcely keep hold of the spoils in his hand. The vanquisher of Medusa was vanquished by Andromeda. He envied the very rocks and called the chains lucky to hold such limbs.

> (Manilius *Astronomica* 5.542–73 (+514))

Andromeda is dressed as a bride as if waiting for her longed-for first time. Attention is given to the softness of her flesh against the hard rock. A hint of sado-masochism creeps in with Manilius' observation that Andromeda's tortures become her. We are put in mind of the eroticism that strangely attends many medieval images of Christ writhing on his 'virgin cross'. Not least, Andromeda's dress and hair become dishevelled in her suspended position, and her breasts exposed, only to be covered in fey fashion by halcyon wings. Lucian subsequently inverts the suspended Andromeda's state of undress, for a yet more direct erotic effect. The Triton reports that Perseus 'espied Andromeda exposed on some prominent rock, pegged to it, exceptionally beautiful, by the gods, with her hair loose, and half naked, mainly below the breasts' (*Dialogues in the Sea* 14).

Artists also exploited the erotic potential of the suspended Andromeda. Vase painters and wall painters often preferred to represent her clothing diaphanously (e.g. *LIMC* Andromeda I no. 23, a Sicilian calyx-crater of *ca.* 350–25 BC, and no. 32, a Roman wall-painting from Boscotrecase). And as with the writers, wardrobe malfunction could be deployed to enhance the effect. One notable example of this is found in the case of a fragment of a Lucanian bell-crater of the early fourth century BC, on which a voluptuous Andromeda holds her thin *peplos*-dress up in her teeth to preserve her modesty (*LIMC* Andromeda I no. 22). In *ca.* 340 BC the female nude entered the canon of Greek sculpture, and this seems to have had an impact on the ways in which Andromeda could be shown. A nude Hellenistic statue, preserved only in the form of a Roman copy reduced to little more than a torso, indicates what could be done. The delicate chain that rests across the top of the girl's right thigh offers little to her modesty (*LIMC* Andromeda I no. 157, from Alexandria). No doubt this was the sort of thing Roman writers had in mind when they compared the suspended Andromeda to a statue. Full nudity was too much for the vase painters, and the only completely nude Andromeda to be found on a vase is a burlesque figure of *ca.* 340–30 BC on a Campanian *hydria* (*LIMC* Andromeda I no. 20). From the third century BC and onwards Etruscan and Roman relief-sculptors and wall-painters were less reticent about going all the way (e.g. *LIMC* Andromeda I nos. 53, 55, 75, 146a, 152).

Roman artists favoured three tender vignettes with little or no correlate in the literary tradition, and all of these are to be found in profusion in Pompeian wall-paintings. In one Perseus is shown helping Andromeda down from her place of suspension, with a miniaturised dead *kētos* sometimes lying at their feet (e.g. *LIMC* Andromeda I nos. 67–71, 73–4, 78, 83–9, 209–11, 222). In the second, completely absent from the written record, we catch a now fully relaxed Perseus and Andromeda, their troubles behind them, sitting together and gazing at the reflection of the Gorgon-head in a rock-pool. Perseus is evidently recounting his earlier adventures to his new fiancée, perhaps still on the shore where the *kētos* was killed (*LIMC* Andromeda I nos.102–4, 109–10, 118, 120, Perseus nos. 66–73). In the third we find Perseus transporting Andromeda through the air, presumably back to Seriphos (*LIMC* Perseus nos. 229–30).[14]

The most striking aspect of Perseus' relationship with Andromeda, in the context of Greek myth, is its solidity. Nowhere do we hear of any difficulties within the marriage, nowhere do we hear of any other women with whom Perseus fell in love or with whom he slept. Nor, for that matter, do we hear of any boyfriends for Perseus, although Hyginus speculates that Hermes loved him and gave him his winged sandals as a love gift (*De Astronomia* 2.12). The contrast with the unnumbered casual sexual conquests and difficult home life of Perseus' great rival Heracles could not be more marked. Of course, many of Heracles' sexual conquests and ensuing children were foisted upon him by peoples or cities who wished to derive their own genealogies from him. But as we shall see (chapter 5), Perseus, too, had no shortage of peoples and cities wishing to share in his glory, and so the fact that he was allowed to remain chaste is remarkable from this perspective, too.[15]

FROM ARCADIA TO INDIA: BLACK ANDROMEDA?

One of the greatest points of instability in the Perseus cycle's relatively conservative tradition relates to the siting of Andromeda's homeland and Perseus' battle with the sea-monster. Cepheus and his family seem to have started life adjacently to Perseus' own Argos in Arcadian Tegea (Pausanias 8.47.5; cf. chapter 5). However, land-locked Tegea could hardly have been threatened by a sea-monster, or have been a matter of concern to marine deities like Poseidon and the Nereids. So if a narrative broadly resembling the *kētos*-episode ever was associated with Tegea, then the monster was presumably a landlubber dragon (as found in the story of Eurybatus and Alcyoneus discussed below), and the divine personnel somewhat different.

If Apollodorus' account of the Andromeda episode reflects Pherecydes' faithfully, then the mythographer will have located it in Ethiopia. As we have seen, iconography may suggest that Sophocles' *Andromeda* was produced *ca.* 450 BC and had an African and therefore an Ethiopian setting. Although it has been doubted, the Ethiopian setting of Euripides' *Andromeda* of 412 is certain. We have explicit testimony to the fact, 'As Euripides says, this king of the Ethiopians was the father of Andromeda' (Scholiast to Germanicus' *Aratus* p. 77 Breysig), and 'Ethiopians' are actually mentioned in a surviving, though admittedly corrupt, fragment (*fr.* 147 *TrGF*). Ancillary indications are provided by the fact that Aristophanes' parody of Euripides' play was also set in Ethiopia (*Thesmophoriazusae* 1098), and that a fragment of Euripides' *Archelaus* of 408/7 also locates Andromeda in Ethiopia (*fr.* 228a *TrGF*). But what kind of Ethiopia are we talking about? As we have noted, another fragment of the *Andromeda* speaks of the *kētos* speeding from the Atlantic to devour the girl (*fr.* 145 *TrGF*). This entails that the Ethiopians in question were those that lived in the extreme west of Africa on the Atlantic coast. Already Homer speaks of the Ethiopians as 'the remotest of men, divided into two communities, one where the sun sets, the other where it rises' (*Odyssey* 1.23–4; cf. Apollonius *Argonautica* 3.1191–2, Strabo C120). And indeed Palaephatus explicitly locates Perseus' own Ethiopians in the extreme west beyond the Pillars of Hercules (*FGH* 44 *fr.* 31). Such Ethiopians of course are conveniently adjacent to the Hesperidean Gorgons. Henceforth Ethiopia was to remain the favoured setting for literary accounts of the Andromeda episode ([Eratosthenes] *Catasterisms* 1.15, Strabo C42–3, Ovid *Metamorphoses* 4.669, Pliny *Natural History* 6.182, Antiphilus at *Greek Anthology* 16.147, Lucian *Dialogues in the Sea* 14, *The Hall* 22, Philostratus *imagines* 1.29, Heliodorus 4.8, etc.). If a desire to associate the Andromeda episode with the Gorgon episode is insufficient to justify the transfer of location to Ethiopia, which we have no particular reason to suppose began with Pherecydes or Sophocles, then the reason for it must remain a mystery to us.[16]

Perseus had some sort of association with Persia at least from the period of the Persian wars (chapter 5), but we first hear that Andromeda and her family were based there from Herodotus (7.61, 150). He tells us that Andromeda bore Perseus his first son Perses in her homeland, that of the Cephenes, and left him there for Cepheus to rear and in due course give his name to 'Persia'. Hellanicus, Herodotus' rough contemporary, put the Cephenes visited by Perseus rather in Babylon (*FGH* 4 *fr.* 59). Some reasons for this transfer of location to the Near East are clear. It was based on the superficial similarities between the names of Cepheus and the Cephenes on the one hand and the names of Perseus (and Perses) and of the Persians on the other. It was also based on the Greek desire to integrate the Persians into their familiar mythology.

We do not find Phoenician Joppa (Jaffa/Tel Aviv) identified as Andromeda's home until the *Periplus* attributed to Scylax, which was composed in the late fourth century BC (104). Compatibly, the Augustan Strabo held that Ethiopa's claim to the Andromeda story preceded Joppa's: 'And there are some who transfer Ethiopia to the Phoenicia near us and they say that the Andromeda story took place in Joppa' (C42–3; cf. C759, Tacitus *Histories* 5.2.3). What can have justified the transfer of the tale to Joppa? It may have been a corrective one. Phoenicia could be imagined to have been on Perseus' return route to Greece from the Gorgons (especially if he hugged the Mediterranean coast, as sailors might), in a way that Ethiopia, western or eastern, could not. It may then have been selected because of the resemblance between the names of Ethiopia and Joppa in their Greek forms (*Aith-iopē, Iopē*). But, however the tale of Andromeda and her *kētos* first found its way to Joppa, the city in due course actively appropriated it for itself, just as at a later date it appropriated – and indeed continues to do so – the story of Jonah and the whale (see chapter 5).

In the third century BC the Argive historian Deinias embarked upon a patriotic project to resolve the conflicting claims of Ethiopia and Persia to Andromeda. He did this in three ways. First, he made Perseus travel on from one to the other. Secondly, he transferred the Cephenes from their traditional Persian location to Ethiopia. And thirdly, he gave an integral role in the Perseus myth to the sea-system that linked (Eastern) Ethiopia with Persia, the Red (*Erythra*) Sea, by deriving its name from a (newly invented?) son of Perseus, Erythras. For the Greeks the Red Sea extended far beyond the boundaries of the sea which we now know by that name: the term covered the (modern) Red Sea, the Persian Gulf, and the Indian Ocean between. Scorn was poured on Deinias' work in the following century by the geographer Agatharchides of Cnidus (Photius *Bibliotheca* no. 250 = Deinias *FGH* 306 *fr.* 7). The association of Perseus with the Red Sea was to be a long and successful one (see, e.g. Nonnus *Dionysiaca* 31.8), so successful, indeed, that one of its fierce fish was named after the hero (Aelian *Nature of Animals* 3.28). In due course Phoenician Joppa too, with its own claim to Andromeda, also had to be brought to the Red Sea, and Conon, writing at the turn of the eras, found a way: 'The kingdom of Cepheus was later renamed Phoenicia, but at that time it was called Joppa, taking its name from the seaboard city of Joppa. Its original borders stretched from our sea as far as the Arabs that live beside the Red Sea' (*FGH* 26 *fr.* 1).

But the fact that the 'Red Sea' also embraced the Indian Ocean allowed Andromeda to be re-sited in yet another exotic location. Philodemus, writing in the earlier first century BC, ends a rude epigram with the declaration that Perseus fell in love with the Indian Andromeda (at *Greek Anthology* 5.132). Two centuries later Philostratus paid tribute to – but agonistically rejected – both the Red-Sea tradition in general and the Indian tradition in particular by opening his Andromeda *ekphrasis* with the words: 'But this is not the Red Sea, nor are these Indians, but we have Ethiopians and a Greek man in Ethiopia' (*Imagines* 1.29). He goes on to explain that the sea only seems to be red because it is tinged with the blood of the slain *kētos*.

Philostratus (*Imagines* 1.29) is the first to crystallise explicitly for us a paradox latent in the artistic and literary tradition of the Ethiopian Andromeda, although he does not offer to resolve it: if Andromeda is an Ethiopian princess, why is she portrayed as

white? The question already occurs as we look at the supposedly
Sophoclean vases on which a white Andromeda is pinned out by
black functionaries (*LIMC* Andromeda I nos. 2–6). And it occurs
again when Euripides' Perseus initially mistakes his Andromeda for
a marble statue (*fr.* 125 K-A; cf. Ovid *Metamorphoses* 4.675). We find
consideration of a similar problem in Heliodorus' fourth-century
AD *Aethiopica* (4.8), although the focus is deferred to the case of
Andromeda's descendant, another Ethiopian princess, the novel's
romantic heroine Charicleia. She, too, is strangely born white. It
is explained that the royal palace was decorated with frescoes of
Perseus and Andromeda, the family's ancestors. At the moment of
conception Charicleia's mother Persinna had been gazing at the
fresco on her bedroom wall in which Perseus was shown, after his
labour, releasing a completely naked – and white – Andromeda from
her rock. This vision imprinted itself on the gestating embryo and
gave Charicleia the precise form and colour of Andromeda. It was a
common notion in antiquity that foetuses should be moulded into
the form of whatever was in their mother's vision at the point of
conception (cf., e.g., Soranus *Gynaecology* 1.39). When the baby was
born, Persinna feared that she would be accused of adultery and her
child stigmatised as bastard (*nothou*), and so she told her husband
Hydaspes that the child had died, whilst exposing it with recognition
tokens for someone else to find and rear. Whether we are to assume
that Andromeda had herself in turn been born white as the result of
a similar process is unclear.[17]

How far back into the tradition does a consciousness of this paradox go? It may have been Euripidean in origin. His Perseus' misap-
prehension seems to speak of an ostentatiously white Andromeda,
and as we have seen, Philostratus points up the white-Ethiopian
paradox in a text that draws heavily on Euripides' *Andromeda*. An
anxiety that Andromeda may be seen as an adulterine bastard, parallel to that expressed for the Charicleia she moulded, provides a
good context for an otherwise puzzling fragment of Euripides' play:
'I do not permit the taking up of bastards (*nothous*). Although they
are in no way inferior to legitimate children, they ail under the law.
This you must guard against' (*fr.* 141 *TrGF*). Cepheus' suspicions
about Andromeda's origins may have permitted him to sacrifice her

more readily to the *kētos*, and these suspicions in turn may have strengthened Andromeda in her eventual resolve to abandon her parents.[18]

So how did an Ethiopian Andromeda first become white? The question itself is probably misconceived. If the earliest versions of the Andromeda tale did indeed locate her in Arcadian Tegea, then she will have been white to start with. In this case the more appropriate question would be: why didn't Andromeda become black when she was transferred to Ethiopia? The answer may lie in part in conservatism. Those with minds attuned to the issues of modern political life may contemplate other explanations.

THE *KĒTOS*: A NATURAL HISTORY

The Greeks applied the term *kētos* equally to mythical sea-monsters and to the actual massive creatures of the sea, principally whales. And if Andromeda's *kētos* is to be compared at any level with an actual sea creature, then whales are the only candidates for that comparison. There certainly were whales, even massive ones, in the waters of ancient Greece. The scapula of a fin whale, the second largest species, found its way down an Athenian well in *ca.* 850 BC. Procopius reports the tale of a 30-cubit-long whale that acquired the name of Porphyrios, 'Purple boy', which terrorised Byzantium and its coast for fifty years in the sixth century AD before finally becoming stranded (*Wars* 7.29.9–16). He is thought to have been a sperm whale. In modern times all the larger species of whale, including even the blue whale, the largest creature on earth, have been sighted in Greek waters, with sperm whales still becoming beached from time to time. But for the ancient Greeks the distance between mythical sea-monsters and real whales will no doubt have been shorter than it is for us. Few of them would have had the chance for a calm and uninterrupted view of the fully intact body of a whale, dead or alive, and we may note that nothing that can be described as a significantly realistic representation of a whale survives from the ancient Greek world.[19]

What did Andromeda's mythical *kētos* look like? It is difficult to get a clear idea from the extant literary sources, which never set out to give us a systematic description of the creature's form. This may be for reasons of poetic style and narrative flow. It may be because the authors wanted to exploit their readers' imaginations. It may be because, for all its mythical nature, it could be understood that everyone knew what a *kētos* looked like. But whatever the cause, one senses a general lack of interest in the creature on the part of the ancient authors, a surprising realisation for us today, for whom it is the most fascinating feature of the Andromeda episode. For ancient authors the beauty of Andromeda, together with her psychology, and the heroism of Perseus are much more interesting subjects. Nor is there ever any attempt to convey even a most begrudging empathy with the creature. This comes across most strikingly in Lucian's gently satirical dialogue in which a Triton tells the Nereids of Perseus' killing of their *kētos* (*Dialogues in the Sea* 14). These reasonable and sympathetic women show pity for Andromeda herself, even for Cassiepeia, who wronged them, but none for the *kētos*, even though it was acting as their champion. And this is despite the fact that there is a special affinity between *kētē* and Nereids in art, where the latter are often decorative portrayed happily riding on the backs of the former (e.g. *LIMC* Ketos nos. 30–4; and cf. no. 35 for a *kētos* with a Triton).[20]

The fullest set of literary indications of the form of Andromeda's *kētos* is found in Ovid's account:

> And lo, just as a swift ship cuts a furrow through the waters, prow first, impelled forwards by the sweating arms of youths, so did the wild creature, driving the waves apart with the force of its breast. Its distance from the crags was equivalent to the amount of air across which a Balearic sling can cast the leaden bullet it hurls. At once, the young man soared aloft into the clouds, his feet driving him up from the earth. As a shadow of the man appeared on the surface of the sea, the wild creature attacked the shadow it saw. And as Jupiter's bird [i.e. an eagle], when it sees a dragon-snake (*draco*) offering its dark back to Phoebus [i.e. the sun] in an open field attacks it from the rear and fixes its greedy talons in the scaly neck to prevent it from twisting back its savage mouth, so, hurtling headlong in swift flight through the open air, Inachides [i.e. Perseus] attacked the wild creature's back and buried his sword in its right shoulder, up as far as

the curving hilt, as it bellowed. Damaged by the deep wound, it repeatedly raised itself aloft into the air, buried itself in the waters, and twisted around in the fashion of a wild boar that a pack of barking hounds has at bay. Perseus avoided its greedy bites with his swift wings. Where the beast was exposed, he repeatedly struck it with his sickle-shaped sword, first the back, covered over with hollow shells, then its ribs, on its flanks, then at the point at which its tail tapered off narrowly into a fish. The beast belched forth from its mouth waves mixed with ruddy blood. His feathers grew heavy with moisture from the spray. He no longer dared trust his soaked ankle-wings. He espied a rock, the topmost part of which jutted from the waters when they were calm, but was covered over with water when it was upheaved. Getting a firm foothold on this and holding onto the highest part of the ridge of the rock with his left hand, he drove his sword repeatedly, three times and four times, through the animal's flank.

(Ovid *Metamorphoses* 4.706–34)

From this we learn that the *kētos* has a breast, back and flanks with ribs, and that it is covered in barnacles. More informatively, we learn that it has a shoulder, which implies a forearm or a substantial fore-fin of some sort, and a fish-tail. The *kētos* is also compared, albeit indirectly, with a dragon-snake, *draco*, and a wild boar. Manilius' description of his monster focuses on its massive coils, which cover the entire sea. It is able to propel itself high into the air, serpent-like, by rising up on these coils to bring the attack to Perseus as he flies through the air (*Astronomica* 5.584–5, 595–7). Achilles Tatius describes his painted *kētos* in the following words: 'But the shadow of its body had been painted beneath the salty water, the ridges of its scales, the curves of its neck, its crest of spines, the coils of its tail. Its jaw was massive and long. It gaped open all the way down to the join of the shoulders, and then immediately came its belly' (3.6–7). Descriptions of the *kētos* encountered by Hesione in the closely parallel tale we shall consider below are compatible and help to fill out our mental picture. Valerius Flaccus repeatedly emphasises his monster's long tail, neck and coils. It also has flickering eyes, a curving mouth with triple rows of teeth and a craggy back (*Argonautica* 2.497–549). Philostratus the Younger gives us a good account of the *kētos* in his *ekphrasis* devoted to Hesione (12): it has large, glaring eyes beneath an overhanging, spiny brow, a sharp snout with three rows of teeth, some of which are barbed, others of which project like fangs. Its evidently serpentine body projects from the sea at different points, like a series of islands (in Classic Loch Ness Monster style), and it has a tail with which it can throw the sea aloft. The pseudo-Lycophronian *Alexandra* interestingly twice applies the term 'dog' to Hesione's *kētos* (34, 471; see below).[21]

These indications broadly conform with what might be regarded as the canonical form of the *kētos* in art, whether appearing in the context of Andromeda and Hesione scenes, on its own, or in the context of more general scenes of marine fantasy. This canonical form, which begins to appear in *ca.* 650 BC, may be described as follows. The creatures have a body that is fundamentally serpentine, and this is clearly true of all its manifestations in archaic art save one (*LIMC* Ketos no. 18). They also often exhibit secondary features of snakes in Greek art, forked tongues and beards. The head itself is usually animalian, with long muzzle and upturned snout, and most often recalls (to our eyes) that of a dog, boar or even horse. But in origin the animalian head seems to have been a lion's, and the affinity between snakes and lions in archaic art is in general a strong one. The long snout may also owe something to the crocodile. Often, too, the *kētos* has forearms that, compatibly, resemble a lion's. It also often has long, even hare-like, ears. It can have spiny crests, horns or tusks, and bristles, and, appropriately to the sea, a fish-tail and fins or flippers.[22]

There is no consistency in the indication of the overall size of Andromeda's *kētos*. The pseudo-Lycophronian creature was evidently large enough for Perseus to enter (*Alexandra* 834–46). Manilius' was seemingly the largest, inconceivably large, in fact, able as it was to cover the entire sea with its body, dead or alive, and to vomit spray over the stars themselves (*Astronomica* 5.834–46). One of the most striking developments in the imperial-period artistic representation of the *kētos* is the artists' relative lack of interest in it, which chimes in with the lack of interest devoted to it in literary texts. Consequently it often appears in the form of a tiny figure, whether appropriately so as relegated to the remote background, or, more bizarrely, shown in the foreground. In many images it resembles nothing more threatening than a drowned pet laid out at

Andromeda's feet (*LIMC* Andromeda I nos. 69, 73, 75, 84, 86, 89, 91). Artists of this time seem to have been embarrassed by the necessity of portraying the creature, and uninterested in the opportunity offered for bravura invention and composition. Their interest, again in parallel with that of ancient writers, tended to follow rather the form of Perseus and in particular that of Andromeda, and the psychology of the latter.

Over time the method employed by Perseus to kill the *kētos* changes. In our earliest attestation of the episode, the Corinthian black-figure amphora of *ca.* 575–50 BC (*LIMC* Andromeda I no. 1 = Fig. 4.1), Perseus merely pelts the creature with rocks or, probably, pebbles, as we have seen. In this respect his weapon matches that deployed by Hesione in the earliest surviving illustration of her story, a Corinthian column-crater of *ca.* 575–50 BC (*LIMC* Hesione no. 3 = Fig. 4.3).

A Caeretan *hydria* of *ca.* 520–10 BC depicts a hero facing up to a

Figure 4.3 Heracles drives off the *kētos* with arrows, Hesione with stones.

splendid *kētos* attended by a chirpy seal, octopus and dolphins, with his *harpē* (*LIMC* Ketos no. 26 = Perseus no. 188 = Herakles no. 2844). It is not clear whether we have here Perseus or Heracles, or even a third, nameless slayer. If it is not Perseus, then our earliest evidence for his using the *harpē* against the *kētos* will be a pair of Italian vases of *ca.* 350–40 (*LIMC* Perseus nos. 189–90). Perseus goes on to use his *harpē* (alone) in this way in the accounts of Ovid (*Metamorphoses* 4.691–734) and Manilius (*Astronomica* 5.834–46).[23]

When did Perseus first deploy against the *kētos* the super-weapon that lay ready to hand, the Gorgon-head? Perhaps already from the point at which the Perseus-related constellations were first developed, since these incorporated the *kētos* and Perseus himself brandishing the Gorgon-head. But the first explicit testimony to Perseus using the head against the monster is found on a fourth-century BC Etruscan cup (*LIMC* Perseus no. 192). Here he threatens the *kētos* with the *harpē* in his right hand whilst swinging the Gorgon-head in his left. The notion that Perseus used the Gorgon-head against the *kētos* first surfaces in literature at the turn of the eras in the rationalising account of Conon, which speaks of Perseus' metaphorically petrifying the crew of the ship 'Ketos' when attacking them (*FGH* 26 fr. 1 at Photius *Bibliotheca* no. 186). The notion was taken up avidly in Greek literature of the AD period, in which Perseus is said to have transformed at least part of the monster to stone (Antiphilus at *Greek Anthology* 16.147, Achilles Tatius 3.6.3–3.7.9, Lucian *The Hall* 22, *Dialogues in the Sea* 14, [Libanius] *Narrationes* 35, at viii p. 55 Förster, Nonnus *Dionysiaca* 30.264–77, 31.8–25). A third-century AD mosaic from Coimbria shows Perseus facing a rather pathetic *kētos* with Gorgon-head in right hand and spear in left. The colours tell us that the fore part of the creature has already been petrified (*LIMC* Perseus no. 194).[24]

In the second-century BC *Alexandra* alone, the erudite and obscurantist Alexandrian poem pseudonymously ascribed to Lycophron, Perseus uses a killing-method shared with the Hesione tradition, that of allowing the *kētos* to devour him so that he can attack its internal organs with his weapons from the inside. Cassandra prophesies:

And Menelaus will see the bastions of Cepheus, and the kick-traces of Hermes Laphrius, and the twin rocks at which the monster leapt, in desire for its meal. But he came and snatched up in his jaws instead of the female [i.e. Andromeda] a male, the golden-fathered 'eagle' [i.e. Perseus], the winged-shoed liver-wrecker. The hateful whale will be slain by the blade of the reaper, its innards stripped out.

([Lycophron] *Alexandra* 834–42)[25]

THE ANDROMEDA TALE IN CONTEXT: HESIONE AND THE DRAGONS

The tale of Perseus' delivery of Andromeda from her *kētos* did not develop in isolation. It developed alongside the closely congruent tale of Heracles' delivery of Hesione from her *kētos*, and the narratives and iconographic traditions bearing upon both of these episodes constantly influenced each other.[26]

In its most canonical form, the tale of Heracles and Hesione proceeds as follows (Homer *Iliad* 20.145–8, Hellanicus *FGH* 4 *fr.* 26b, [Lycophron] *Alexandra* 31–6, 470–8, Diodorus 4.32, 42, Ovid *Metamorphoses* 11.199–215, Valerius Flaccus *Argonautica* 2.451–578, Apollodorus *Bibliotheca* 2.5.9.2.6.4, Hyginus *Fabulae* 31 and 89, Philostratus the Younger *Imagines* 12). Poseidon helped Laomedon build the walls of Troy, but Laomedon cheated him of his promised pay. In revenge Poseidon sent a *kētos* against Troy, which destroyed the people and ruined the land by belching a flood of brine over it (or according to Ovid, the flood came first and the *kētos* second). Apollo instructed Laomedon to rid himself of the creature by putting a daughter of the Trojans out for it. His plan to compel Phoenodamas to sacrifice one of his daughters failed when he enlisted popular pressure to compel Laomedon himself to sacrifice his own daughter Hesione instead. She was duly put out for the monster in royal dress, chained to rock. In the meantime, Laomedon offered his immortal horses to anyone that could slay the *kētos* for him. Heracles took up the offer, and managed to get himself inside the creature. He remained inside for three days and killed it by attacking its liver or its flanks from within, but when he emerged the creature's digestive juices had dissolved all his hair. He got inside either by luring the creature to insert its head through the entrance of a defensive bulwark or by donning Hesione's dress and substituting himself for her. Laomedon then cheated Heracles too of his reward, by palming him off with mortal horses. In revenge Heracles sacked Troy. He killed Laomedon and all his children except for Hesione, who was given as a prize to his champion soldier Telamon and became mother to Teucer by him, and Podarces, whom Hesione bought (*epriato*) from Heracles at the cost of a mirror or veil and who was consequently renamed Priam. In contrast to the Andromeda tale, there are only vague indications of any erotic interest between Heracles and Hesione, this in Diodorus.[27]

The coincidence between the central vignette of the Hesione tale and that of the Andromeda tale, in which an innocent virgin is tied to a rock as a sacrifice for a sea-monster, which is then destroyed by a hero, is evident. The tale of Hesione is likely to have been fully developed by the time of the *Iliad*, a century before our earliest attestation of the Andromeda tale, and this may, but need not, indicate the Hesione tale's priority. The poem does not mention Hesione herself, but it does allude to Athena and the Trojans building a wall for Heracles to hide behind when the *kētos* chased him from the shore to the plain. Because of the general congruence between the central vignettes of the two tales, it is hard to know what to think when the excellent Tzetzes accuses the author of the *Alexandra* of being drunk on his patron Ptolemy's wine and so confusing the two stories when telling that Perseus killed his *kētos* by getting inside it and hacking away at his liver (on [Lycophron] *Alexandra* 839). Has the author indeed assimilated the traditional Andromeda narrative to the traditional Hesione narrative, which he himself also gives us? Is he deliberately emphasising the parallelism between them? Or is he (also) giving us a lesser known but established variant of the Perseus episode?

Three vase illustrations of the Hesione episode may be noted. The earliest representation of Hesione's *kētos* is found on the Corinthian column-crater of *ca.* 575–50 BC mentioned above (*LIMC* Hesione no. 3 = Fig 4.3). Here Heracles has dismounted from his chariot, driven by Iolaus, and strides towards the *kētos*, seemingly firing three arrows at once from his bow at it. Andromeda stands in advance of him before the *kētos*, pelting it with round stones of different colours. Of the *kētos* itself we see only an odd, elongated white head, with a large eye, long rows of teeth, and a lolling tongue. Arrows and stones thrown by its antagonists cling to it. The conventional wisdom has read the dark vertical strip of paint from which the head emerges to indicate that the monster is emerging from a cave and being driven back into it by Heracles and Hesione. Admittedly no such lair is referred to in the literary sources, and it remains a problem that the head does not so much emerge from the cave as float, bodilessly, before it. But in an important book Adrienne Mayor has recently advanced a challenging new reading of this admittedly curious imagery. She reads the admittedly skeletal-looking *kētos*-head as a fossil skull, and sees the dark strip of paint as representing a rock face from which the fossil is projecting. She can even identify the fossil as that of a giant Miocene giraffe ('Samotherium'). If she is right, the image becomes a strangely compressed and sophisticated one, in which the artist is attempting to make, as it were, a palae-ontological argument, and to explain the monstrous fossil skulls he saw around him by associating them with the sort of mythical *kētos* faced by Heracles and Hesione. And in this case her reading would have important implications for the way in which the ancient Greeks thought about their *kētē*. But perhaps her reading remains, in the end, just too challenging. Perhaps the simplest solution is to read the strip of black paint to represent the surging wave of the flood that Poseidon sent against Troy, somehow in association with the *kētos* (we may compare the waves beneath the head of the *kētos* on the first Andromeda vase, *LIMC* Andromeda I no. 1 = Fig. 4.1). This reading, which pays great respect to the literary sources for the episode, also supplies us with a head that is no longer disembodied: it merely projects from the surging wave.[28]

Also of interest is a black-figure cup of *ca.* 520 BC. Here a particularly serpentine *kētos* gapes before Heracles, who grabs its tongue by the root in preparation for reaping it with his *harpē* (*LIMC* Hesione no. 4 = Ketos no. 25). And on a fourth-century BC Etruscan red-figure crater, the name vase of the Hesione Painter, a veiled Heracles strides into the gaping mouth of the *kētos* whilst unsheathing a sword

(*LIMC* Hesione no. 6). The veil no doubt salutes the version of the myth hinted at in the *Alexandra* account, in which Heracles has disguised himself as Hesione and substituted himself for her in order to facilitate getting inside the creature.[29]

More generally, the Andromeda and Hesione episodes alike bear a strong resemblance to a series of Greek myths in which heroes rescue innocent victims from land-based dragons. The most pressing parallels, both first recorded for us in the second century AD, feature an innocent victim who is not a girl, but a boy in whom the liberating hero develops an erotic interest, as was often the way. Pausanias tells us about Menestratus of Thespiae:

> In the city at Thespiae there is a bronze statue of Zeus the Saviour. They explain that a dragon-snake (*drakōn*) was once devastating the city, and the god gave the command that the ephebe chosen by the lot each year should be given to the beast. They say that they do not remember the names of those that were killed. But they tell that when the lot fell upon Cleostratus his lover Menestratus devised a plan. He had a bronze breastplate made with a fish-hook pointing upwards on each of its little segments. He put this breastplate on and handed himself over willingly to the dragon. His purpose was, in handing himself over and being killed, in turn to kill the beast. In return for this Zeus has acquired the epithet 'Saviour'.
>
> (Pausanias 9.26.7–8)

Antoninus Liberalis preserves in his *Metamorphoses* (8) the similar but happier tale of Eurybatus of Delphi from the second-century BC *Metamorphoses* of Nicander. A monster called Lamia (NB) or Sybaris would venture out of its cave to attack the Delphians and their flocks. Apollo told the Delphians they could deliver themselves from the monster by exposing a citizen lad to it. The lot fell upon the fair Alcyoneus. Eurybatus caught sight of him as he was being led off to his doom and fell in love. So he substituted himself for the boy, taking on his sacrificial garlands, overwhelmed the monster, and threw her down the mountain. The wounded creature disappeared and a spring, which the locals called Sybaris, appeared in her place.[30]

Here it is worth remembering that Andromeda may originally have been associated with land-locked Tegea in Arcadia, and therefore that the monster she faced may originally have resembled the Thespiae dragon or Lamia-Sybaris.

FOLKTALE COMPARANDA

A great many international folktales correspond closely in theme and structure with the tales reviewed in the foregoing section. The motif of a dragon-slayer, typically wearing a suit of armour studded with blades or hooks, feeding himself to the dragon so that he can destroy it from within, for example, is a common one in British dragon legends, such as that of the White Snake of Mote Hill in Kirkudbright and that of the Bisterne Dragon. And in a tale from Shetland Assipattle delivers the princess Gemdelovely from a massive sea-monster known as the Stoorworm by sailing a boat into its mouth, digging a hole in its liver and inserting a clod of burning peat into it. The monster spits him out in its agonies as it dies, and he marries the princess.[31]

But the folktale of greatest potential interest for the Andromeda episode – and indeed for the wider Perseus cycle – is that found most famously in Gottfried von Strassburg's *Tristan* of 1210 AD (books 12 and 14; no. 300 in the Aarne-Thompson catalogue). Here the country and people around Wexford are being burned up by a terrible fiery dragon. The king of Ireland promises his daughter Isolde to whoever can slay it. After a mighty fight in which the dragon eats half of his horse, Tristan tracks and kills the creature and cuts out its tongue, snapping the mouth back shut. He stumbles away from the scene but is temporarily overcome by exhaustion, the heat from the dragon, and the noxious fumes the tongue continues to exude. In the meantime the king's cowardly steward discovers the dragon's body, cuts off its head, and runs back claiming to have killed the dragon and demanding Isolde for his bride. Eventually there is a show-down at court in which the steward produces the head as evidence for his slaying but is confuted when Tristan produces the tongue. Tristan is awarded Isolde, and the steward humiliated. A version of this tale with yet greater resonance for the Perseus cycle is found in the Swedish folktale of *Silverwhite and Littlewarder*.

Silverwhite is a young man born to a princess locked in a tower but impregnated by an enchanted apple (cf. Danae). On his journeys he delivers not one but three princesses exposed to sea trolls, and cuts out the vanquished sea trolls' eyeballs. A courtier of their father the king claims to have done the deed, and is to be given the youngest princess to wife as reward, but on the wedding day Silverwhite produces the eyeballs to prove himself the rightful groom and gets the girl.[32]

This folktale-type strikingly mirrors not only the principal arc of the Andromeda tale but also its coda with Phineus, the wrongful competing claimant for the bride. Is it possible that the Andromeda tale could once have resembled this type even more closely? Perhaps so. It is clear that the type was known in antiquity. A fragment of the fourth-century BC Dieuchidas of Megara (*FGH* 485 *fr.* 10, amplified by Pausanias 1.41) tells how Megara was ravaged by the Cithaeronian lion, which killed many. King Megareus promised his daughter and kingdom to the one that should subdue it. Alcathous killed it and put its tongue in his wallet. Others, sent by the king to do the job, claimed that they had done the deed, but they were confuted when Alcathous produced the tongue. Furthermore, we have noted the iconographic evidence for Heracles' apparent removal of the *kētos*' tongue in the Hesione tradition that is so heavily congruent with the Andromeda tradition. Particularly intriguing is the fact that the motifs of the removal of a head from a body (Medusa) and the removal of an eye from a head (the Graeae), as in the Silverwhite narrative, are to be found in Perseus' other monster episodes. We have noted already the structural and thematic parallels that link the Graeae episode with the Medusa episode, and the Medusa episode with the Andromeda episode (chapter 3). Could such a folktale lie deeply buried beneath the Perseus cycle as we know it? Were its constituent motifs, once unified, subsequently differentiated and distributed across two separate episodes? Or did the Perseus cycle as a whole merely gravitate towards the imagery of the folktale in question, without ever completely assimilating it?

OVERVIEW

The tale of Andromeda, first attested in the sixth century BC, was popular throughout the remainder of antiquity. The ancient tradition seems to have been heavily shaped by the tragedies of Sophocles and Euripides. Writers and artists alike tended to be more interested in the erotic potential of Andromeda's distress than in the figure of the serpentine sea-monster. Similar Greek tales, such as those of Heracles and Hesione, Menestratus and Alcathous, and international folktales of dragon-slaying, such as those of Tristan and Silverwhite, have more to bring to our appreciation of the tale and its motifs than any supposed archetypes from the Near East.

5

THE USE AND ABUSE OF PERSEUS

PERSEUS IN THE ARGOLID

The myth of Perseus was repeatedly appropriated and adapted by cities and peoples and sometimes even individuals as they sought to make claims about their antiquity or identity or to express relationships with others. Perseus was a hero in east and west, as Nonnus noted (*Dionysiaca* 30.264–77), and by the end of antiquity a remarkable swathe of the ancient world had laid some sort of claim to the man.

The notion that Perseus was in origin a historical king of Mycenae in the age to which that city gave its name is simplistic. Nonetheless, the earliest and the most vigorous claims to Perseus came from the Argolid, from Argos and Mycenae above all, and if any region of Greece is to be identified as the cradle of Perseus, then it must be this one. Mycenae was destroyed in around 468 BC (Diodorus 11.65, Pausanias 2.16.5), and enjoyed only a brief revival in the third and second centuries BC. It is hardly surprising, therefore, that Argos' claim to Perseus should be the more insistent one in the extant sources. Some have supposed that Argos took advantage of Mycenae's fifth-century destruction to appropriate Perseus for herself. But Perseus' association with Argos is already attested in the mid sixth century ([Hesiod] *Catalogue of Women frs* 125, 129.10–15 MW), whereas the literary and epigraphic association of Perseus with Mycenae only emerges in around 500 BC. Of individual Argives who worked to appropriate Perseus for the city we can name only one, the third-century BC historian Deinias, who sponsored the by then old idea that Persia had been named after Perses, son of Perseus, and the possibly new idea that the Red Sea (i.e. our Red Sea, the Persian Gulf and the Indian Ocean) had been named after another one, Erythras (*FGrH* 306 *fr.* 7).[1]

Perseus had left numerous physical signs of his presence in Argos for Pausanias to find when he toured the city in the second century AD. One could still see the subterranean remnants of the bronzed chamber in which Acrisius had imprisoned Danae, which the tyrant Perilaus was said to have demolished (2.23.7). Demolition by the tyrant, who seems to have belonged to the sixth century, may imply that Perseus had a symbolic value for his rivals in the Argive aristocracy. Some have imagined the structure concerned to have been a bronze-age tholos-tomb (of which there are such fine examples in the Argolid), with its bronze rosettes on the walls and its relieving triangle opened by robbers forming a skylight above. Perseus' Cyclopes had left a stone head of Medusa in the city (Pausanias 2.20.7). Medusa's actual head (somehow escaping Athena's aegis) was said to lie buried under a heap of earth adjacent to the city's marketplace, and adjacently to that was situated the tomb of Perseus' daughter Gorgophone (2.21.5–7). Argos also boasted the tombs of Choreia and the 'Haliae' women slain by Perseus among the casualties of Dionysus' maenad-army (2.20.4 and 2.22.1). The coffin of Ariadne, who according to Nonnus also died in the battle, had been discovered in the city beneath the temple of Cretan Dionysus (Pausanias 2.23.8; cf. Nonnus *Dionysiaca* 25.98–112, 47.664–713). In the imperial period the city minted coins with images of Perseus under a range of emperors from Antoninus Pius (138–61 AD) to Valerian (253–60 AD) (*LIMC* Perseus nos. 23 and 58).[2]

By the Roman period at any rate, and no doubt long before, Perseus had acquired a cult in Argos. An inscription honouring a local worthy, one Tiberius Claudius Diodotus, celebrates him for, *inter alia*, financing games, the Sebasteia and the Nemeia, and bestows upon him 'the honours of Perseus and Heracles, and the privilege of wearing gold and purple' (*IG* iv. 606). The honours of Perseus and Heracles were a graceful tribute to this man, since both these heroes had famously been founders of games (Hyginus *Fabulae* 273).[3]

Mycenae held Perseus to have been its founder, and projected the origin of its name into his mythical adventures (Pausanias 2.15.4). Already in *ca.* 500 BC Hecataeus knew that Perseus had founded the city (*Mukēnai*) where the pommel (*mukēs*) had fallen from his *harpē* (*FGH* 1 *fr.* 22). Nicander amplifies this: the spot was also the one in which a nymph showed him the spring of Langeia, and Perseus planted the city with a variety of tree given to him by Cepheus, which came to be known as *perseai* (*Alexipharmaka* 98–104, *ca.* 130 BC). The variety in question may be *Mimusops Schimperi*. Pausanias speaks of the pommel and the spring too. He tells that the spring was also named after Perseus, *Perseia*, and adds that he discovered it when, in thirst, he picked a mushroom (*mukēs* again; Pausanias 2.16.3; cf. Stephanus of Byzantium s.v. *Mukēnai*). Ctesias of Ephesus derived the name of the city rather from the fact that it was founded on the hill on which the Gorgons Stheno and Euryale came to rest as they gave up the pursuit of Perseus, and let forth a bellow (*mukēma*) of despair (Ctesias of Ephesus *ap.* ps.-Plutarch *On rivers* 18.6). One would give much to know more about Ctesias and his work. His *Perseis* would appear to have been an epic poem devoted to our hero, but we know nothing more of him or it, and even his date remains obscure. It helps little to note that he is mentioned by and therefore antedated a work, the psuedo-Plutarchean *On rivers*, which is itself of uncertain date, but not prior to the second century AD.[4]

A cult of Perseus is attested at Mycenae by a pair of inscriptions from the late sixth and early fifth centuries. They seem to have been associated with an archaic fountainhouse constructed in the ruins of the bronze-age citadel, which was then rebuilt in the Hellenistic period and subsequently shown to Pausanias as the Perseia spring. The earlier text is highly fragmentary but includes the phrase 'are to be judges'. The later text, apparently a supplement to it, stipulates that, 'If there is no office of demiurge, the sacred-recorders for Perseus are to be judges for the parents in accordance with what has been decided' (*IG* iv 493). We infer that the earlier inscription had prescribed for the demiurges to act as the regular judges. Jameson speculates far beyond this evidence to reconstruct a dramatic *rite de passage* in which adolescents proved their manhood before their parents and the judges by re-enacting the Gorgon mission. In this they would have to seize Medusa's head and elude pursuers in the role of her sisters. Such a hypothesis begs many questions, not the least of which is why Perseus' sacred-recorders should only have been employed exceptionally, as it seems, in the rite to which the hero was supposedly central.[5]

Despite the failure of Mycenae's Hellenistic revival, Perseus' rebuilt fountainhouse survived into the late second century AD for Pausanias to see (2.16.3). At this point, too, Pausanias found a heroon or hero-shrine of Perseus on the road from Mycenae to Argos, where he received honours from the then locals, if not as great as those he received from the Seriphians and the Athenians (2.18.1). In the previous century Statius had imagined that heroic Mycenae had had a cult statue of Perseus, and that this had wept as a prophecy of doom, in the fashion of ancient statues (*Thebaid* 7.418). Did the heroon possess such a statue in Statius' age? From at least the first century BC and into the second century AD Dionysus was worshipped at Argos and at nearby Lerna as having been slain by Perseus (see chapter 2). Was Perseus himself also worshipped in the context of this cult?[6]

Mycenae's citadel could display magnificent bronze-age 'Cyclopean' walls, and so, too, could two other Argolid cities that also laid claim to Perseus as founder, Tiryns and Midea. It will doubtless have been these cities that championed the notion that Perseus returned to the Argolid from Seriphos with the Cyclopes in tow (Bacchylides 11.77–81, Pherecydes *FGH* 3 *fr.* 26; Euripides *Iphigenia at Aulis* 152, 1498–1501; Apollodorus *Bibliotheca* 2.4.4; Pausanias 2.16.4–5, 8.25.6; Stephanus of Byzantium s.v. *Midea*; Tzetzes on [Lycophron] *Alexandra* 838). How and where did Perseus encounter these ferocious one-eyed giants, and what was the nature of his dealings with them? Our sources leave the conceit frustratingly unelaborated, but perhaps it was ever so. In a variant tradition, it was rather his great uncle Proetus that brought them from Lycia to fortify Tiryns (Apollodorus *Bibliotheca* 2.2.1). The notion that Perseus should have swapped the kingship of Argos for that of Tiryns after the accidental killing of Acrisius may have originated in an attempt to negotiate between these two cities' competing claims to the hero (Apollodorus

Bibliotheca 2.4.4; Tzetzes on Lycophron 838; Pausanias 2.16.2–3). We recall that a series of terracotta helmet-masks deriving from the seventh century BC and partly resembling Gorgons have been found in the city (chapter 3). Jameson would like to relate these, too, to a similar *rite-de-passage* contest. Elsewhere in the Argolid, Cynoura held itself to have been founded by Perseus' son Cynouros (Stephanus of Byzantium s.v. *Cynoura*). And in the imperial period Asine minted Perseus coins on the model of Argos' own.[7]

Pausanias tells of two towns just beyond the borders of Argolis that also made claims to Perseus. Nemea in Phliasia to the north knew that Perseus first sacrificed to Apesantian Zeus on Mt Apesas above the city, and launched himself into the air from its summit (Pausanias 2.15.3; Statius *Thebaid* 3.464 is wrong to suggest that the mountain is adjacent to Lerna).

The case of Tegea, in Arcadia to the west, is more complex. In a sanctuary of Athena Poliatis called the 'Bulwark' the city kept a defensive talisman ostensibly from the heart of the Perseus myth, a lock of the Gorgon's hair (Pausanias 8.47.5). It was given to the city by Heracles when he came to Arcadia in the course of his campaign against Sparta:

> He asked Cepheus with his twenty sons to fight in alliance with him. But Cepheus feared that if he abandoned Tegea the Argives would march against it, and so refused to participate in the campaign. But Heracles received from Athena a lock of the Gorgon in a bronze water-jar and gave it to Sterope the daughter of Cepheus and told her that if an army attacked, she should hold the lock up three times from the walls without looking forwards herself, and she would thus rout the enemy. This taking place, Cepheus joined the campaign with his sons.
>
> (Apollodorus *Bibliotheca* 2.7.3)

The bronze water-jar evidently contained the lock's awful power, its role being similar to that of the *kibisis*. The most striking feature of this tale is the extrusion of Perseus himself from the midst of his familiar company: we have Athena, Cepheus and the Gorgon. This Cepheus, king of Tegea, is the son of Aleus (cf. Apollodorus *Bibliotheca* 3.9.1), and he and his father are strongly rooted in Arcadia, as the eponymous heroes of the Arcadian towns of Caphyae and Alea respectively. But we can not doubt that this Cepheus is to be identified as the original Cepheus of Perseus' myth, who was subsequently sent out to Ethiopia, Persia, Phoenicia and India. We might suspect that Heracles has come to supplant Perseus' orginal role in this particular tale, and this makes sense in context, for the Gorgon's lock is needed in war against none other than Perseus' own city of Argos. Tegea, it seems, may at some point have embraced Perseus within its own myth before writing him out again as a gesture of hostility against Argos. The figure of Heracles could be used as counterweight to that of Perseus at Sparta too. Even so, the Tegean tale intriguingly suggests that the Cepheus of the canonical version of the Perseus myth may in origin have been no exotic Ethiopian or Phoenician, but a homely Arcadian, and this is plausible. Where was a more natural place for a prince of Argos to seek a bride than in this neighbouring land?[8]

PERSEUS IN SERIPHOS AND LARISSA

A number of other cities were hallowed with a role in Perseus' myth, the first of which was Seriphos, where Dictys had brought the boy and his mother safely ashore. From around 300 BC the island struck coins with Perseus' image, which indicates that he was at that point playing a major role in its state ideology. These types were imitated by the neighbouring islands of Gyaros and Melos. Pausanias tells that, alongside Athens, Seriphos exceeded Mycenae in the honours it paid the hero (2.18.1). Seriphos was one of the many places to claim that Perseus and his adventures had left a permanent mark on their landscape and environment. The island's rocky nature was said to have resulted from the devastating work of the Gorgon's head upon it, no doubt in association with Perseus' vengeance on Polydectes (Eustathius on Dionysius Periegetes 525). A more charming take on Perseus' effect on the landscape of Seriphos was preserved by Aelian in the early third century AD. He tells that the frogs of Seriphos are silent, but make a piercing or grating noise if removed from the island. This is because they had disturbed the sleep of the exhausted

Perseus when he returned from his adventures, and in answer to his prayer they were silenced by his father Zeus (*Nature of Animals* 3.37).[9]

The 'Larissa' to which Acrisius originally withdrew for his own safety before the returning Perseus would have been none other than his own fortified acropolis, for the Argive acropolis did indeed bear the name of 'the Larissa' (Pausanias 2.24.1, Scholiast Apollonius 1.40, etc.). Indeed, according to the fifth-century AD Hesychius, Acrisius was named after Athena Akria ('of the peak'), who had her sanctuary on the Larissa. However, not one but two cities of the name Larissa seized the opportunity offered by Acrisius' withdrawal to insert themselves into the Perseus myth. The literary tradition preferred the claim of Larissa in Thessaly, which could boast the heroon-tomb of Acrisius outside its walls (Pherecydes *FGH* 3 *fr.* 26, Sophocles *Larissaeans frs* 378–83 *TrGF*, Apollodorus *Bibliotheca* 2.4.4; Scholiast Apollonius *Argonautica* 4.1091, Tzetzes on [Lycophron] *Alexandra* 838) or, more curiously, within the temple of Athena on its acropolis (Clement of Alexandria *Protrepticus* p. 39 Potter). Hellanicus indeed told that Acrisius had founded the city, perhaps with the implication that he had named it after his home acropolis (Hellanicus *FGH* 4 *fr.* 91). A little closer to Argos was Larissa Cremaste in Phthiotis, and it, too, asserted its claim to a piece of Perseus by striking coins with his image.[10]

PERSEUS IN ATHENS AND SPARTA

Other Greek cities also aspired to the glamour that Perseus could bestow, and this included its greatest ones. The Athenians had no role in the canonical Perseus myth, but they were fascinated by him, perhaps in part because of his role in decorating their patron goddess' aegis or shield with the Gorgon-head. A large proportion of the images of Perseus and his myth that survive to us from antiquity of course do so on pots made in Athens, and this must be indicative of a significant degree of Athenian interest in the hero, whatever the value of the current fashion for interpreting the images on Attic pots in the contexts of the markets for which they were destined. One of the two earliest identifiable images of Perseus of any kind comes to us on an Attic pot of *ca.* 675–50 BC (*LIMC* Perseus no. 151), and by the middle of the following century he had become a very popular theme. In due course, Perseus was celebrated also in public art at the heart of the city. Pausanias reports that Myron's statue of Perseus 'after he had done the deed to Medusa' was displayed on the Acropolis (1.23.7). This may have been erected to celebrate the alliance made with Argos in 461 BC. As we have seen, Perseus earned a comprehensive treatment from the Athenian mythographer Pherecydes in *ca.* 456 BC, and he was a firm fixture on the Attic stage throughout the Classical period.[11]

Athens was fortunate to have a namesake hero of its own that it could identify with the Argive Perseus. This man, whose name was expressed as Perrheus in the Attic dialect, was the eponymous hero of the deme and harbour of Perrhidae (Harpocration s.v. *Thyrgōnidai*; Hesychius s.vv. *Perrheus, Perrhidai*; Stephanus of Byzantium s.v. *Perseus, Perrhidai*). Pausanias noted that Athens, alongside Seriphos, outstripped Mycenae in the honours it paid Perseus, and that the Athenians had a sacred precinct dedicated to him and an altar of Dictys and Clymene, called the saviours of Perseus (2.18.1). The presence of Dictys indicates a full identification with the Argive hero by this stage. But who is Clymene, found only here in association with Perseus? She may have been the Nereid named by Homer (*Iliad* 18.47) and Hesiod (*Theogony* 351), and she may have brought Perseus' chest safely into Dictys' fishing net, as Thetis and the Nereid Doris resolve to do in Lucian's charming sketch (*Dialogues in the Sea* 12).[12]

In Sparta Perseus could be a more contentious figure. He was being admired there already in *ca.* 500 when the famous temple of Athena Chalkioikos was decorated with its bronze reliefs (Pausanias 3.17.3). No doubt he was already considered an ancestor of some of the Spartans at any rate. When Ion of Chios toasted the ancestors of the Spartan king Archidamus in the mid-fifth century BC, he spoke of 'Libating in sacred fashion to Heracles and Alcmene, to Procles and the Perseids, and let us start from Zeus' (*fr. eleg.* 27.5–7 West/ Campbell = Athenaeus 463a–c). A second-century AD inscription of the city honours one Lucius Volusenus for his virtue and goodwill towards the city and notes that he is 'a descendant of Heracles and Perseus' (Tod and Wace 1906: no. 281 = *IG* v.1 477). It is not unusual to find Perseus paired with his great-grandson Heracles in this way as a worthy ancestor of the Spartans. But sometimes the 'Perseids' could be taken to represent not Sparta's internal strength but its external threats, in contrast to its own 'Heraclids', as in the oracle preserved by Herodotus and supposedly given to the Spartans before the great Persian invasion of 480 BC (7.220.3): 'Inhabitants of broad-lawned Sparta, it is destined for you either that your great and famous city is sacked by Perseid men, or that, alternatively, the territory of Lacedaimon will mourn the death of a king from the family of Heracles.' Herodotus goes on to affirm that it was in the light of this oracle that King Leonidas sacrificed his life delaying the Persians at Thermopylae. One might suspect that the oracle and the attendant story of Leonidas were only composed post-eventum. But it is also conceivable that the oracle was of greater antiquity than the Persian war, and that at its point of delivery or composition it referred, by the term 'Perseids', to not the Persians but the original Perseids, i.e. the Argives. Argos had been Sparta's great perennial enemy in the Peloponnese from the seventh century onwards, and Sparta contrived to find herself at war with the city in every generation. Anyone composing such an oracle with Argos in mind might reasonably have expected to find it fulfilled eventually.

In 366 BC Isocrates referred to the Spartan claim to be overlords of Argos on the basis that they were the sole surviving descendants of Perseus, a claim which interestingly presents Perseus as at once a symbol of an external enemy and a symbol of an internal ancestor (*Archidamus* 17–19). Sparta may have legitimated other acts of imperialism by making appeal to Perseus' children. The claim to fame of Perseus' sole daughter, the appropriately named Gorgophone or 'Gorgon-slaughter', was that she had been the first widow to remarry. After the death of her first husband, Perieres of Messenia, she had become the wife of the Spartan Oebalus (Apollodorus *Bibliotheca* 1.9.5, 2.4.5, 3.10.3–4, Pausanias 2.21.7, 4.2.4). Was Messenia her dowry? No doubt the notion that Helos had been founded by the youngest son of Perseus, Heleios, also served Spartan imperialist ambitions (Pausanias 3.20.6).

Samos, too, found a small way to write itself into the Perseus legend. Tzetzes preserves the information that Athena drew pictures for Perseus to explain to him what the Gorgon looked like at a place that was accordingly to become the Samian city of Deikterion, 'Demonstration' (on [Lycophron] *Alexandra* 838).

PERSEUS IN PERSIA

The ostensible similarity between the name of Perseus and that of the Persians could not have gone unremarked for long after the Persians brought themselves to the attention of the Greeks through the conquest of Lydia (*ca.* 550 BC), but it will have taken something rather more powerful than mere wordplay to sustain a connection between the two terms. A strong mythical connection had been forged between them at least by the time that Aeschylus produced his *Persians* in 472 BC. Here the Persian king Xerxes is described as 'of a gold-born race', i.e., as descended from Perseus (79–80). We have just seen the oracle that Herodotus, who published his work *ca.* 425 BC, tells us was given to the Spartans in the build-up to the Persian invasion of 480. Of importance here, too, is another story he relates of the same period (7.150). According to this, Xerxes sent a herald to Argos and advised the Argives that he was kindred, being descended from Perses, the son of Perseus and Andromeda, whom Herodotus elsewhere tells that Perseus and Andromeda left behind with Cepheus so that he could have a male heir (7.61). He therefore asked them to sit quiet during the invasion, and promised to honour them appropriately after a successful outcome. After some deliberation, sit quiet the Argives did. We can be sure that the notional link between Perseus and the Persians originated with the Greeks rather than the Persians. Had the Greeks of Asia Minor already developed the link to assuage their subjection to the Persians in the sixth century? Did Argos develop it during or after 480 to apologise for remaining neutral during the great invasion, as Herodotus himself almost suggests? Or did the Greek allies develop it after the repulse of the Persian invasion as they carried the war to the Persians, as a means of now laying claim to their territory? Perses ostensibly constitutes a redundant doublet of Perseus himself. But the familiar arc of Perseus' myth could not allow him to remain in Persia, and so the generation of an all-but homonymous, matrilocal son was evidently held to be the most convenient solution. Herodotus also reports another tradition, evidently Greek in origin but attributed by him to the Egyptians, that Perseus himself was an Assyrian who became Greek (6.54; cf. Cephalion *FGH* 93 *fr.* 1).[13]

For the Greeks Persia was the home of the Zoroastrian fire-religion, the magi and magic. It was only appropriate, therefore, that in due course Perseus should also become the founder of Zoroastri-anism and of the magi, and himself a great magical adept. Such a development will also have been given a fillip by the assimilation of Perseus and his son Perses with another mythical figure, Perses, king of the Taurians. This Perses was the son of Helios (the Sun), the brother of Aietes, and the father of the witch-goddess herself, Hecate. Hecate was mother, by Aietes, of the great witches Circe and Medea. Medea then became mother to Medus, the founder of the magical race of the Medes and father to another Perses (Hesiod *Theogony* 409, Dionysius Scytobrachion *FGH* 32 *fr.* 1a *ap.* Scholiast Apollonius *Argonautica* 3.200; Diodorus 4.45–6 and 56; Stephanus of Byzantium s.v. *Persai*). When the Ps.–Lycophronian *Alexandra* (early second century BC) refers to Hecate's father under the name of Perseus, it is probably alluding to an exisiting assimilation with our hero (1175). In the twelfth century AD Eustathius tried to sum up the confused traditions he inherited from antiquity: 'the Persians, so called after Perses the son of Medus, but according to others after Perseus or after Perses the son of Perseus and Andromeda, as Herodotus says' (on Dionysius Periegetes 1059).[14]

A separate mythological mutation also contributed to the devel-opment of a magical Perseus. Euhemerising Graeco-Roman writers ('euhemerism' denotes the historicising of myth) contrived to iden-tify Perseus' father Zeus with a minor Italian deity, Picus ('Picus a.k.a. Zeus', *Pikos ho kai Zeus*), and to find beneath the myths of both figures the history of a long-dead Assyrian prince, a brother of Ninus. Diodorus tells how this Assyrian prince had come to Italy, seduced many fine women there by deploying the 'mystical illusions' associated with the Near East, and sired many children by them, including another Graeco-Roman meld, Faunus-Hermes. Upon his death his children buried him, as he had commanded, in a tomb in Crete, with the names Picus and Zeus upon it (6.5).[15]

The fifth–sixth-century AD Christian chronographer John Malalas, building on the work of the fourth-century Pausanias of Antioch, explains how Perseus invented the Zoroastrian religion. He had come to the city of Iopolis in Syria (also known as Ione), where he had recognised kindred men of Argive descent. The river Orontes, then called the Drakon ('Dragon'), flooded disastrously, and Perseus advised the Iopolitans to pray. In answer to their prayers a ball of fire came down from heaven which dried up the flood. Perseus founded a sanctuary 'Of the Immortal Fire' for the Iopolitans, and took some of the heavenly fire back to Persia, where he had a palace, and there taught the Persians to revere it, appointing trustworthy men to tend the flame, to whom he gave the name of 'magi' (Malalas p. 38 Dindorf = Pausanias of Antioch *fr.* 3 at *FHG* iv pp. 467–8). This story reconfigures an earlier tradition in which the bed of the river Orontes was created when Zeus hurled his thunderbolts down on the primeval dragon Typhon. As Typhon fled he cut the riverbed with his coils, before releasing its source as he dived into the earth. The river initially took Typhon's name for its own (Strabo C750–1; cf. Pausanias Periegetes 8.29). Like his father Zeus before him, Perseus, famous destroyer of snake-form monsters, fights the dragon-river with fire from the sky.[16]

Malalas has much to say of Perseus' magical enterprises, perhaps also derived from Pausanias of Antioch (Malalas pp. 35–9 Dindorf; cf. John of Antioch *fr.* 1.8, *fr.* 6.10, *fr.* 6.18 [*FHG* iv pp. 539–44], [Lucian] *Philopatris* 9, George Cedrenus 1.30–41). He offers a partly rationalised and deeply unsympathetic version of the Medusa tale that is strongly influenced by the familiar magical culture of his own age, that was found in the grimoires of the Greek Magical Papyri. Perseus' father Picus-Zeus instructs him in the sorcery of the abominable 'skull-cup' (*skyphos*). Perseus manufactures one of these for himself by decapitating with his sickle a wild-haired and wild-eyed but evidently harmless Libyan girl by the name of Medusa, seemingly selected at random. He consecrates her skull with mystic rites, and so produces an instrument of power with which to subject and slay his opponents. Using this to seize the throne of Assyria he covets, he then teaches the skull-cup rite to the Persians, and so calls them 'Medes' (*Mēdoi*) after 'Medusa' (*Mĕdousa*). The Gorgon-head as described aligns well with a series of recipes for skull-cups (*skyphoi*) found in a magical papyrus of the fourth century AD (*PGM* iv, 2006–2125), and these give a good indication of the sort of rites that Malalas will have envisaged. The recipes are incorporated into a fictional letter to a Persian mage Ostanes from a Thessalian sorcerer Pitys, who praises the skull-cup technique as the spell of choice for the great magi of the past. One is to take a dead man's skull and deploy some obscure words of power to summon up the relevant ghost, which will then present itself in one's dreams, and which can be employed as an all-purpose familiar. The ghost can instil sexual desire, send dreams, or strike people down sick. How far does the notion that the Gorgon-head was a magical object of this sort go back in the tradition? It may already lurk behind Ovid's *Metamorphoses*, where Eryx, one of Phineus' supporters, refers to the Gorgon-head with the phrase 'magical (*magica*) weapons' (5.197, of 8 AD).

In a further development Perseus himself became a figure of magical power to be conjured with. An imperial-period sardonyx gemstone amulet against gout, in the Hermitage, shows Perseus flying through the air with *harpē* and Gorgon-head. On the reverse is inscribed: 'Flee, gout, Perseus pursues you.'[17]

It has been precariously contended that Perseus had an impact on an indirect outgrowth of Zoroastrianism, the Mithraic mysteries, the practice of which we first encounter in Cilicia in 67 BC (Plutarch *Pompey* 24), an area, in subsequent centuries at any rate, strongly devoted to Perseus. The central Mithraic cult image is of Mithras killing the bull, the 'tauroctony': he turns away as he kills it, as Perseus does when he kills the Gorgon, and, as Perseus sometimes does, he wear a Phrygian cap. The cult image as a whole supposedly reflects the fact that the constellation of Perseus hovers above the constellation of Taurus. The name 'Perses' was given to the fifth grade of initiation. Perseus' myth is further held to have influenced other aspects of Mithraic imagery, including its *harpē*, its lion-headed god, supposedly recalling an early Gorgon, and its under-ground chambers.[18]

PERSEUS IN EGYPT

Herodotus and other Greeks, struck by the magnificence and antiquity of Egypt, sought to derive much of their religious and mythological repertoire from the country. Perseus cried out for iden- tification with an Egyptian figure, not only because he was a major and ancient hero, but also because of his established connections with Africa. By the time Herodotus published, *ca.* 425 BC, the Gorgon episode was already established in Libya, whereas the Andromeda episode had been located in some kind of Ethiopia at least since Sophocles' *Andromeda* of *ca.* 450 BC (Chs 3 and 4).

Herodotus makes record of a 'Watchtower of Perseus' adjacent to the Canobic mouth of the Nile Delta (2.15; cf. Euripides *Helen* of 769, Strabo C801). Whatever the age and nature of the building in ques- tion, the manner of his reference may suggest that he took his infor- mation about it from Ionian logographers of the earlier fifth century BC. Projecting Greek notions onto the Egyptians themselves, he indi- cates that the Greeks found Perseus in the Horus worshipped at Chemmis, the modern Ahkmîm (2.91). This Perseus had a square temple with a massive gatehouse and surrounded by trees. His statue was within. He was honoured in a supposedly Greek fashion (a clue, no doubt, to the identification), with athletic competitions including every event, at which animals, cloaks and skins were offered as prizes. The Chemmitans supposedly claimed that Perseus was born in their city but sailed from there to Greece, apparently as a baby and apparently with his mother (cf. the canonical chest epi- sode). When he came back to Africa on the Gorgon mission, he visited Chemmis, having learned the name from his mother, and recognised the Chemmitans as kin. From that time they celebrated the athletic competition for him in accordance with his instructions. Games for Perseus at Chemmis are attested still – or again – in the Roman period by an inscribed advertisement: 'Sacred Olympian competition of Perseus of the sky [i.e. Horus], open to all, celebrated with triumphal entry, in the Great Games of Pan [i.e. Min].' Herodo- tus reports also that Perseus would frequently manifest himself to the Chemmitans, often inside his temple, that he would leave behind a single sandal (winged?), and that this boded well for Egypt.[19]

PERSEUS IN THE MACEDONIAN AND HELLENISTIC DYNASTIES

The Argead kings of Macedon had claimed ancient descent from Argos from at least the reign of Alexander I (r. *ca.* 498–454), when they had sought recognition as part of the Greek community by requesting admission to the Olympic Games (Herodotus 5.22). The similarity between the family name 'Argeadae' and 'Argos' may have inspired the choice of city.

Persean imagery lurks within the Argead foundation legend recorded by Herodotus (8.137–9). The last king of the previous dynasty, disturbed by omens, dismissed his servant Perdiccas. When he demanded his pay, the king contemptuously gave him the patch of sunlight that fell on the floor through his smoke vent. Perdiccas, to his surprise, accepted the gift, cut around the patch with his knife and gathered up the sunlight three times into his robe. This enabled him, in due course, to return and seize the kingdom for himself. Here the sunlight, flowing down from an overhead aperture and being scooped up into Perdiccas' robe, correlates strikingly with Perseus' father Zeus flowing down from the overhead skylight of Danae's prison and into her *kolpos*, her 'lap' or the fold of her dress. The sunlight and Zeus alike confer kingship. And here it may be relevant that the name that the Macedonians chose from their royal family's onomasticon to project back upon their mythical founder was *Per*-diccas, recalling Perseus in its first syllable.[20]

In 407/8 Euripides recast a namesake of his patron, King Archelaus, as the founder of the Argead dynasty. A substantial papyrus fragment of the *Archelaus* preserves part of the prologue spoken by the founding Archelaus, in which he proudly traces his descent from his Argive ancestors and amongst them places particular emphasis on Perseus, and his great-grandson Heracles is there too (*fr.* 228a *TrGF = P.Hamburg* 118a). The pair had seemingly come to constitute important paradigms for Alexander the Great by the time he visited the oracle of Zeus-Ammon in Siwah in 332–1 BC:

> Thereafter a longing seized him to go to Ammon in Libya, partly to consult the god, because the oracle of Ammon was said to be infallible, and it was said that

Perseus and Heracles had consulted it. Perseus had consulted it when he was sent against the Gorgon by Polydectes. Heracles consulted it when he was travelling to Antaeus' home in Libya, and to Busiris' home in Egypt. Alexander was possessed by a rivalry towards Perseus and Heracles. He was descended from both of them, and he himself referred some part of his own birth to Ammon, just as myths referred the births of Heracles and Perseus to Zeus. Anyway, he set out for Ammon's oracle with the notion that he would either know about his affairs with greater certainty, or that he would at any rate say that he had found the knowledge.

(Arrian *Anabasis* 3.3.1–2 (cf. Strabo C814, Plutarch *Moralia* 332a))

Alexander moved in the footsteps of Perseus and Heracles. He claimed descent from them both, as his ancestors had done before him. More particularly, he could also claim that like them both he had been directly sired by Zeus-Ammon, whom his earthly father Philip had supposedly found sleeping with his mother Olympias in the form of a gigantic snake (Plutarch *Alexander* 2, Justin 11.11.3). The curious phrase 'referred some part of his own birth to Ammon' probably indicates that he held himself to have been sired jointly by Philip (upon whom he depended for his Persean blood) and Zeus. Further indications of Alexander's devotion to Perseus are to be found in his ability to recite Euripides' *Andromeda* from memory (Nicobule *FGH* 127 *fr.* 2), and perhaps, too, in the Gorgon-head he sported on his breastplate, as seen in the famous Alexander mosaic from the House of the Faun at Pompeii, which is thought to preserve much accurate historical detail. For Alexander Perseus, the scion of old Argos and conqueror of Persia, came to have massive symbolic value as, in Lane Fox's phrase, 'a hero of integration between east and west'. Nor did Perseus' Egyptian associations inconvenience the conqueror of Egypt.[21]

The Argead line expired shortly after Alexander himself, but the dynasty that eventually took its place in Macedon, that of the Antigonids, was also to turn to Perseus as an icon. Coins of the last two Antigonids, Philip V (r. 221–179 BC) and Perseus (r. 179–168 BC), are illustrated with heads of the hero Perseus in winged helmet, or full figures of him with *harpē* (*LIMC* Perseus no. 18). Nothing can speak more strongly than the fact that Philip actually called his son and heir

Perseus. The name was particularly appropriate for the child, since his mother appears to have been the Argive Polycrateia (Plutarch *Aratus* 49.2 and 51.2 and *Cleomenes* 16.5, Livy 27.31.3, 32.21 and 32.24 and Aelian *Varia historia* 12.42). The adoption of this imagery presumably entails that the Antigonid family too claimed descent from Perseus, although the details of the connection remain obscure.[22]

The Antigonids were not the only Hellenistic dynasty to lay claim to the heritage of Alexander. For the Seleucids, who eventually took over Alexander's Persian conquests, Perseus' Persian connections were of particular value too. As a preliminary to the adjacent foundation of the great city of Antioch in 300 BC, Malalas tells us, Seleucus I Nicator went up to Iopolis on Mt Silpion and made sacrifice to Zeus of the Thunderbolt in the temple Perseus had built there for his Argive kin (pp. 37–8 [incorporating Pausanias of Antioch F3 at *FHG* iv pp. 467–8], 199–200 Dindorf). It is likely that Perseus' association with the region began with Seleucus, although we can not be completely sure of this, as Greeks had frequented the mouth of the Orontes since *ca.* 800 BC, when the mysterious Al Mina trading post had been established. Seleucus celebrated Perseus further by decorating coins from his Antioch mint with gorgoneia. Later, the hero himself was to decorate the medallions struck contemporaneously by the rivals Antiochus II Theos and Antiochus Hierax. Did the Seleucids actually claim descent from Perseus? If they did, it may have been via Apama, Seleucus I's noble Persian wife (Arrian *Anabasis* 7.4.5–6, Strabo C578).[23]

Perseus was also an attractive figure for the Ptolemaic dynasty that took over Egypt after Alexander's death, for his established associations with Alexander, Egypt and of course Greece alike. Perseus' association with Egypt was taken up by Callimachus, court poet of Ptolemy II, who told that he planted the trees named *perseai* for him there (*fr.* 655 Pfeiffer; cf. Malalas p. 37 Dindorf). At some point prior to the fourth century AD the orator Aphthonius implied that a (Hellenistic?) court of the Alexandrian acropolis was decorated with images of Perseus' achievements (12.48). Long after the Ptolemies were gone, in the reign of Antoninus Pius (138–61 AD), their capital Alexandria still considered it worthwhile to issue coins displaying Perseus with the *kētos* (*LIMC* Perseus no. 213).[24]

The Seleucids and the Ptolemies may also have found themselves attracted to Perseus because the border-territory they perpetually disputed with each other hosted one of the canonical locations of his myth, Phoenician Joppa. The Andromeda episode, as we have seen (chapter 4), had already been connected with Joppa by the time that the pseudo-Scylacian *Periplus* was composed in the late fourth century BC. That the Joppans themselves soon recognised that the tale belonged to them is indicated by the fact that Ptolemies II and III (r. 282–46, 246–22 BC) minted coins in the city decorated with Perseus' *harpē*. In 58 BC Marcus Scaurus celebrated his aedileship (an annual magistracy) by mounting a show in Rome that included the bones the Joppans had been exhibiting as those of the *kētos* (Pliny *Natural History* 9.11). The skeleton was 40 feet long, the spine one-and-a-half feet thick, and the ribs were larger than those of an Indian elephant. These were no doubt the remnants of a beached sperm whale, or perhaps the fossilised bones of a pre-historic animal. When Pomponius Mela published in 43–4 AD, he referred to the bones of the *kētos* as exhibited again in Joppa (1.11). Perhaps Scaurus had duly returned them after his aedileship, or perhaps the resourceful locals had found a replacement set. Mela noted also that the Joppans kept altars dedicated to Cepheus and Phineus with great reverence.[25]

We often have cause to note the impact that Perseus' adventures left on the landscape. Joppa was rich in such marks. In the 70s AD Josephus noted that one could still observe the marks of Andromeda's chains on its sea crags (*Jewish War* 3.420). In the following century Pausanias reported that the spring 'in the land of the Hebrews' in which Perseus had washed his hands after killing the *kētos* had turned permanently red (4.35.9). The tradition in accordance with which Perseus used the Gorgon-head to transform at least part of the *kētos*' vast bulk into rock seems to imply that the monster was remembered in some striking coastal feature. However, we do not find this motif explicitly associated with Joppa. Lucian associates it rather with Ethiopia (*The Hall* 22). Pliny, writing around the same time as Josephus, similarly notes the marks left by Andromeda's chains on Jaffa's rock, and tells also that 'the Ceto of the myth is the object of cult there' (*Natural History* 5.69; cf. 5.128 and 6.182). The local goddess identified here as Ceto (*Kētō*) is thought to have been

Astarte/Atargatis, also known in Greek as *Der-kĕtō*, who resembled a mermaid in form (Diodorus 2.4, Lucian *Syrian Goddess* 14). The association of Jonah's whale (Jonah 1:3 and 1:17) with Joppa-Jaffa, where today it is celebrated in a bronze statue, may be secondary to the Perseus myth.[26]

It is hardly surprising that the Pontic dynasty of the Mithra- dateses should have embraced Perseus. He had been a favourite of the two great dynasties to east and west that the Pontic dynasty aspired to supersede, the Antigonids and the Seleucids, and he was the mythical founder of the Persian nation in which the Mithridatic dynasty had its roots. Perseus decorated the dynasty's coins in the reigns of Mithridates IV (169–150 BC; *LIMC* Perseus no. 41) and Mithridates VI (121–63 BC; *LIMC* Perseus nos. 19, 20, 42, 123), in the latter case in a wide variety of types.[27]

PERSEUS IN ROME AND ITALY

North of Rome Perseus was a popular subject in Etruscan art. He is found in bronze statuettes and on bronze mirrors, bronze cistae, intaglios, scarabs and painted plaques from the sixth century BC onwards into the third century BC (*LIMC* Perseus nos. 4, 46–9, 74–5, 97–9, 107–10, 126–9, 150ab, 164ab, 170–1, 192). Some of these arte- facts, mirrors and scarabs and a cista foot, are inscribed with the Etruscan variants of his name, *Pherse* and *Perse* (*LIMC* Perseus nos. 47–8, 75, 97, 110, 127). South of Rome he flourished on Apulian and other South Italian red-figure vases in the fourth century BC (*LIMC* Perseus nos. 32–5, 66–72, 93–5, 180–4, 189–90).

In due course Perseus was welcomed into learned Rome as an important part of the repertoire of Greek myth appropriated by its poets. Tragedies, all lost, were devoted to the various legs of his myth by Livius Andronicus, Naevius (both second half of third century BC), Ennius (third–second century BC) and Accius (later second century BC (*TRF* i, pp. 3, 30–2, 172–4)). Thereafter he featured prom- inently in the work of the extant Latin poets, notably Horace, Ovid, Manilius and Lucan, as we have seen. From the end of the first century BC and up until their city's destruction in 79 AD, the residents of Pompeii took Perseus and Andromeda to their hearts: countless images of the couple survive amongst the rich frescoes with which they decorated their houses (*LIMC* Andromeda I nos. 33–41, 67–72, 91–3, 100–1, 103–12, 129–31, 147).[28]

But the Romans also attempted to make Perseus their own more actively. Virgil's *Aeneid* (of 19 BC) alludes to a version of Danae's story in which Acrisius had put her to sea in a boat still pregnant with Perseus and she had given birth to Perseus afloat. Upon their arrival in Italy King Pilumnus, whose name perhaps vaguely recalls Polydectes', had married Danae. Together they founded Ardea and became ancestors to Turnus, Aeneas' principal antagonist in Italy (Virgil *Aeneid* 7.372, with Servius *ad loc.*, Scholiast Germanicus *Aratus* p. 147 Breysig). A compatible notion found in the Vatican Mythographers, though doubtless of older vintage, served to weave Perseus further into the history and culture of the peninsula: he was named after the Dictys-like Italian fisherman that saved him from the sea (First Vatican Mythographer 137 Bode = 2.55 Zorzetti, Second 110 Bode). We have also seen how, by the time of Malalas at least (fifth–sixth centuries AD), Perseus had also been Italianised through the identification of his father Zeus with the minor Italian deity Picus (Malalas pp. 35–6, 199 Dindorf; George Cedrenus 1.30–2; John of Antioch *fr.* 6.18, *FHG* iv p. 544).

PERSEUS IN ROMAN ASIA MINOR

Perseus made his very first appearance on a coin in Cyzicus in *ca.* 500 BC (*LIMC* Perseus no. 16). After this he disappears from the coinage of Asia Minor for 600 years. When Lucan's *Pharsalia* was published in 65 AD Perseus was sufficiently well established as the founder of Tarsus in Cilicia for the poet to attribute the epithet 'Persean' to it (3.255; cf. Ammianus Marcellinus 14.8.3). From the reign of Hadrian (117–38 AD) Perseus' image came to appear on the city's coinage and it doggedly retained him there into the reign of Decius (249–51 AD). The city displayed him in a range of contexts: he could be given the epithet *boēthos*, 'helper'; he could appear along-side a fisherman (Dictys?); he could be shown holding bulls in honour of Apollo Lycaeus, or sacrificing to him in the company of the emperor (*LIMC* Perseus nos. 5, 6 and 59). Perseus was popular with other cities in Cilicia too, where he appeared on the Hadrianic coins of Aigai, Iotape, Anemourion and Mopsos. In Lycaonia he appeared on the coins of Iconium, Laodicea and Coropissos; in Isauria on the coins of Carallia, in Cappadocia on the coins of Tyana; in Phrygia on the coins of Sebaste; and in Lydia on the coins of Hierocaesarea and Daldis (*LIMC* Perseus nos. 22, 60, 111, 215).[29]

An inscription and a literary text lay some flesh on these numismatic bones. An imperial-period decree of Argos in honour of one Publius Antius Antiochus of Cilician Aigai affirmed that the peoples of the two cities were anciently related, since 'Perseus, on his way to fight the Gorgons, came to Cilicia, the remotest part of Asia on the eastern side'. John Malalas narrates Perseus' progress through Asia Minor as a sort of mythological projection of a Hellenistic king's campaign of conquest and foundation (pp. 36–7 Dindorf; cf. John of Antioch *fr.* 6.18, *FHG* iv p. 544, George Cedrenus 1.40–1). On arrival in Lycaonia Perseus founds a city on the site of the village of Amandra. The new city takes its name, Iconium (modern Konya) from the 'image' (*eikōn*) of the Gorgon-head he sets up on a pillar there. Progressing on through Isauria he comes to the village of Andrasus in Cilicia, where he hurts the sole (*tarsos*) of his foot as he dismounts from his horse. An oracle has foretold that this portends victory. He duly prevails with the Gorgon-head, and founds the city of Tarsus on the site, sacrificing a simple girl called Parthenope to purify it. We may presume that Tarsus preserved the imprint of Perseus' foot to exhibit, in a further example of Perseus' lasting impact on the physical environment.[30]

It was into an Asia Minor saturated with Perseus and his tracks in this fashion that Alexander of Abonouteichos (in Paphlagonia) was born in the early decades of the second century AD. Lucian devoted an excoriating biography to this (in his view) shamelessly fraudulent prophet, who came to fame as the human sponsor of Glycon, 'Sweety', a snake endowed with a humanoid head and the gifts of speech and prophecy, and a reincarnation of Asclepius. Lucian tells that in the first phase of his great deception Alexander carried a sickle (*harpē*) whilst claiming descent from Perseus on his mother's side (*Alexander* 11). It is intriguing to find this latter-day, sickle-wielding Perseus on such good terms with a snake. Evidently the name of Perseus had become a great one to conjure with in the region, and conferred a remarkable degree of legitimacy on Alexander's enterprises. After achieving fame, Lucian tells us, Alexander even prevailed upon the Roman emperor to change the name of his home town from Abonouteichos to Ionopolis and to strike coins with Glycon on one side and his own image, carrying Perseus' sickle, on the other (*Alexander* 58). No coins with the image of Alexander as Perseus survive, although coins with the image of Glycon himself do, including one type from the reign of Lucius Verus (161–9 AD) that bears the legend 'Glycon of the Ionopolitans', which brings us very close to Lucian's claim. The rebranding of the city, which survives in its modern name of Inéboli, was designed to present Abonouteichos as the mother-city of Ionia. We may conjecture that a bond of kinship with Perseus was claimed for the inhabitants of Ionopolis, as it was for the town's most famous son, and just as it had been for the inhabitants of Syrian Iopolis or Ione.[31]

PERSEUS RATIONALISED

We turn now to a very different sort of exploitation of the Perseus figure, a more disinterested and deflationary one. In parallel with the development of the Perseus cycle as a living myth, there developed a series of rationalising exegeses of it. Like the myth-proper, these rationalising versions formed a tradition of their own, with their own repeated themes, variations and innovations. In due course some of these themes were curiously fed back into the mainstream tradition.

It was the Gorgon episode that first attracted the attention of the rationalisers. Palaephatus, Aristotle's contemporary in the later fourth century BC, has left us a detailed rationalised version of the Perseus myth (*On unbelievable things, FGH* 44 *fr.* 31). Phorcys was king of the gold-rich Ethiopians of Cerne, an island in the extreme west beyond the Pillars of Hercules, and his rule extended over a pair of neighbouring islands too, one of which was Sarpedonia. He made a golden statue of Athena with the epithet 'Gorgon', but died before he could dedicate it. His three daughters Stheno, Euryale and Medusa each took the rule of an island, dividing up his property between them, but keeping the statue in store. Perseus, an Argive pirate, was attracted to the rich kingdom run by seemingly weak women. He contrived to capture the women's trusted adviser, Ophthalmos, 'Eye', as he sailed between their separate islands, and he compelled him to tell him of the statue, which Perseus then demanded from the women in ransom for Ophthalmos. Stheno and Euryale cooperated and so Perseus returned Ophthalmos to them, but Medusa resisted, and so he killed her. He mounted the statue's head on his ship and renamed the vessel 'Gorgon'. Thereafter he sailed around the islands extorting money. When the Seriphians were confronted with his demands, they abandoned their island, leaving human-sized stones in their marketplace. Thereafter Perseus urged his victims to avoid the fate of the Seriphians, who had been turned to stone on seeing the head of the Gorgon.

Here we may already identify four striking characteristics of the wider rationalising tradition. First, the new story-line is meandering and arbitrary: why, for instance, did the Seriphians put stones in the marketplace? Secondly, and relatedly, there is no attempt to preserve admiration for the heroic figure, whose undermotivated actions now seem random, amoral and brutal. Thirdly, fabulous details of the original story are cheaply neutralised by deferral into personal names. The detachable eye becomes a man called 'Eye'. The monstrous Gorgon becomes the epithet of a goddess in statue form. Fourthly, fabulous details are explained as deriving from the exaggerated or metaphorical utterances of participants or onlookers, as in Perseus' threat to his victims after Seriphos. Noteworthy too is Palaephatus' merging of the Graeae and the Gorgons. This amalgamation, which may or may not knowingly salute the archaeology of the myth-proper (chapter 3), was to become popular in the rationalising tradition, surviving even into the work of the Vatican Mythographers (First Vatican Mythographer 130 Bode = 2.28 Zorzetti; Second 112–14 Bode, Third 14.1–4 Bode).[32]

Writing at some point after the fourth century BC, Heraclitus builds on Palaephatus' themes and techniques alike. He allows the

Graeae to remain separate from the Gorgons, but identifies them in turn with the Hesperides as guardians of the golden apples. They remain blind too, but use a man called 'Eye' to help them walk, in the manner of a guide-dog (*On unbelievable things* 13). Hermes was Perseus' humble track coach, and onlookers said that wings had been attached to his feet (9; cf. John Malalas p. 34 Dindorf, George Cedrenus 1.39–41). Medusa was a courtesan so beautiful that she stopped men in their tracks, so that they were metaphorically said to have been 'turned to stone'. But, falling in love with Perseus, she wasted away, lost her looks and came to resemble a horse. In depriving her of her youthful beauty, Perseus deprived her of her 'head' (1). The notion that Medusa came to resemble a horse is presented here as an explanation of the motif of the birth of Pegasus, but we cannot help but recall that one old version of Medusa's myth-proper had made her a centaur (*LIMC* Perseus no. 117 = Fig. 3.1).

The notion that Medusa metaphorically 'petrified' men with her beauty was to become a popular one in the rationalising tradition (e.g. Pausanias 2.21.5–7, quoted below, John of Antioch *fr.* 1.8, *FHG* iv p. 539). Lucian's Lycinus gives the conceit a rude twist by suggesting that a woman whose beauty has given him an erection must be a Gorgon who turns men to stone (*Portraits* 1). The third-century AD Latin poet Septimius Serenus built on this notion to produce a novel explanation for the eye of the Graeae, again identified with he Gorgons: 'the Gorgons were girls *of a single beauty*, which rendered young men motionless when they saw them' (Serenus *fr.* 25 Büchner; cf. Scholiast Germanicus *Aratus* p. 147 Breysig, First Vatican Mythographer 130 Bode = 2.28 Zorzetti, Second 112 Bode, Third 14.1 Bode). So popular did the concept of petrifying beauty become, in fact, that its influence even fed backwards into literary renderings of the Perseus myth-proper. Manilius, writing at the beginning of the first century BC, tells that, 'Perseus had not been frozen by the Gorgon, but he was frozen by the sight of Andromeda' (*On Astronomy* 5.570).[33]

The work of the rationalising mythographer Dionysius Scytobrachion, who wrote in the second century BC, is reflected in Diodorus, who wrote *ca.* 30 BC (3.52.4–55.3; cf. Pliny *Natural History* 6.36). Diodorus gives us an extended rationalising account of the Gorgons faced by Perseus. They have mutated from three monstrous sisters into an entire race of Libyan warrior women. These lived in the west of Libya adjacently to Atlas and the city of Cerne, which, however, in contrast to Palaephatus' account, was not theirs. Though they tried to take it for themselves, they were eventually defeated and almost extirpated in a great war by another race of warrior women, the Libyan Amazons, who had come into alliance with the Cernaeans. In later times, the Gorgons grew strong again under their queen Medusa, and this time it was Perseus' turn to subdue them. Eventually both the Gorgon race and the Amazon race were wiped out by Heracles as he travelled west through Libya to set up his 'Pillars'. An interesting facet of this rationalisation is that it seemingly draws on another established motif within the Perseus myth-proper, that of Perseus' war against a female army as seen in his war against Dionysus' maenad army.

Writing in the following century the paradoxographer Alexander of Myndos took a radically different approach to the Gorgons (Athenaeus *Deipnosophists* 211). His Gorgon is a variety of wild sheep that live amongst the Numidians of Libya. Normally its gaze is fixed on the ground, and kept there by a heavy fringe that falls down over its eyes, and hence it is called the 'downward-looker'. But if it can shake its hair aside, it kills whoever it sees with the beam from its eyes. Its breath is also fatal. On the one hand here the Gorgons have been cut down to size even further: no longer broadly humanoid even, they are now merely part of the exotic fauna of Africa. But on the other hand the fauna described are so bizarre that one feels that one has left the world of rationalisation far behind.[34]

Pausanias the Periegete, writing in the later second century AD, satisfyingly weaves together the strands of the Heraclitan tradition of Medusa as a stunningly beautiful woman, the Palaephatan tradition of Medusa as a queen who inherits her role from her father Phorcys, and the Diodoran tradition of Medusa as the warrior-queen of a wild race.

> Medusa was the daughter of Phorcus and after her father's death she ruled over those who lived around lake Tritonis. She went out to hunt and she led the

Libyans into battle. At the time in question she encamped her army opposite Perseus' force (for Perseus was accompanied by picked men from the Peloponnese), and she was killed by a ruse during the night. Perseus was amazed at her beauty even though she was dead, so he cut off her head to show the Greeks. But this other account seemed to be more plausible to the Carthaginian man Procles, son of Eucrates [*FHG* iv p. 484 *fr.* 1]. The desert parts of Libya produce various beasts the reports of which are incredible. Amongst them are wild men and wild women. Procles said that he had seen one of these men brought to Rome. So he conjectured that one of these women had strayed from her people and, arriving at lake Tritonis, destroyed the locals, until Perseus killed her.

(Pausanias 2.21.5–7)[35]

Here we may turn once again to the fifth–sixth century AD John Malalas' account of Perseus and Medusa (pp. 35–9 Dindorf). We might dispute whether the substitution of a mythical monster for a magical implement ultimately constitutes a move in the direction of rationalisation, though it can certainly be said that Malalas is recasting Perseus' actions in a fashion that would be readily intelligible in his own day. But Malalas' work also reflects the more established aspects of the rationalising tradition: the amoral Perseus who butchers a seemingly innocent Medusa almost at random, and the wild-woman Medusa. The cruelty of Perseus implicit in the rationalising tradition serves Malalas well as a means to discredit an otherwise popular and respected pagan hero.

We first find Zeus' impregnation of Danae rationalised in an ode of Horace of *ca.* 23 BC, where the shower of gold is an elaborate image for the bribing of Danae and her guards with money for sexual access (*Odes* 3.16.1–11; cf. John Malalas p. 34 Dindorf, George Cedrenus 1.39–41). Horace's notion became integrated into the mainstream reception of the Danae tale from the high Renaissance onwards, with painters, such as Titian, Tintoretto, Tiepolo, Boucher and Klimt, depicting the golden shower as a rain of tumbling gold coins, and so transforming Danae from a violated innocent into an experienced and expensive courtesan.[36]

With Conon, who wrote at the turn of the eras, we first encounter a rationalised version of the Andromeda episode (*FGH* 26 *fr.* 1 *apud*

Photius *Bibliotheca* no. 186). Two suitors competed for the hand of Cepheus' daughter Andromeda, Cepheus' brother Phineus and one Phoenix. Cepheus chose Phoenix, but attempted to avoid his brother's opprobrium for deciding against him by arranging for Phoenix to snatch the girl in his ship named 'the Kētos', i.e. 'Seamonster', 'either because it resembled the creature or by chance'. Perseus was sailing past, took pity on the wailing girl, sank 'the Kētos', slew its crew, 'who were all but turned to stone with amazement', and took her back to Greece as his wife. The rendering of the *kētos* as a ship here is of some interest. For all that it may initially seem an arbitrary gesture, ancient ships often used *kētos*-heads as battering rams from the later archaic period onwards. Images of ships so decorated are preserved in ancient art: they often resemble what we think of as a Viking ship (e.g. *LIMC* Ketos nos. 46–50). This in turn suggests an archaeology for Palaephatus' rather odd Gorgon ship: was that itself a reworking of an established rationalised tradition about a *kētos*-ship?[37]

OVERVIEW

The figure of Perseus could be used to adorn and legitimate states, dynasties and individuals in various ways. He could also be used to negotiate claims of sameness and difference, be it between Greeks or between Greeks and non-Greeks. On the one hand, Perseus was the most Greek of heroes, whose adventures could be read out of the local landscapes he had shaped with trees, walls, stones or even animals. On the other, he was the progenitor of the race that constituted the greatest threat to all that was Greek: the Persians. And as a stridently Greek hero with a history of travels, Perseus was an ideal figurehead for the displaced Greeks of the Hellenistic diaspora. His visits to Persia and Syria made the Greek denizens of the Seleucid empire feel at home, whilst his visits to Egypt and Libya comforted the denizens of the Ptolemaic empire. The rationalisers exploited the figure of Perseus in a different way. They worked in their own tradition, one that ran in parallel with that of myth-proper, but sometimes their work could have an impact even on accounts in the straight tradition. The work of the rationalisers prepared the ground for the allegorisation of the myth in the medieval period. It is to this, and to the wider reception of the Perseus myth after antiquity, that we now turn.

PERSEUS AFTERWARDS

PERSEUS AFTER ANTIQUITY

FROM FULGENTIUS TO FREUD: THREE AGES IN THE ALLEGORISATION OF THE MEDUSA TALE

The previous chapters have attempted to give broadly synoptic coverage to the Perseus cycle in ancient literature and art. Such treatment is not feasible for Perseus' massive impact upon the more recent western tradition, and so we will confine our focus to three themes: first, the indefatigably persistent custom of allegorising Perseus' story, which began in the early medieval period and is with us still; secondly, the mutation of Perseus into the Christian knights St George and Roger; and thirdly, Perseus' greatest moment in western art, Burne-Jones's *Perseus Series*.

From the early medieval period stems a Latin tradition that was to flourish until the twelfth century. This paradoxically combined a rationalisation of Perseus' myth with an allegorisation of it. The processes of rationalisation and allegorisation share a notion that a myth is an obscure text that requires a rational form of decoding, but in other ways they are highly antithetical. Rationalisation supposes that a myth transmits a series of historical events that have become randomly perverted as they are handed down, as it were, through a series of 'Chinese whispers'. Allegorisation supposes that a myth accurately transmits a mystical and abstract truth wrapped in decorative imagery. If a myth can be successfully interpreted according to one of these processes, it should not be susceptible to interpretation by the other. Furthermore, rationalisation seeks out the banal in its subject matter, as we have seen, whereas allegorisation relishes the exotic in it.

Writing in late fifth century AD Fulgentius begins with a rationalising account of the Gorgon episode firmly in the tradition of Palaephatus, which he attributes to one Theocnidus (*Mitologiae* 1.21). King Phorcys died leaving his three daughters wealthy. Among these the powerful Medusa increased her wealth through agriculture, and so acquired the surname 'Gorgon' modelled on the Greek word *geōrgoi*, 'farmers'. She was described as having a snake-like head because of her cunning. Perseus, arriving by ship, and so said to be 'winged', took a fancy to her land, slew her and took it. He carried off her capital, and in so doing was said to be carrying off her head. As he expanded the wealth of the captured kingdom he also invaded the kingdom of Atlas and forced him to take refuge inside a mountain, and so was said to have changed Atlas into a mountain by using the head, i.e., the capital, of Gorgon. At this point Fulgentius passes over to allegorisation to explain what the 'embroidering' Greeks meant by this story. The Gorgons are emblematic of three kinds of Terror. Stheno represents the Terror that weakens the mind, and her name is taken to derive from *asthenia*, 'weakness'. Euryale represents a Terror that occupies the full breadth of the mind, and her name is taken to signify 'breadth'. Medusa represents the Terror that not only clouds the mind but also the vision, and her name is taken to derive from the phrase 'not seeing' (*mē idousa*). Perseus, representing Virtue or Manly Courage, aided by Athena, representing Wisdom, destroys these Terrors. He turns his face away because Virtue never contemplates Terror. He has a mirror because Terror is reflected in one's external appearance. Pegasus, born from Medusa's blood, represents Renown, and is accordingly 'winged'. Pegasus' creation of the spring of Hippocrene for the Muses represents the passage of Renown into commemorative art.

The allegorising portion of the text holds the various figures of the myth to represent abstract principles. But the journey from mythical figure to the quality it represents is made in different ways. Athena represents Wisdom, and the Muses the arts, because these are fields over which these goddesses were patrons. Perseus was no patron of Manly Courage, nor were the Gorgons patrons of Terror, but these are certainly qualities that the figures uncontroversially embody within the context of the myth (already in the Hesiodic *Catalogue of Women* Perseus is described as a Master over Terror, *fr.* 129.15 MW). But the meaning given to Pegasus, for all that it is nicely judged within the context of the allegory, had no obvious point of contact with the mythical figure in its own terms. The different processes by which meaning is derived from the Gorgons' names is a curious one. Medusa's name, recast as *mē idousa*, is taken to convey her significance directly. Euryale's name means 'Broad Leap'. The second part of the name is ignored, but significance is derived directly from the first. Stheno's is simply stated to mean in itself 'weakness' and the Greek word *asthenia* is called in for support. In fact it means the opposite, 'strength' (deriving from *sthenos*, to which *asthenia* plays negatived complement). We may suspect that the tradition underlying Fulgentius had more explicitly invoked a logic of opposites. Fulgentius' reading was taken up avidly in the Latin west, and is reflected strongly in the work of the three Vatican Mythographers, who wrote between the ninth and twelfth centuries, the third of whom actually cites him by name (First Vatican Mythographer 130 Bode = 2.28 Zorzetti, Second 112–14 Bode, Third 14.1–4 Bode).

Writing in the same century as the Third Vatican Mythographer, but in the Greek rather than the Latin tradition, Tzetzes gives us a wholly different kind of allegorisation of the Gorgon myth (on [Lycophron] *Alexandra* 17). According to this the myth encapsulates not moral truths but meteorological ones. The sun (Perseus) is caused by air (Athena) to evaporate (decapitate) the finest elements of the sea (Medusa), which in themselves resemble air. But it can not evaporate (decapitate) the stable (immortal) heavier elements of the sea (Stheno and Euryale). The heavier part of the evaporated water 'streams' (*pēgazein*, Pegasus) back down to earth again as rain, whilst its lighter part becomes shiny ether (the 'golden-sworded' Chrysaor).

With the Italian Renaissance we come to the second age of the allegorisation of the Medusa tale. The Renaissance allegories tend not to strike out completely afresh, but to ground themselves at least partly in the Fulgentian tradition. Thus in the late fourteenth century the Chancellor of Florence Coluccio Salutati read the Gorgons as allegories of prose style (*On the Labours of Hercules*). As in Fulgentius, Stheno still signifies weakness, but now she represents more specifically weak prose style. Medusa continues to signify a kind of blindness or oblivion because she now represents the rhetoric that makes men forget their former thoughts. Her snakes represent the cunning rhetorical arguments that transmit wisdom. For Leone Ebreo in the late 1490s (*The Philosophy of Love*), Perseus' victory over the Gorgons symbolises the triumph of spirituality over earthly vice, and for this reading Fulgentius' association of 'Gorgon' with the working of the earth itself is called in for support. Moving across to Elizabethan England, a clearer break with the Fulgentian tradition is found in Francis Bacon's elaborate reading of the Gorgons as allegories of war (*The wisdom of the ancients* 1609 [Latin version], 1619 [English version]). Medusa, as the mortal Gorgon, represents a war that can be completed and won, in distinction to the others. To succeed one needs alacrity (winged sandals), secrecy (the Cap of Hades) and espionage (the mirror-shield).[1]

The third age of the allegorisation of the Medusa tale we inhabit still. The conviction that Medusa must somehow represent something beyond herself continues to flourish. Gorgon myth and imagery is seen as a cunning conundrum handed down from antiquity, a defined mystery to be resolved with a single brilliant insight and from which some profound truth of the human condition can be unlocked. The attitude can become explicit in titles, as in Elworthy's 'A Solution of the Gorgon Myth' and Wilk's *Medusa: Solving the Mystery of the Gorgon*. These brilliant insights, some of them rooted in remarks in ancient texts or in the earlier allegorical tradition, include the discoveries that the Gorgons symbolised fear, the sun, the moon, the sea, volcanoes, deserts, storm-clouds, lions, goats, owls, gorillas, octopuses, and underworld demons. Of these, let us confine ourselves to noting, first, that the absurd octopus theory has proven unaccountably popular and, secondly, that the storm-cloud theory is more respectable than one may at first imagine.[2]

But of modern allegorisations of the Gorgon myth it is Freud's that has had the greatest impact. His brief essay on the subject was composed in 1922, but not formally published until 1940. For him the myth's function is to allay male fears of castration. The act of decapitation in itself symbolises castration, whilst Medusa's head represents an adult vulva, the first sight of which gives rise to castration anxiety in boys. Medusa's snakes represent the vulva's pubic hair, but at the same time they also represent a host of reassuring, compensatory phalluses. Medusa's petrifying gaze further reassures boys that they can still harden in erection. This arbitrary theory, worth less than the cheap joke of Lucian of which it is oddly reminiscent (chapter 5), is without explanatory value, but has nonetheless been warmly received by Freud's psychoanalytical disciples, anthropologists, historians and feminists. Amongst the latter Cixous contends that the myth speaks not simply of male castration anxiety, but also of a corresponding female decapitation anxiety: in response to their castration anxiety men supposedly attempt to deprive women of voice and identity. Freud's work even persuades, amazingly, some Classical scholars, who have finessed it in various ways. Slater reassigns Medusa's snakes from phalluses to vulvas. Vernant compares the Gorgon with Baubo, an obscure ancient figure whose iconography does indeed combine face with vulva. And Csapo adds to Freud's compensatory phalluses the boars' teeth and lolling tongues exhibited by some gorgoneia, as well as Medusa's children, Chrysaor, 'Golden Sword', and Pegasus, the flying horse that 'gushes forth'.[3]

Another allegorical reading of the Medusa episode, published by Sartre in 1943 shortly after the publication of Freud's theory, has also been influential. In *L'être et le néant* (*Being and Nothingness*) he took the action of the Medusa head as emblematic of his notion that a person – a 'subject' – is 'objectified' by the gaze of another. In other words, another's gaze brings one from an unreflecting and unselfconscious state into a state of paralysing self-consciousness. As, in the wake of Sartre, the gaze has become a matter of concern to theoreticians of art and film, so the imagery of Medusa has retained centre-stage in their work. Some of this art-theory has been fed back into the interpretation of Classical archaeology.[4]

THE CHRISTIAN PERSEUS: ST GEORGE AND PRINCESS SABRA, ROGER AND ANGELICA

The figure of Perseus lived on in the Greek world in different forms. A folktale recorded in Lesbos in the nineteenth century seems to derive ultimately from the pagan myth (though not necessarily directly from antiquity). In this a young man with a special colt conquers forty dragons and a seven-headed beast from which he cuts the tongues. A sorceress then advises him that he will come to the castle of another sorceress who will attempt to petrify him with a drink of enchanted wine. On arrival at the castle he finds his brothers already petrified, avoids the wine, compels her to restore his brothers to life and kills the sorceress. This intriguing tale seems, from an ancient perspective, to wrap up together Perseus' divine advisers, his mission against the *kētos*, his mission against the Gorgon, and Pegasus. But it also wraps up Odysseus' encounter with the witch Circe, in which he escapes transformation into a pig by avoiding the potage she offers him and so compels her to revert his already changed companions to human form (Homer *Odyssey* 10).[5]

The Andromeda episode may have helped to shape what has become our best loved dragon-slaying legend, that of St George and the Dragon. St George's wider legend goes back to the sixth century AD, but his association with the dragon is not attested until the twelfth-century version of the *Miracula Sancti Georgii* (*Codex Romanus Angelicus* 46, pt. 12, written in Greek), by which time other Christian saints had already been slaying dragons for some eight hundred years. In summary, the fair city of Lasia was presided over by an idolatrous king, Selbius, whom God decided to punish. He caused an evil dragon to be born in the adjacent lake, and it ate anyone who came to fetch water. The king's armies were useless against it. The king and his people decided to placate the dragon by offering it a child, and the lot fell upon the king's own daughter (who in later versions acquires the name Sabra). She was duly decked out in purple and linen, gold and pearls, and sent off to the monster by her tearful father, whose attempts to redeem her life from his people with gold and silver came to nothing. George, en route back to his home of Cappadocia, encountered the girl as she sat waiting to be devoured by the dragon, and asked her the reason for her tears. On hearing the story, George prayed to god for help in subjecting the dragon and ran to meet it whilst making the sign of the cross. The dragon fell at his feet. George fitted the girl's girdle and her horse's bridle to the dragon and gave it over to the girl to lead back to the city. Overcoming their initial fear of the creature, the king and his people loudly declared their faith in the Christian God, whereupon George killed the dragon with his sword, and handed the girl over to the king. George summoned the archbishop of Alexandria to baptise the king and his people. They built a church in George's name, in which George called forth a sacred spring. In the wider text St George's legend is chiefly centred in Palaestine, with Joppa as well as neighbouring Lydda and Tyre being featured. The site of the dragon-slaying itself, Lasia, is seemingly a fictional city with a speaking name, 'Rough place.' In later redactions of the text it, too, is explicitly located in Palaestine, but it is less clear where the original author imagined it to be. Still, there may be enough here to support to the notion that St George's adventure originates, at one level, in a rewriting of Perseus'. Certainly the myth of Perseus had been kept alive in the Greek East, with the twelfth-century scholars Tzetzes and Eustathius both exhibiting close familiarity with it, as indeed in the Latin west, where the Vatican Mythographers do likewise. The version of George's slaying of the dragon that was to become the canonical one in the Latin west is that of Jacobus de Voragine's thirteenth-century *Legenda Aurea* or *Golden Legend* (58), in which the dragon-slaying is located rather in Libya.[6]

Ludovico Ariosto published the greatest epic of the Italian Renaissance, *Orlando Furioso*, in several versions between 1516 and 1532. It is of course deeply indebted to the Classical tradition and nowhere more so than in one of its best known episodes, that in which Roger (Ruggiero) delivers Angelica from a sea-monster (cantos 10.92–11.9). The narrative dizzyingly kaleidoscopes the motifs of the traditional Persean tale. The Isle of Tears off the Breton coast is inhabited by pirates who plunder the area of damsels to expose for a visiting sea-monster known as an orca. Roger flies overhead on his hippogryph (horse-gryphon) and espies Angelica chained naked to a rock on the shore. He first imagines her to be made of alabaster or marble, before falling in love with her and forgetting his long-time love Bradamant. No sooner has he addressed her than the orca arrives for its meal. It is described very much after the fashion of an ancient *kētos*, with a mass of twisting coils and a boar-like head. Roger returns to the air on his hippogryph and swoops to attack the monster with his lance, but he is unable to break through its hard carapace. The thrashing monster churns the waters so high that Roger no longer knows whether his hippogryph is flying or swimming. He decides he must use the deadly flash of his enchanted shield against the monster. He first protects Angelica from its power by slipping an amuletic ring onto her finger, then unveils the device which emits the light of a second sun that stuns the monster as soon as it hits its eyes. Roger is still unable to pierce its skin, so he gives up, liberates Angelica, puts her on the back of his hippogryph and flies off with her to a neighbouring shore, where he hopes to consummate his desire. But before he can get his armour off Angelica has put the ring in her mouth, making herself invisible, and she eludes him. His enchanted shield makes an easy substitute for both Perseus' mirror-shield and indeed the Gorgon-head he took with it, whilst the amuletic ring of invisibility pays tribute to Perseus' Cap of Hades.

The fates of Perseus and Andromeda, St George and Princess Sabra and Roger and Angelica were to remain intertwined, particularly in the fine-art tradition, where the iconographies of the three episodes tended to merge and feed off each other. The early medieval confusion between Bellerophon and Perseus, together with the defining requirement that a knight should have a mount, meant that Perseus must normally be shown rescuing Andromeda from the back of Pegasus. And this in turn required that Roger should have his hippogryph.

BURNE-JONES' *PERSEUS SERIES*

The myth of Perseus has naturally flourished again since the Renaissance in the literature, drama and music of the west, and particularly so in its art. The impregnation of Danae and the rescue of

Andromeda have proved more popular themes with painters than the decapitation of Medusa, perhaps because of the obvious opportunities they both provide for a nude dignified by Classicism. The tradition of Perseus' iconography is in fact a continuous one from antiquity. Even through the depths of the Dark Ages it was perpetuated in the illustrated codices of the principal Latin astronomical treatises, the Latin translations of Aratus' *Phaenomena* by Cicero and Germanicus and Hyginus' *On Astronomy* (see chapter 4). We have fine examples of these from as far back as the Carolingian period. In the codices imagination is given free rein, despite the basic strictures of representation enforced by the fixed relationships of the star patterns with body parts and attributes. And it was this tradition that ultimately inspired the world's single most famous image of Perseus, Cellini's 1545–54 bronze in Florence's Loggia dei Lanzi.[7]

The most elaborate Perseus project in western art is the unfinished *Perseus Series* of Edward Burne-Jones. Burne-Jones first came to the subject with a plan to illustrate the substantial 'The Doom of Acrisius' episode of his colleague William Morris' heroic-couplet epic *The Earthly Paradise* in 28 woodcuts. The poem opens memorably with an intrigued Danae watching the construction of a (Horatian) bronze tower before she is suddenly locked within as she wanders through it out of curiosity (pp. 172–3). The description of the act of impregnation, with Zeus as sunlight turning into golden rain, may offer a rare Victorian description of a female orgasm (pp. 180–2). Morris' Arthurianising tendency becomes clear when we meet the rescuing Dictys, transformed from humble fisherman to knight hunting with hawk (p. 188). Perseus' progress to the Gorgons is streamlined: Athena, initially disguised as an old woman, is his sole divine helper and gives him his equipment directly, and we encounter no Nymphs or Naeads. The handling of Medusa is distinctive: she is a tragic woman, fair but blighted by Athena with a (seemingly unattached) nest of snakes in her hair. Perseus' decapitation is presented as a compassionate deliverance of her from her misery (pp. 200–5, 217). The sea-monster sent against 'sweet Andromeda' (the name rhyming with 'play', p. 228) is fully serpentine in form, a 'worm', and Perseus is able to dispatch it relatively easily with a single blow of the sword (pp. 211, 214–15). The portrayal of the aged Acrisius in the moments before his accidental death, anxiously peering as if looking for a foe (p. 235), is particularly effective.

Although Burne-Jones' plans to provide woodcuts for this text were abandoned, the influence of Morris' poem remained strong when in 1875 he agreed to decorate a room for Lord Balfour, the future Prime Minister, with a series of ten images on the Perseus theme. The work, with some images destined for rendering in painted gesso relief, remained incomplete at the artist's death in 1898. Much preparatory material survives, but the project's most important remnants consist of ten watercolour and body-colour cartoons (1885), held by Southampton City Art Gallery, and six oil paintings, four of them complete, held by the Staatsgalerie in Stuttgart (1885–8). The series disregards the 'family saga' parts of the story to concentrate on the monster episodes, although Burne-Jones made a separate painting of *Danae* or *the Brazen Tower* (1888), which is strongly influenced by the compelling opening sequence of Morris' treatment.[8]

Burne-Jones brings to the works the medievalising inclinations he shared with Morris at many levels. The images are cropped close over the heads of his principal figures, to produce the distinctive 'low-ceiling' effect of much medieval art. Medieval too is the technique of representing a subordinate episode in the background, redeploying the foreground characters (Picture 1). The composition of figure-groups can salute the classics of early Renaissance art: his three 'Sea Nymphs', for example (Picture 3: Naeads and Nereids have been either identified or confused), recall the three Graces of Botticelli's *Primavera*. And his figures' clothing is a predominantly medieval confection, saluting in part the world of early Italian Renaissance painting, and in part the world of King Arthur: Perseus is presented as a (horseless) Arthurian knight.

On display here too is Burne-Jones' interest in symbolism, and this is particular clear in Picture 5, destined for gesso, which illustrates the birth of Pegasus and Chrysaor from Medusa's severed neck. The artist actively tries to frustrate our attempts to read the picture as a coherent image. First, the names of the characters are inscribed adjacently to them, as we might find on an icon. Secondly, the individual characters are drafted in contrasting styles and textures in a way that suggests that they exist in separate overlaid plains, and have been unnaturally superimposed through a sort of scrapbook technique. No doubt this effect would have been further enhanced in the gesso. For all that Pegasus' hard-musculatured final hoof is still emerging from Medusa's languid decapitated body, drawn in the soft style of the painter Albert Moore, it seems to belong to a different world. This picture, incidentally, is also one of few to illustrate the generation of the snakes of Libya from the drops of blood from Medusa's head.[9]

The Andromeda paintings (Pictures 8–10) seem to have been the focus of Burne-Jones' interest. As Perseus battles the fully serpentine or eel-like sea-monster (Picture 9, see Fig. 6.1) and is caught up in its arabesque coils, he appears to merge with it. His armour and the monster's skin share the same colour (more grey in the cartoon, more green in the painting) and metallic effect, and Perseus' long limbs echo the monster's coils in their arrangement. His winged sandals, scale-like armour and elaborate helmet echo in their configuration the barbs of the monster's head. Burne-Jones had tried a version of the same trick in his *St George Series* of 1868, in which the dragon is seemingly clothed in a shiny black-plated armour that mirrors St George's.

In contrast to the dark figures of Perseus and the sea-monster and the muted background, the figure of the starkly pale nude Andromeda, her back turned towards us, stands out. Burne-Jones has clearly followed the Ovidian hint (*Metamorphoses* 4.675) that Andromeda resembled a marble statue in her exposed state, and she duly reminds us of the Galatea of Burne-Jones' *Pygmalion Series* (1868–70). Her delicate chain is coincidentally reminiscent of that draped across the thigh of the Hellenistic-Roman Andromeda torso in Alexandria (*LIMC* Andromeda I no. 157).[10]

Some have seen phallic imagery in the rock to which the naked Andromeda is tied (Pictures 8–9) and particularly in the serpentine monster (Picture 9) with which, as we have seen, Perseus tends to merge. Its massive thick tail shoots upright between Perseus' legs, to hang over his shoulder. And so, it seems, we have Perseus ready

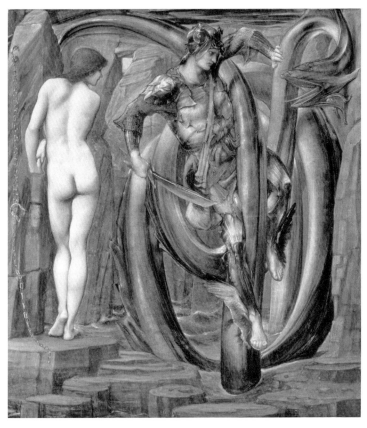

Figure 6.1 Sir Edward Burne-Jones (1833–98), *Perseus Series: The Doom Fulfilled.*

to deflower the naked and defenceless Andromeda with his monstrous, gargantuan member. This presumably countermands the androgyny that some have precariously detected in the figures of the Series.[11]

As Anderson winningly observes, 'Even [Burne-Jones'] knights in shining armour and damsels in distress seem to suffer from "ennui", a sort of bored indifference, even when faced with the immediate plight of being eaten by a sea-monster'. And indeed throughout the series Perseus, Gorgons and Andromeda alike are suffused in face, figure and even movement with a characteristic Burne-Jonesian quality that seems to combine calm, stillness, passivity, languidity, world-weariness, melancholy, lovelornness and spiritual contemplation. In this respect, too, the figures can seem strangely unintegrated into the scene of which they are a part: they are more symbols than engaged actors.[12]

Evidently with Perseus now at the front of his mind, Burne-Jones returned to the St George theme his *Saint George* of 1877 and produced in this a perfect amalgamation of the two slayers. In this full-length portrait a calm and unhurried St George stands resting on his lance and holding a Persean mirror-shield before him. In this we see the reflection of Princess Sabra with a heavily serpentine dragon coiling around her. She recalls Andromeda, chained by her wrists from above, in her pose and in her nakedness.[13]

OVERVIEW

The Perseus myth has spoken to us continuously since antiquity. Certainly, it engages us with its central irresolvable conundrum, the nature of the Gorgon. But ultimately more powerful is the fact that it is a story, or nested set of stories, with everything to offer: a faultless hero, a classic quest structure, gratifying acts of revenge, romance charged with eroticism, compelling folktale motifs and, last but not least, a pair of intriguing and terrible monsters.

CONCLUSION: THE PERSONALITY OF PERSEUS

Perseus is an easy hero to admire, but a hard one to like. Of all the major Greek heroes he is the only one to whom it is difficult to attribute a personality. For the most part, we can only see him as a cypher action-hero. This is the function of two related phenomena. First, there is little in the surviving traditions about Perseus to suggest the hero ever had to grapple with any dilemma or emotional conflict of the sort to allow him to express a personality. Unlike Acrisius, he is not faced with the problem of what to do with an only daughter whose son is destined to kill him. Unlike Cepheus, he does not have to come to terms with sacrificing his only daughter to save his people. His uncomplicated bourgeois love life presents him with no unrequited love, spurned lovers, or hard choices. Perseus merely does what is right, defeats unpleasant monsters and hostile gods with relative ease (if he has any nerves before battle, we hear little of them), and goes home with his loving wife. The nearest we come to a potential dilemma on his part is the question whether to take up the kingship of Argos acquired through the accidental killing of his own grandfather, but even in this case a happy solution presents itself. Secondly, no ancient work of literature survives for us of the sort to construct a personality for him. He is the Achilles to no *Iliad*, the Heracles to no *Madness of Heracles*, the Jason to no *Medea*. But perhaps this is in part because ancient authors of epic or tragedy similarly found it hard to find a third dimension for this figure. The only extended and sustained artistic narrative of Perseus' canonical adventures to survive to us is Ovid's in the *Metamorphoses*. This is a good read, but Perseus' personality as such is not Ovid's concern.[1]

APPENDICES

LITERARY SOURCES FOR THE PERSEUS CYCLE

The key literary sources for the myth of Perseus and its manipulation in antiquity are listed here in something akin to chronological order. Many dates remain approximate or conjectural. Most of these texts may be found in English in the Loeb Classical Library. A translation of the Pherecydes fragments is given in chapter 1. The more important or substantial texts are indicated by an asterisk. Ovid offers the best point of entry. Iconographic sources are listed at Roccos 1994a.

ca. 700 BC	Homer *Iliad* 8.348–9, 14.319–20, *Odyssey* 11.633–5
ca. 700	*Hesiod *Theogony* 270–94
mid vi	*[Hesiod] *Shield* 216–37
mid vi	[Hesiod] *Catalogue of Women frs* 129, 135, 137
later vi	*Cypria fr.* 30 West
ca. 500	Hecataeus *FGH* 1 *fr.* 22
ca. 500	*Simonides *fr.* 543 Campbell
498	Pindar *Pythian* 10.29–48
490	*Pindar *Pythian* 12.6–26
earlier v	Aeschylus *Phorcides frs* 261–2 *TrGF*
earlier v	Aeschylus *Dictyoulkoi frs* 46a–47c *TrGF*
467	Pratinas *Perseus*, at Aristias no. 9 T1 *TrGF*
mid v	Aeschylus (?) *Prometheus Bound* 792–809
ca. 456	*Pherecydes of Athens *FGH* 3 *fr.* 26
468–06	Sophocles *Acrisius frs* 60–76 Pearson/*TrGF, Larissaioi frs* 378–83 Pearson/*TrGF, Danae frs* 165–70 Pearson/*TrGF*

ca. 450	Sophocles *Andromeda frs* 126–36 Pearson/*TrGF*
431 BC	Euripides *Dictys*
ca. 425	*Herodotus 2.15, 91, 6.53–4, 150, 220
ca. 423–2	Cratinus *Seriphians frs* 218–32 K–A
later v	Hellanicus *FGH* 4 *frs* 59, 60, 91
later v	Euripides *Danae frs* 316–330a *TrGF*
412	*Euripides *Andromeda frs* 114–56 *TrGF*
411	*Aristophanes *Thesmophoriazusae* 1009–1135
407–8	Euripides *Archelaus fr.* 228a *TrGF*
ca. 398	Polyidus *fr.* 837 Campbell
iv	Ps.-Scylax 104 = *GGM* p.79
iv or before	Dinarchus of Delos *FGH* 299 *fr.* 1
late iv	*Palaephatus *De incredibilibus FGH* 44 *fr.* 3
after iv?	Heraclitus *De Incredibilibus* 1, 9. 13
276–4	Aratus *Phaenomena* 248–53, 484, 685, 711
ca. 270–40	Apollonius *Argonautica* 4.1513–17
iii	Deinias of Argos *FGH* 306 *fr.* 7
later iii	Euphorion *fr.* 18 Powell = *Supplementum Hellenisticum fr.* 418.
later iii	Livius Andronicus *Danae, Andromeda*
later iii	Naevius *Danae*
iii–ii	*[Eratosthenes] *Catasterismi* 1.15, 16, 17, 22 and 36
late iii/early ii	Ennius *Andromeda*
early ii	*[Lycophron] *Alexandra* 834–46
earlier ii	Agatharchides of Cnidus at Photius *Bibliotheca* no. 250
ii	*Greek Anthology* 3.11 (Cyzicene temple epigram)
ca. 130	Nicander *Alexipharmaka* 98–105
later ii	Accius *Andromeda*
earlier i	Philodemus *Greek Anthology* 5.132.8
ca. 30	Diodorus 3.52–55
ca. 23	Horace *Odes* 3.16.1–11
19 BC	Virgil *Aeneid* 7.372
i BC/i AD	Conon *FGH* 26 *fr.* 1 at Photius *Bibliotheca* no. 186
8 AD	*Ovid *Metamorphoses* 4.607–5.268 and 6.119–20
ca. 20	Strabo C19, 42, 759, 814
ca. 20	*Manilius *Astronomica* 5.504–634

ca. 43–4	Pomponius Mela 1.11
i	Antiphilus *Greek Anthology* 16.147
65	*Lucan 9.619–99
75–9	Josephus *Jewish War* 3.420
79	Pliny *Natural History* 5.69, 128, 6.182, 9.11
91/2	Statius *Thebaid* 3.460–5
i/ii	*[Apollodorus] *Bibliotheca* 2.4.1–5, 2.7.3
early ii	Zenobius *Centuriae* 1.41
130s–150s	Arrian *Anabasis* 3.3.1–2
mid ii	Achilles Tatius 3.6.3–3.7.9
mid ii	*Pausanias 1.21.3, 1.22.6–7, 1.23.7, 2.15.3–4, 2.16.2–6, 2.18.1, 2.18.7, 2.20.4, 2.20.7, 2.21.5–7, 2.22.1, 2.27.2, 3.1.4, 3.2.2, 3.17.3, 3.18.11, 3.20.6, 4.2.4, 4.35.9, 5.18.5, 8.47.5, 10.10.5
ii	Hyginus *On Astronomy* 2.9–12, 31, *Fabulae* preface 9, 63, 64, 151, 244, 273
ca. 170	*Lucian *Dialogues in the Sea* 12, 14, *Alexander* 11, 58, *De Domo* (*The Hall*) 22, 25, *How to Write History* 1
later ii	Artemidorus of Daldis *Oneirocriticon* 4.63
ca. 190	Clement of Alexandria *Protrepticus* p. 39 Potter
ca. 200	Athenaeus 211, 537d
Soon after 212	Oppian *Cynegetica* 2.8–13
early iii	Hippolytus *Refutations* 4.35
early iii	Aelian *Nature of Animals* 3.28, 3.37, 13.26
early iii	*Philostratus *Imagines* 1.29
iii	Septimius Serenus *fr.* 25 Büchner = Servius on Virgil *Aeneid* 6.289
iii	Scholia on Germanicus *Aratea* pp. 77–8, 82, 98, 137–9, 147, 173
iv	Servius *Aeneid* 6.289, 7.372
iv	Pausanias of Damascus *FGH* 854 *fr.* 3
later iv	Heliodorus *Ethiopica* 4.8, 19.6, 10.14
iv or later	[Libanius] *Narrationes* 35–6, at Förster *Libanius* viii pp. 55–6
450–70	*Nonnus *Dionysiaca* 25.31–142, 30.264–77, 31.8–25, 47.498–741
late v	*Fulgentius *Mythologies* 1.21

v–vi	Lactantius Placidus *Commentary on Statius'* Thebaid 1.25.5
v–vi	Lactantius Placidus *Narrationes* 4.19–20, 5.1–2
v–vi	*John Malalas *Chronicle* pp. 34–9, 199 Dindorf
vi	John of Antioch *frs* 1.8, 6.10, 6.18 (*FHG* iv pp. 539–44)
vi	Stephanus of Byzantium s.vv. *Kynoura, Midea, Mykēnai, Persai, Perseus, Thasos*
ca. 875–1075	*First Vatican Mythographer 71, 73, 130, 131, 137
ix–xi	Second Vatican Mythographer 110–14
xi	George Cedrenus 1.30, 32, 39–41
x	Suda *s.v. monokrēpidi*
xii	*Tzetzes on [Lycophron] *Alexandra* 17, 836, 838, 839, 842–6, 879, 1175
xii	Eustathius on Dionysius Periegetes 38, 211, 525, 767, 857, 910, 1059
late xii	Third Vatican Mythographer (= Master Alberic of London) 14.1–4

UNDATEABLE

Ctesias of Ephesus *Perseis* apud [Plutarch] *On Rivers* 18.6
Scholia on Homer *Iliad* 14.319, 19.116
Scholia on Apollonius *Argonautica* 1.747, 3.200, 3.1035, 4.1091

FAMILY TREE

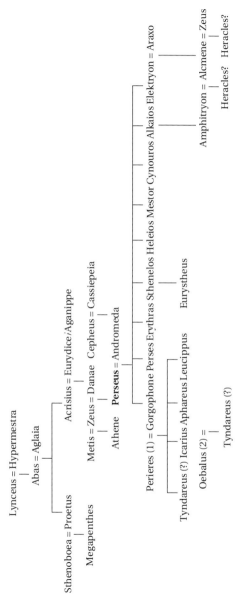

NOTES

1 INTRODUCING PERSEUS

1 Pherecydes and Apollodorus: Frazer 1921: i 153, Woodward 1937: 8, Gantz 1993: 307. The Apollodoran material in turn forms the basis for Zenobius *Centuriae* 1.41 and Tzetzes on [Lycophron] *Alexandra* 838.
2 For the narrative's shell structure see Aélion 1984: 202–8 and Dillon 1990: 5.

2 THE FAMILY SAGA

1 For the four Aeschylean plays see Gantz 1980: 149–51, 1993: 302. The *ca.* 490 theory: Howe 1952: 172–6, 1953. Baby Perseus on the pots: Schauenburg 1960: 3–12, Maffre 1986: 336–7. The *ca.* 460 theory: Oakley 1982, 1988, Simon 1982: 139. For a comprehensive review of all fragmentary dramas bearing on the Perseus cycle, see Dillon 1990: 201–43.
2 For discussion of the Sophoclean Perseus plays see Howe 1952: 198–227. For the various Greek myths concerning accidental killing with a discus see Dillon 1990: 60–2.
3 Discussion in Howe 1952: 228–49.
4 Discussion of the relevant comic fragments at Dillon 1990: 234–5. For Cratinus see Dugas 1956: 9–10, with observations on the placenames in the fragments, and Ruffell 2000: 492–3.
5 See the commentary on these images in Maffre 1986: 335–6. Radermacher 1917 contended that the imagery was inspired by shooting stars.
6 See Hartland 1894–6: i, with a wealth of folktale parallels for the Danae

episode, close and remote, Segal 1990, a collection of classic essays, amongst which Rank's is of particular importance, Binder 1964: 123–250, Dillon 1990: 34–52. For Cypselus see Ogden 1997: 87–94.

7 The myth is discussed at Handley and Rea 1967, Bauchhenss-Thüriedl 1971, 1986, Burkert 1979: 6–7, Gantz 1993: 428–31, Heres and Strauss 1994, Collard *et al.* 1995: 17–52.

8 Dillon 1990: 14 reads divine 'fosterage' as an initiatory motif.

9 See Ogden 1997: 53–61.

10 See the discussions in Glotz 1904: 69–97, Delcourt 1938: 37–43, Bremmer and Horsfall 1987: 26–50, Dillon 1990: 43–5, Sissa 1990: 101–3 and 119–21, Ogden 1997: 13, 28, 31–2, 53–4, 58, 60.

11 The theory of Hyginus' dependence on Ovid: Gantz 1993: 310.

12 With Pindar *fr.* 284 compare Apollodorus *Bibliotheca* 2.4.1, where a non-Pherecydean source is indicated but not named. For further speculation on the possible role of a supposed seduction by Proetus in the myth, see Gantz 1993: 300–1.

13 See Gantz 1993: 303.

14 The metre of Simonides' text baffled even the ancients themselves: West 1981.

15 For reconstruction of the *Dictyulci* see Howe 1952: 191–7, Lloyd-Jones 1957: 531–41, Werre-de Haas 1961 (especially 72–4), Dillon 1990: 208–12.

16 See also chapter 5 for Aelian's account of the adult Perseus' dealings with the frogs of Seriphos.

17 For the Telemachus comparison, cf. Dillon 1990: 19.

18 For discussion of the workings of Polydectes' trick, see Halliday 1933: 131, Vernant 1991: 135, Napier 1992: 78–9, Gantz 1993: 303, Wilk 2000: 243 n.1.

19 Cf. Howe 1954: 214.

20 The only substantial modern discussion of this episode is that of Dillon 1990: 161–200; see 165 for Apollodorus of Athens.

21 For the Perseus-maenad vases, see Dugas 1956: 11–13, Schauenburg 1960: 93–6, 139–40, Dillon 1990: 171–9, 235–6, Schefold 1992: 90, Roccos 1994a: 346. For Dionysus' tomb at Delphi, see the discussion in Fontenrose 1959: 388 (with care).

22 For the *Arg(i)ania* see Dillon 1990: 185–7. For the *Agriōnia* see Schachter 1981–94: i, 173–4, 179–81, 181–91.

23 For the killing of Dionysus in other contexts see above all Linforth 1941: 306–64, with further references at 310 n.3; cf. also Detienne 1979: 68–94, Dillon 1990: 169–70, Seaford 2006: 115–18. For Dionysus 'In the Marshes' see Burkert 1985: 237.

24 See Gigli 1981, Dillon 1990: 193–5.

25 For the daughters of Proetus see Frazer 1921 at 2.2.2 and Gantz 1993: 117, 311–13, both with further sources. Note also Halliday 1933: 126. For the significance of these myths, see Burkert 1983: 176–7, 1985: 165; cf. also Dugas 1956: 12.

3 MEDUSA AND THE GORGONS

1 Cf. Krauskopf and Dahlinger 1988: 285–6. Halm-Tisserant 1986 notes that the Gorgon-head bearing aegis is only associated with Athena in art from ca. 550 BC, whether in the form of a shield of a bolero, and so concludes that the passages of the *Iliad* which incorporate the aegis into Athena's panoply are later interpolations.

2 For the date of the *Theogony* see West 1966: 40–78.

3 For gorgoneion and Gorgon iconography in general see Furtwängler 1886–90 (a classic article), Glotz, G. 1877–1919a, Blinkenberg 1924, Hampe 1935–6, Besig 1937, Riccioni 1960, Howe 1952: 91–166, 1954, Feldman 1965, Sparkes 1968, Von Steuben 1968: 13–17, 1979, Karagiorga 1970, Phinney 1971, Stern 1978, Napier 1986: 83–134 (with care), Floren 1977, Belson 1981 (on architecture: a very clear piece of work), Halm-Tisserant 1986, Krauskopf and Dahlinger 1988 (esp. 316–19 for the earliest material), Jameson 1990, Wilk 2000 (with care). For the rare and challenging nature of the frontal face in two-dimensional Greek art, see Vernant and Ducroux 1988, Frontisi-Ducroux 1989, 1993, 1995, Vernant 1991: 111–38.

4 See the discussions of the images at Howe 1952: 33–46, Carpenter 1991: 104, Gantz 1993: 304, Roccos 1994a: 345. For further centaur Gorgons (without Perseus), see the series of sixth century BC engraved gems, Boardman 1968 nos. 31–3. It is conceivable that Medusa is found represented in almost inverse form, with humanoid body and horse's head, on an archaic Chaldician-style amphora from Rhodes, illustrated at Smith 1884 plate xliii. This a puzzling image: perhaps we are looking at Pegasus being born head-first from the severed neck, or even a human-bodied Pegasus (I thank Emma Aston for drawing this image to my attention). For the date of the *Shield*, see Cook 1937.

5 Medusa tale first: e.g. Jameson 1990: 216, Heubeck and Hoekstra 1989 on *Odyssey* 11.633–5. Gorgoneia first: e.g. Hopkins 1934: 341–5, Howe 1954: 214–15, Gantz 1993: 304.

6 For the apotropaic function of gorgoneia, see Roscher 1879: 46–63, Harrison 1903: 183–97, Feldman 1965, Benoit 1969, Vernant and Ducroux 1988: 191–2, Frontisi-Ducroux 1989: 159, Dillon 1990: 75–81, Carpenter

1991: 105 (noting that name of the 'gargoyle' that began to appear on medieval churches from ca. 1200 AD may ultimately be cognate with 'Gorgon'), Wilk 2000: 151–81 (for the critical split-second theory, and also supposing that gorgoneia on temples served to deter birds from roosting under the rooftiles), Mack 2002: 572–4, 585, 592. For gorgoneia specifically on shields, see Chase 1902.

7 See Harrison 1908: 187, Halliday 1933: 138–8, Howe 1952: 29–30, 1954, Croon 1955, Riccioni 1960: 144, Boardman 1968: 38–9, Napier 1986: 83–134, 1992: 80, Krauskopf and Dahlinger 1988: 316–17, Jameson 1990, Vernant 1991: 111–16.

8 For the Near-Eastern background to the Gorgon see above all Burkert 1987: 26–33, 1992: 82–7, and also the discussions at Hopkins 1934, 1961, Howe 1952: 72–6, 1954: 217–18, Croon 1955: 12–13, Schauenburg 1960: 34–5, 134, Barnett 1960, Riccioni 1960: 135–43, Goldman 1961, Boardman 1968: 37–9, Napier 1986: 83–134, Krauskopf and Dahlinger 1988: 317, West 1997: 453–5, Wilk 2000: 64–5. For Gorgon imagery of the Mistress-of-Animals type, see Frothingham 1911, Marinatos 1927/8, Howe 1952: 47–66, 1954: 215, Kantor 1962, Karagiorga 1970, Phinney 1971, Vernant 1991: 115–16.

9 See the discussions at Roscher 1879: 117, Robert 1920: 245, Howe 1952: 68–9, 1954: 216, Schauenburg 1960: 131–2.

10 Athena as Perseus' divine helper: Deacy (forthcoming).

11 See Jameson 1990: 221, Gantz 1993: 305, Larson 2001: 151, 262. Schefold 1992: 86 confuses the Naeads with the Graeae.

12 Aristias: cf. Dillon 1990: 203. The South Italian vases: Carpenter 1991: 107.

13 Cf. Gantz 1993: 306.

14 This argument runs counter to the established trend, which is to view the Aeschylean plot as a simplification of the Pherecydean one, designed to suit the stage's unity of action: thus Halliday 1933: 132, Howe 1953: 270 and Gantz 1993: 305. Halliday notes the awkwardness of Pherecydes' jostling divine helpers.

15 Roccos 1994a: 341 detects winged boots on Perseus' feet (the only part of him to survive) on the ca. 657–50 Proto-Attic neck amphora with the wasp-bodied Gorgons, but this seems ambitious. Boardman 1968: 39 argues that Perseus' winged boots originated in an artistic elaboration of curling boot-tongues.

16 For the Cap of Hades see Hermann 1853, Roeger 1924. Phinney 1971: 449–50 disputes that the Cap of Hades played a role in enabling the decapitation itself.

17 The sickle in Perseus' (and Heracles') iconography: Milne 1956: 301,

Roccos 1994a: 347. Sickles deployed against monsters: Schmidt 1958 (anguiforms), Boardman 1968: 39, Jameson 1990: 28 (more generally). Argos originally a dragon: Watkins 1995: 316, 383–4. Uranus: Zeitlin at Vernant 1991: 136.

18 Pherecydes' account: but Phinney 1971: 458–9 suspects that the reference to a mirror derives from a Byzantine interpolation. The reflected head and the aetiology of the shield blazon: Vernant 1991, Gantz 1993: 306–7, Frontisi-Ducroux 1993, Wilk 2000: 148.

19 Perseus and the Hyperboreans: discussion at Howe 1952: 170–1, Dillon 1990: 22–7.

20 See Roscher 1879: 23–30.

21 For Atlas, see Gantz 1993: 410–11. Ancient images of Atlas and Perseus: De Griño *et al.* 1986: 3, 7.

22 The notion that the Gorgon is an underworld demon and emblem of death is argued with vigour by Croon 1955 (unpersuasively), Baldi 1961, Feldman 1965: 491–2, Hughes and Fernandez Bernades 1981, Dillon 1990: 94–7, Wilk 2000, especially 183–91. See also Krauskopf and Dahlinger 1988: 285, Frontisi-Ducroux 1989: 157, Vernant 1991: 121–34.

23 Polydectes: Halliday 1933: 129. Sea-monster: Schmidt 1907: 155–87, Vermeule 1979: 179–96.

24 Dillon 1990: 30 is wrong to assert 'in no case does Perseus use the *gorgoneion* to kill Acrisius'.

25 Cf. Phinney 1971: 453, Vernant 1991: 135, 147.

26 See, importantly, the material collected at Roscher 1879: 64–5, 74–7. *Drakōn* and *derkomai* as cognate: so Chantraine 1968–80 s.v. *derkomai*, but Frisk 1960–73 s.v. *drakōn* has doubts.

27 For the petrifaction process see also Schauenburg 1960 plates 37–8; cf. Frontisi-Ducroux 1993, Roccos 1994b. For Ovid's statues see Hardie 2002: 178–80.

28 Cf. Phinney 1971: 451–2.

29 For the bellowing of Euryale see Roscher 1879: 85–99. Etymology: Roscher 1879: 93–4, Howe 1952:12–17, Feldman 1965: 487–8, Phinney 1971: 447, Napier 1986: 88, Vernant 1991: 116–18, 125–7, Mack 2002: 588 n.5. Linguistic literature: Frisk 1960–72 and Chantraine 1968–80 s.vv. *gorgos*.

30 For the development of the beautiful Gorgon in art, see Krauskopf and Dahlinger 1988: 324–5. For the Medusa Rondanini see Phinney 1971: 452–3, Belson 1980.

31 Gantz 1993: 305–6. For the Graeae in art, see Kanellopoulou 1988, Oakley 1988, and more generally Drexler and Rapp 1886–90 and Mack 2002: 590.

32 Cf. Halliday 1933: 134, Phinney 1971: 446

33 Cf. Vernant 1991: 123, 145.
34 For the Hesperides see Simon 1990 and Gantz 1993: 6–7. For the image of Perseus, the Hesperides and Ladon see Schauenburg 1960: 88–9 and plate 35.2.
35 For female triads and dyads in Greek myth (they extend far beyond the Perseus cycle), see Hansen 2004: 306–9.
36 For the Eurymedon-Medusa congruence, cf. Dillon 1990: 14–15.
37 The parallelism between Perseus' two monster fights: cf. Wilk 2000: 26–7. For the possibility that the Gorgons could be conceived of as sea-nymphs, see Krauskopf and Dahlinger 1988: 286. The identity between Andromeda's *kētos* and Ceto mother of the Gorgons is sponsored by Mack 2002: 588, 601 n.23. For Ceto as a sea-monster in art, see Boardman 1987: 78, Papadopoulos and Ruscillo 2002: 207.
38 For Bellerophon see Robert 1920: 179–85, Schefold and Jung 1988: 115–27, Gantz 1993: 312–16, Lochin 1994a, 1994b.
39 For the associations between Perseus and Bellerophon, see Aélion 1984, Schefold 1992: 90–1, Gantz 1993: 312–16, Wilk 2000: 135–7, the last with care. For Euripides' *Sthenoboea* and *Bellerophon* see Collard *et al.* 1995: 79–120. For the conformity of the Sthenoboea/Anteia episode to the 'Potiphar's wife' story-type, see Hansen 2002: 341.
40 See Gantz 1993: 340–73. The exchange between Pelias and Jason: see Halliday 1933: 131.
41 For *monokrēpides* see above all Brelich 1955–7; also Brunel 1934, Deonna 1935, Lambrinoudakis 1971: 241–301, Robertson 1972, Edmunds 1984, Ogden 1997: 32.
42 For the Gorgon adventure as an initiation rite projected into myth see especially Hughes and Fernandez Bernades 1981, Dillon 1990 and Jameson 1990. Dillon's general notion that Perseus significantly progresses in the course of his story from *oikos* (family) to *polis* (city) seems contrived, but his comparison (16) of the archaic gorgoneion's typical boar's tusks with the boar a Macedonian youth must kill before reclining with the men (Athenaeus 18a) gives pause for thought. Jameson's notion that the myth of Perseus served as a sort of performance-text for boys' initiation rites in Mycenae is highly speculative. Further contentions that Perseus' myth is essentially one of maturation are to be found at Croon 1955, Burkert 1987: 27, 1992: 85, Napier 1986: 83–6, 181, 1992: 85, Mack 2002: 579–80. It is often held that dragon-slaying more generally idealises trials of initiation too: Röhrich 1981: 813.

4 ANDROMEDA AND THE SEA-MONSTER

1 Schauenburg 1960: 56 disputes that Andromeda's hands are tied.

2 For the case: Gaster 1952, Fontenrose 1959: 275–306, 390, 467; Morenz 1962, Burkert 1983: 211, 1987: 28, 1992:85, Schefold 1992: 90. Much is made of the 'Astarte Papyrus' (*ANET* 17–18), an Egyptian account of the Canaanite myth.

3 See Burkert 1987: 28, 33, including an image of the seal; cf. Fontenrose 1959: fig. 18 for a similar image. Marduk uses a sickle against Tiamat: Hopkins 1934: 348.

4 For Sophocles' *Andromeda* and its iconography see Petersen 1915: 606–17, Pearson 1917 and *TrGF* ad loc., Woodward 1937: fig. 29, Howe 1952: 218–27, Schauenburg 1960: 97–103, 1967b, Phillips 1968, Dillon 1990: 206, Klimek-Winter 1993: 23–54, Roccos 1994a: 346, Balty 1997, Collard *et al.* 2004: 137, 147. The notion that the play was satyric does not carry much support.

5 For reconstructions see Müller, E. 1907, Howe 1952: 253–80, Dillon 1990: 226–31, Von Bubel 1991, Klimek-Winter 1993: 55–315, Austin and Olson 2004: lxii–lxiii, Collard *et al.* 2004: 133–68, Wright 2005: 121–2.

6 See Klimek-Winter 1993: 108–18 and Collard *et al.* 2004: 139–40. Phillips 1968 rather sees the development of the rock-arch iconography as originating in Italian vase painting, but he seems to underestimate the significance of Euripides' Echo.

7 For the Latin Andromeda tragedies see Klimek-Winter 1993: 317–75.

8 Perseus and the zodiac: Goold 1959: 11. More generally, see Rathmann 1938.

9 Eudoxus etc.: Klimek-Winter 1993: 19–21.

10 For further parallels between the figures of Danae and Andromeda, see Csapo 2005: 101.

11 The *King Kong* (1933) scene actually inspired in turn Ray Harryhausen's treatment of the Andromeda sequence in the only significant movie to have been made of the Perseus story, the generally worthy *Clash of the Titans* (1981). This accounts for the disappointingly humanoid appearance of his *kētos*, rechristened as a 'Kraken'. See Harryhausen and Dalton 2003: 260–82, esp. 265; cf. Wilk 2000: 209–15 (unsympathetic) and Llewellyn-Jones 2007.

12 Putti and Nereids ride *kētē* in decorative scenes: Boardman 1997: 731, 735–6.

13 For the *Thesmophoriazusae*'s parody of Euripides' *Andromeda*, see Rau 1967: 65–89, 1975 and Austin and Olson 2004 *ad loc.* For the plank see Collard *et al.* 2004: 142.

14 For the images discussed here see Roccos 1994a: 346–7.

15 Wright's notion, 2005: 68, that Pherecydes had Perseus 'abandon' Andromeda when he pursued Acrisius to Larissa is based on a counter-intuitive interpretation of Pherecydes *FGH* 3 *fr.* 26 = *fr.* 12, Fowler. It is difficult to know what to make of the Scholiast to Germanicus' claim that Eros (Cupid) had fallen in love with Andromeda prior to the Perseus episode (Breysig 1867: 139).

16 Doubt that Euripides' *Andromeda* was set in Ethiopia: Wright 2005: 129. The western Ethiopians: cf. Klimek-Winter 1993: 258.

17 For discussion of the Heliodoran episode in folkloric context, Billault 1981.

18 The traditional suppositions about the role of *fr.* 141 *TrGF* in Euripides' play, for which see Collard *et al.* 2004: 165, are unpersuasive.

19 For the term *kētos* and its application and for ancient encounters with whales, see Boardman 1987, 1997 and Papadopoulos and Ruscillo 2002, especially 199–201, 206, 216.

20 See Boardman 1997: 733–5 for the affinity between Nereids and *kētē* in art.

21 Coleman 1983 unpersuasively views Manilius' description as a largely realistic one of an actual whale of the mystoceti class.

22 For the canonical form of the *kētos* in art see above all Boardman 1987, especially 74, 78, 1997, especially 731–5, Papadopoulos and Ruscillo 2002, especially 216–22. See also, more generally, Shepard 1940, Vermeule 1979: 179–209.

23 For the Caeretan *hydria* see Boardman 1987: 80, 1997 *ad loc.*, Papadopoulos and Ruscillo 2002: 218.

24 Dillon 1990: 134 is therefore wrong to date the notion that the sea-monster should have been fossilised only from the first century AD.

25 Milne's notion, 1956: 301, that Perseus had attacked the *kētos* with spears alone on (lost) fifth-century BC Attic vases is speculative.

26 Cf. Brommer 1955, Oakley 1997: 628–9.

27 For the myth and iconography of Hesione see Drexler 1886–90, Robert 1920: ii, 349–58, Weicker 1912, Brommer 1955, Milne 1956, Lesky 1967, Burck 1976, Gantz 1993: 400–2, 442–4, Oakley 1997, the last with further bibliography.

28 See Boardman 1987: 77, 1997: 732, Mayor 2000: 158–62, Papadopoulos and Ruscillo 2002: 219.

29 For *LIMC* Hesione no. 4 see cf. Alexiades 1982: 51–3, Boardman 1987: 80, Papadopoulos and Ruscillo 2002: 216–17. For *LIMC* Hesione no.6 see Papadopoulos and Ruscillo 2002: 218.

30 For Menestratus cf. Hartland 1894–6: iii, 37.

31 See Hetzner 1963: 12–21 for a catalogue of folktales in which a hero delivers a maiden from a dragon. For the British dragon-legends referred to, see Hartland 1984–6: iii, 14–15 and Simpson 1980: 40–1, 61–4, 70–5, 78–81, 109, 118, 133–41.

32 For the tale of *Silverwhite and Littlewarder* see Cavallius and Stephens 1848: 78, Lüthi 1976: 47–57. For folktale comparanda for the Andromeda tale, see Hartland 1894–6: i, 20–1, iii, 32–3, 47–9, AT 300, Bolte and Polívka 1913–32: i 547–56 (parallels for no. 60 Grimm, *Die zwei Brüder*), Schmidt 1958, Liungman 1961: 38–47, Röhrich 1981, Alexiades 1982 (modern Greek tales), Scherf 1982: 61–4, Ashliman 1987: 51–3 (English language tales), Hansen 2002: 119–30. Milne 1956: 301–2 speculates that Perseus may also have been thought to have cut off the tongue of his *kētos*.

5 THE USE AND ABUSE OF PERSEUS

1 Perseus as a Mycenean king: Nilsson 1932: 26, 40–3, Mylonas 1957: 15 (specifying that Perseus ruled '*c.* 1310 or 1340 BC'!), Schauenburg 1960: 137–8, Napier 1992: 79–80. The Perseus myth's origin in the Argolid: Glotz 1877–1919b: 400, Halliday 1933: 116, 126. Howe 1952: 76–8, 1954: 217. The notion that Argos appropriated Perseus from Mycenae: West 1985: 152 (in the Dark Ages), Jameson 1990: 213 (in the Classical period). Date of Perilaus: Berve 1967: 35–6.

2 Danae's prison as a tholos-tomb: Halliday 1933: 120, 127–8, Howe 1952: 79–80, Napier 1992: 83, Janko 1994: 14.319–20. The coins: see further Imhoof-Blumer and Gardner 1888, Glotz 1877–1919b: 400 n.8, Frazer 1898: 2.18.1, Head 1911: 440.

3 Cf. Jameson 1990: 222.

4 The *Perseis*: Davies 1986: 97–8 and Dillon 1990: 3, 158 curiously assert that no *Perseis* poem was ever composed. Yialouris 1953: 320–1 contended, on the basis of iconography, that a *Perseis* epic thrived in the late seventh century BC. He makes no reference to Ctesias, and proposes that it may have been composed by Eumelos. Halliday 1933: 122 postulates the existence of a lost 'Argive' epic. For *perseai* as *Mimusops Schimperi* see Gow and Scholfield 1953 *ad loc.*

5 Jameson 1990.

6 Statius: cf. Smolenaars 1994 *ad loc.*

7 The puzzling role of the Cyclopes: Gantz 1993: 310. Proetus and Tiryns: see Dugas 1956: 6–8. The Tirynthian masks: Jameson 1990: 218–19. The

coins of Asine: Glotz 1877–1919b: iv, 400 n.8; Imhoof-Blumer and Gardner 1888: plate I 17–21, plate GG 23, Head 1911: 432.

8 The lock of the Gorgon: see Krauskopf and Dahlinger 1988: 286, Faraone 1991: 138. Original identity of the two Cepheuses: Halliday 1933: 141–2, West 1985: 83–4, 147–8.

9 Seriphos and Perseus: Croon 1955 even supposed that Seriphos was the ancient centre of his cult. The coins: Glotz 1877–1919b: 400, Head 1911: 490, *LIMC* Perseus nos. 18 and 40.

10 Acrisius' Larissa as the Argive acropolis in origin: Glotz 1877–1919b: 400. Coins of Larissa Cremaste: Head 1911: 300.

11 The popularity of Perseus on sixth-century Athenian vases: Milne 1956: 300, Sparkes 1968, and Roccos 1994a. Myron and the Argive alliance: Glotz 1877–1919b: 401.

12 Perrheus: Glotz 1877–1919b: 401, Farnell 1921: 337. Clymene: Dugas 1956: 2–3.

13 The second-century Agatharchides of Cnidus (at Photius *Bibliotheca* no. 250) was to deny the link between *Perseus* and *Persai* on accentual grounds.

14 Tzetzes on [Lycophron] *Alexandra* 1175 upbraids the poet for metrically-induced recklessness. For the various mythological figures named Perses, see Wüst 1937a, 1937b, 1937c.

15 For Picus-Zeus see Cook 1914–40: ii, 693–6, Harris 1916, Rohde 1941: 1217.

16 The theme of Perseus' discovery of long-lost kin in remote lands goes back to Herodotus' Egyptian Perseus (2.91.2–5); see below.

17 Glotz 1877–1919b: 402, Langlotz 1960: 35, 43 (with illustration), Schauenburg 1960: 127.

18 Ulansey 1989: 25–45, building on Will 1947.

19 The 'Watchtower' reference from the Ionian logographers: Lloyd 1969: 81. Strabo locates the Watchtower rather between the Bolbitine and Sebennytic mouths. For the identification of Horus as the Chemmitan god to whom Herodotus refers, see Lloyd 1969, superceding the former belief that Herodotus was referring to Min. For the inscribed advertisement, see Iconomopoulos 1889 = Lloyd 1969: 84.

20 For the rich king-making imagery in this tale see Ogden 1997: 119–23.

21 The Alexander Mosaic: Naples, Museo Nazionale 10020; cf. Stewart 1993 esp.130–50. Lane Fox 1973: 201.

22 Antigonid Perseus coins: see also Hammond and Walbank 1988 plates m and n, Dillon 1990: 175–6. Polycrateia: Glotz 1877–1919b: 402 and Ogden 1999: 183–7.

23 For Perseus, Iopolis and the foundation of Antioch, see Downey 1961: 49–55, 67–8, 75 (coins at 50–1); Grainger 1990: 47–8, 55–6. For the royal medallions: Glotz 1877–1919b: 402.

24 Alexandrian coins: see also Head 1911: 862.

25 Joppan coins: Head 1911: 803. The bones: Mayor 2000: 138–9, Papadopoulos and Ruscillo 2002: 213. Mayor tentatively suggests that fossilised bones may have been connected with Perseus' petrifaction of the *kētos*.

26 Identity of Ceto here: Glotz 1877–1919b: 401, Fontenrose 1959: 282–3. Jonah at Joppa: Schmidt 1907, Boardman 1987: 77, Mayor 2000: 138–9.

27 See further Head 1911: 501–2 for the coins of Mithridates VI; see further Ulansey 1989: 38–9.

28 For these murals see Phillips 1968.

29 Coins of Cyzicus: Head 1911: 526. Imperial-period coins: see further Glotz 1877–1919b: 401–2, Head 1911: 716–17, 721 (Cilicia), 733 (Tarsus), 713, 720 (Lycaonia), 753 (Isauria), 684 (Phrygia), 650–1, 650 (Lydia).

30 The inscription: *BCH* 28 [1904] 421–4 lines 20–1. Perseus at Tarsus: see further Burkert 1983: 210 n.26, 1987: 28, 1992: 85.

31 For Alexander and Glykon see Victor 1997, with 169–70 and plates 2–5 for the coins.

32 For the dating of the three Vatican Mythographers, see Elliot and Elder 1947 and Zorzetti and Berlioz 1995.

33 I thank my colleague Prof. Tim Whitmarsh for the Lucian reference.

34 Wilk 2000: 90–2 ponders whether a gnu or a Barbary sheep underlies this description.

35 Nothing further is known of Procles' date.

36 Titian *Danae receiving the shower of gold* (ca. 1560); Tintoretto *Danae* (ca. 1578), Tiepolo *Zeus and Danae* (1733), Boucher *Danae receiving the golden shower* (1740), Klimt *Danae* (1907–8). See Reid 1993: i, 319–23.

37 For *kētos* ships see Boardman 1987: 81 and 1997: 734–5.

6 PERSEUS AFTER ANTIQUITY

1 Selections from all the works discussed in this section are conveniently gathered in Garber and Vickers 2003.

2 For reviews of Gorgon theories in the nineteenth and twentieth centuries, see Howe 1952: 7–32, 1954: 209–12, Croon 1955: 12, and Wilk 2000: 93–5, and especially Hughes and Fernandez Bernades 1981: 58–69. The octopus theory: Elworthy 1903, followed by Lettvin 1977 and Wilk 2000: 100–4, who add squids and cuttlefish into the mix. The storm-cloud theory:

Roscher 1879, a well-made case, followed by Furtwängler 1886–90. As to the moon theory (most recently Suhr 1965), Clement of Alexandria had observed that Orphics referred to the moon as a *gorgonion*, because of the face in it (*Stromata* 5.8.49.4). Readers may be amused by the indiscriminate series of anthropological comparanda for the Gorgon collected by Kaiser Wilhelm II 1936 (yes: *that* Kaiser Wilhelm II).

3 Freud 1940. His disciples: e.g. Ferenczi 1926: 360 (originally 1923), Coriat 1941, Elwin 1943, cf. Glenn 1976. Anthropologists: e.g. Obeyesekere 1981. Historians: e.g. Hertz 1983. Feminists: e.g. Cixous 1975 (on which cf. Eilberg-Schwartz 1995: 6–8), Kofman 1983: 84–5, Warner 1985: 108–14, Joplin 1991, Wilk 2000: 217–24. Classicists: Feldman 1965, Slater 1968: 17–18, 319–36, Vernant 1991: 112–16, Csapo 2005: 97–103. Csapo also finds Oedipal behaviour in Perseus' killing of the 'father-figures' supposedly constituted by Polydectes and Phineus (though not, oddly, in his killing of his grandfather Acrisius).

4 Sartre 1943, with H.E. Barnes in Sartre 1956. Art theory: Marin 1977, Clair 1989, Owens 1984. Clair's work is extended to music theory by Bernardini 1993. Film theory: Stephen Heath 1978, de Lauretis 1984. Classical archaeology: Frontisi-Ducroux 1993, 1995, Mack 2002. The last is an interesting (if long-winded) application of Sartre's approach to the ancient iconography of Medusa. It is not clear whether the author is aware of his ultimate debt to Sartre.

5 Georgeakis and Pineau 1894: 84, Hartland 1894–6: iii, 100.

6 The relevant part of the *Codex Romanus Angelicus* is reproduced at Aufhauser 1911: 52–69, with 74–6 for the problem of Lasia, and 202–6 for the relevant part of the *Golden Legend*. The last is translated in Ryan 1993. For St George's derivation from Perseus see Hartland 1894–6: iii, 38–47, Fontenrose 1959: 515–20.

7 In short compass it is not possible even to list the texts and artefacts. See the most helpful (but inevitably incomplete) chronologically organised catalogues of Reid 1993: i, 319–23, ii, 870–83 (*s.vv.* 'Danae' and 'Perseus'). For the star-pictures of the medieval codices see Langlotz 1951, 1960, Phinney 1971: 461, Schauenburg 1960: 129–30, Phillips 1968: 16–23 and plates 16–20, *Götter* 1990: 148–51, Roccos 1994a: 348 and, with care, Wilk 2000: 107–28, who also discusses star-maps in the Graeco-Arabic tradition. Cellini's Perseus: Braunfels 1948.

8 For the Perseus Series see above all Löcher 1973 and Anderson and Cassin 1998. Note also Kestner 1984, Bruckmuller-Genlot 1985, Wildman and Christian 1998: 221–33. With *Danae* or *The Brazen Tower* cf. Morris 1968: 172–3.

9 The generated snakes are misintepreted as shorn snake-locks at Anderson and Cassin 1998: 28.

10 Andromeda as the focus of Burne-Jones' interest: Löcher 1973: 105–6.

11 Phallic imagery: Kestner 1984: 113 (with 96, 116 for androgyny), Bruckmuller-Genlot 1985: 61–2, Munich 1989: 123–5 (the last destructively unsympathetic).

12 Anderson and Cassin 1998: 6; cf. Bruckmuller-Genlot 1985: 61–2, Wildman and Christian 1998: 222.

13 Cf. Munich 1989: 127–9.

CONCLUSION: THE PERSONALITY OF PERSEUS

1 For the 'colourlessness' of monogamous Perseus, see Schauenburg 1960: 16, Dillon 1990: 3, 156–7.

FURTHER READING

There are fewer scholarly books in English devoted to Perseus than one might imagine. Edwin Hartland's three-volume *The Legend of Perseus* (1894–6), a classic in its own day and still in print, remains an excellent read and is well referenced by the standards of its age. However, it devotes relatively little space to the Perseus-cycle in its ancient context and is concerned rather with the assembly of a massive phalanx of international folktale parallels, a resource for which it retains its value. Since Hartland, the only scholarly book on Perseus in English has been Woodward's short *Perseus: a study in Greek art and legend* (1937). This offers a gentle and readable introduction to Perseus' iconography, and includes a small selection of the literary sources in translation. Hulst's *Perseus and the Gorgon* (1946) is a 'pyramidiot' text and may be ignored. Fuller and more detailed treatments of the myth are to be found in two Ph.D. theses, Howe's 'An Interpretation of the Perseus-Gorgon myth' (Columbia, 1952) and Dillon's 'The Greek Hero Perseus: Myths of Maturation' (Oxford, 1990). The former is available through UMI and is reflected in the author's subsequent articles; the latter, alas, remains relatively inaccessible, though richly deserving of publication. Focusing on the Gorgon rather than Perseus himself is Wilk's *Medusa: solving the mystery of the Gorgon* (2000), which combines intriguing insight with amateurish speculation.

For most the best recent English-language starting-points on Perseus may, therefore, be Jameson's article 'Perseus, the Hero of Mykenai' (1990), the pages on the early development of his myth in

Gantz's *Early Greek Myth* (1993: 300–11) and the substantial iconographic article on 'Perseus' in *Lexicon Iconographicum Mythologiae Classicae* (Roccos 1994a). This lexicon, a superb but unimaginably expensive publication, may also be consulted also for its articles on 'Danae' (Maffre 1986, in French) and 'Andromeda I' (Schauenburg 1981, in German). Extensive *LIMC* entries are addressed also to the ubiquitous presence of Gorgon imagery in ancient art, principally 'Gorgo, Gorgones' (Krauskopf and Dahlinger 1988, in German), and more limited ones to the minor characters in Perseus' saga.

Indeed much of the good work on Perseus is in German. Schauenburg 1960 should be singled out. See also Robert 1920: 222–45, Hampe 1935–6, Brommer 1955, and Langlotz 1960. Note too the relevant articles in the standard German encyclopedias, *ML* and *RE*, for 'Perseus' (respectively, Kuhnert 1897–1909, Caterall 1937), 'Danae' (Stoll 1884–6, Escher 1901), and 'Andromeda' (Roscher 1884–90, Wernicke 1894). The exceptionally good entry on 'Perseus' in the French *DA* still deserves attention (Glotz 1877–1919b).

The general bibliography and the notes appended to the chapters indicate further reading on matters of detail.

BIBLIOGRAPHY

Aarne, A., and Thompson, S. 1928. *The Types of the Folktale*. Helsinki.

Aélion, R. 1984. 'Les mythes de Bellerophon et Persée: Essai d'analyse selon un schéma inspiré de V. Propp.' *Lalies: Actes de sessions de linguistique et de littérature* 4, 195–214.

Alexiades, M.L. 1982. Οἱ Ἑλληνικὲς Παραλλαγὲς γιὰ τὸν Δρακοντοκτόνο Ἥρωα (Aarne-Thompson 300, 301A καὶ 301B). Παραμυθολογικὴ Μελέτη. Ph.D. diss., Ioannina.

Anderson, A., and Cassin, M. 1998. *The Perseus Series by Sir Edward Coley Burne-Jones*. Southampton.

Ashliman, D.L. 1987. *A Guide to Folktales in the English Language. Based on the Aarne-Thompson Classification System*. New York.

Aufhauser, J.B. 1911. *Das Drachenwunder des heiligen Georg in der griechischen und lateinischen Überlieferung*. Byzantisches Archiv 5. Leipzig (Teubner).

Austin, C., and Olson, S.D. (eds.) 2004. *Aristophanes: Thesmophoriazusae*. Oxford.

Baldi, A. 1961. 'Perseus e Phersu' *Aevum* 35, 131–5.

Balty, J.-C. 1997. 'Kassiepeia' in *LIMC* viii.1, 666–70.

Barnett, R.D. 1960. 'Some Contacts between Greek and Oriental Religions' in *Eléments orientaux dans la religion grecque ancienne (Colloque de Strasbourg 22–24 Mai 1958)*. Strasbourg. 143–53.

Bauchhenss-Thüriedl, C. 1971. *Der Mythos von Telephos in der antiken Bildkunst*. Würzburg.

—— 1986. 'Auge' in *LIMC* iii.1, 45–51.

Belson, J.D. 1980. 'The Medusa Rondanini' *American Journal of Archaeology* 84, 373–8.

—— 1981. The Gorgoneion in Greek architecture. Ph.D. diss. Bryn Mawr. Available through UMI.

Benoit, F. 1969. 'Gorgone et "tête coupée" du rite au mythe' *Archivo Español de Arqueología* 42, 81–93.

Bernardini, P. 1993. 'Il mito di Medusa come metafora della creazione artistica: Osservazioni in margine a un recente volume di Jean Clair' *Quaderni urbinati di cultura classica* 44, 125–30.

Berve, H. 1967. *Die Tyrannis bei den Griechen*. 2 vols., Munich.

Besig, H. 1937. *Gorgo und Gorgoneion in der archaischen griechischen Kunst*. Berlin.

Billault, A. 1981. 'Le mythe de Persée et les Éthiopiques d' Héliodore. Légendes, représentations et fiction littéraire' *Revue des études grecques* 94, 63–75.

Binder, G. 1964. *Die Aussetzung des Königskinders Kyros und Romulus*. Meisenheim am Glan.

Blinkenberg, C. 1924. 'Gorgone et lionne' *Revue archéologique* 19, 267–77.

Boardman, J. 1968. *Archaic Greek Gems: Schools and Artists in the Sixth and Early Fifth Centuries BC*. Evanston.

—— 1987. 'Very Like a Whale: Classical Sea Monsters' in Farkas, A.E. *et al.* (eds.) *Monsters and Demons in the Ancient and Medieval Worlds*. Mainz. 73–84.

—— 1997. 'Ketos' in *LIMC* viii.1, 731–6, viii.2, 496–501.

Bode, G.H. 1834. *Scriptores Rerum Mythicarum Latini*. Cellis.

Bolte, J., and Polívka, G. 1913–32. *Anmerkungen zu den Kinder- und Hausmärchen der Brüder Grimm*. 5 vols., Leipzig.

Braunfels, W. 1948. *Benvenuto Cellini: Perseus und Medusa*. Berlin.

Brelich, A. 1955–7. 'Les monosandales' *La nouvelle Clio* 7–9, 469–84.

Bremmer, J.N., and Horsfall, N. 1987. *Roman Myth and Mythography*. London.

Breysig, A. (ed.) 1867. *Germanici Caesaris Aratea*. Berlin.

Brommer, F. 1955. *Die Königstochter und das Ungeheuer*. Marburger Winckelmann-Programm.

Bruckmuller-Genlot, D. 1985. 'Saint Georges et Persée dans la peinture Victorienne' *RANAM (Recherches anglaises et américaines)* 18, 33–65.

Brunel, J. 1934. 'Jason μονοκρήπις' *Revue archéologique* 4, 34–43.

Büchner, C. (ed.) 1982. *Fragmenta Poetarum Latinorum Epicorum et Lyricorum praeter Ennium et Lucilium*. 2nd edn. Leipzig.

Burck, E. 1976. 'Die Befreiung der Andromeda bei Ovid und der Hesione bei Valerius Flaccus' *Wiener Studien* 10, 221–38.

Burkert, W. 1979. *Structure and History in Greek Mythology and Ritual.* Berkeley.

—— 1983. *Homo Necans.* Berkeley. Trans. of *Homo Necans.* Berlin, 1972.

—— 1985. *Greek Religion.* Translation of *Griechische Religion der arcahischen und klassichen Epoche.* Stuttgart, 1977.

—— 1987. 'Oriental and Greek Mythology: The Meeting of Parallels' in Bremmer, J.N. (ed.) *Interpretations of Greek Mythology.* London. 10–40.

—— 1992. *The Orientalizing Revolution: Near-Eastern Influence on Greek Culture in the Early Archaic Age.* Cambridge, MA. Translation of *Die orientalisierende Epoche in der griechischen Religion und Literatur.* Heidelberg, 1984.

Caillois, R. 1964. *The Mask of Medusa.* New York.

Campbell, D.A. (ed.) 1982–93, *Greek Lyric.* Loeb Classical Library. 5 vols., Cambridge, MA.

Carpenter, T.H. 1991. *Art and Myth in Ancient Greece.* London.

Caterall, J.L. 1937. 'Perseus' in *RE* xix.1, 978–92.

Cavallius, G.O.H., and Stephens, G. 1848. *Schwedische Volkssagen und Märchen.* Vienna.

Chantraine, P. 1968–80. *Dictionnaire étymologique de la langue grecque: Histoire des mots.* 2 vols., Paris.

Chase, G.H. 1902. 'The Shield Devices of the Greeks in Art and Literature' *Harvard Studies in Classical Philology* 13, 61–127.

Cixous, H. 1975. 'Le rire de la Méduse' *L'Arc* 1975, 39–54. Revised and translated as 'The laugh of the Medusa' *Signs* 1 (1976), 875–93.

Clair, J. 1989. *Méduse: Contribution à une anthropologie des arts du visuel.* Paris.

Coleman, K.M. 1983. 'Manilius' Monster' *Hermes* 111, 226–32.

Collard, C., Cropp, M.J., and Gibert, J. 2004. *Euripides: Selected Fragmentary Plays.* ii. Oxford.

Collard, C., Cropp, M.J., and Lee, K.H. 1995. *Selected Fragmentary Plays.* i. Warminster.

Cook, A.B. 1914–40. *Zeus: A Study in Ancient Religion.* 3 vols., Cambridge.

Cook, R.M. 1937. 'The Date of the Hesiodic Shield' *Classical Quarterly* 31, 204–14.

Coriat, I.H. 1941. 'A Note on the Medusa Symbolism' *American Imago* 2, 281–5.

Croon, J.H. 1955. 'The Mask of the Underworld Demon: Some Remarks on the Perseus-Gorgon Story' *Journal of Hellenic Studies* 75, 9–16.

Csapo, E. 2005. *Theories of Mythology.* Oxford.

Daremberg, C., and Saglio, E. (eds.) 1877–1919. *Dictionnaire des antiquités grecques et romaines* (*DA*). 5 vols., Paris.

Davies, M. 1986. 'Prolegomena and Paralegomena to a New Edition (with Commentary) of the Fragments of Early Greek Epic' *Nachrichten der Akademie der Wissenschaften in Göttingen* 2, 91–111.

Deacy, S. (Forthcoming.) *A Traitor to her Sex? Athena the Trickster*. Oxford.

De Griño, B., *et al.* 1986. 'Atlas' in *LIMC* iii.1, 2–16.

De Lauretis, T. 1984. *Alice Doesn't: Feminism, Semiotics, Cinema*. Bloomington.

Delcourt, M. 1938. *Stérilités mystérieuses et naissances maléfiques dans l'antiquité classique*. Liège.

Deonna, W. 1935 'Monokrépides' *Revue de l'histoire des religions* 89, 50–72.

Detienne, M. 1979. *Dionysus Slain*. Baltimore. Translation of *Dionysos mis à mort*. Paris, 1977.

Dillon, J.E.M. 1990. The Greek Hero Perseus: Myths of Maturation. Oxford D.Phil. diss.

Dindorf, L. (ed.) 1831. *Ioannis Malalae Chronographia*. Bonn.

Downey, G. 1961. *A History of Antioch in Syria: From Seleucus to the Arab Conquest*. Princeton.

Drexler, W. 1886–90. 'Hesione' in *ML* i.2, 2591–4.

Drexler, W., and Rapp, A. 1886–90. 'Graiai' in *ML* i.2, 1729–38.

Dugas, C. 1956. 'Observations sur la légende de Persée' *Revue des études grecques* 69, 1–15.

Edmunds, L. 1984. 'Thucydides on Monosandalism (3.22.2)' in Dow, S., hon., *Studies Presented to Stirling Dow on his Eightieth Birthday*. Greek, Roman and Byzantine monographs no. 10. Durham, NC. 71–5.

Eilberg-Schwartz, H., 1995. 'Introduction' in Eilberg-Schwartz, H., and Doniger, W. (eds.) *Off with her Head! The Denial of Women's Identity in Myth, Religion and Culture*. Berkeley. 1–13.

Elliott, K.O., and Elder, J.P. 1947. 'A Critical Edition of the Vatican Mythographers' *Transactions of the American Philological Association* 78, 189–207.

Elwin, V. 1943. 'The Vagina Dentata Legend' *British Journal of Medical Psychology* 19, 439–53.

Elworthy, F.T. 1903. 'A Solution of the Gorgon Myth' *Folklore* 14, 212–42.

Escher, J. 1901. 'Danae (2)' in *RE* 4, 2084–7.

Faraone, C.A. 1991. *Talismans and Trojan Horses: Guardian Statues in Ancient Greek Myth and Ritual*. New York.

Farnell, L. 1921. *Greek Hero Cults and Ideas of Immortality*. Oxford.

Feldman, T.P. [= T.P. Howe] 1965. 'Gorgo and the Origin of Fear' *Arion* 4, 484–94.

Ferenczi, S. 1926. 'On the Symbolism of the Head of Medusa' in his *Further Contributions to the Theory and Techniques of Psycho-analysis*. London. 360. Originally drafted 1923.

Floren, J. 1977. *Studien zur Typologie des Gorgoneion*. Münster.

Fontenrose, J. 1959. *Python: A Study of the Delphic Myth and its Origins*. Berkeley.

Förster, R. (ed.) 1903–27. *Libanii Opera*. 12 vols., Leipzig.

Fowler, R.L. 2000. *Early Greek Mythography* i. Oxford.

Frazer, Sir James G. 1898. *Pausanias' Description of Greece*. 6 vols., London.

—— 1921. *Apollodorus*. 2 vols., Loeb Classical Library. Cambridge, MA.

Freud, S. 1940. 'Medusa's Head' *International Journal of Psychoanalysis* 25, 105–6. Reprinted in *The Standard Edition of the Complete Psychological Works of Sigmund Freud*. London, 1953–74. xviii, 273–4. Originally drafted in 1922.

Frisk, H. 1960–72. *Griechisches etymologisches Wörterbuch*. 3 vols., Heidelberg.

Frontisi-Ducroux, 1989. 'In the Mirror of the Mask' in Bérard, C., *et al. A City of Images*. Princeton. 151–65.

—— 1993. 'La Gorgone, paradigme de création d'images' *Les cahiers du College Iconique: Communications et débats I*. Paris. 71–86. A partial English translation: 'The Gorgon, Paradigm of Image-Creation' in Garber, M., and Vickers, N.J. (eds.) *The Medusa Reader*. New York, 2003. 262–6.

—— 1995. *Du masque au visage: Aspects de l'identité en Grèce ancienne*. Paris. 65–80.

Frothingham, A.L. 1911. 'Medusa, Apollo and the Great Mother' *American Journal of Archaeology* 15, 349–77.

Furtwängler, A. 1886–90. 'Die Gorgonen in der Kunst' in *ML* i.2, 1701–27.

Gantz, T. 1980. 'The Aischylean Tetralogy: Attested and Conjectured Groups' *American Journal of Philology* 101, 133–64.

—— 1993. *Early Greek Myth: A Guide to the Literary and Artistic Sources*. Baltimore. 2 vols. Continuous pagination.

Garber, M., and Vickers, N.J. (eds.) 2003. *The Medusa Reader*. London.

Gaster, T.H. 1952. 'The Egyptian "Story of Astarte" and the Ugaritic Poem of Baal' *Bibliotheca Orientalis* 9, 82–5.

Georgeakis, G., and Pineau, L., 1894. *Le folklore de Lesbos*. Paris.

Gigli, D. 1981. 'Il Perseo nonniano: osservazioni per uno studio dell' ironia nelle Dioniache' *Prometheus* 7, 177–88.

Glenn, J. 1976. 'Psychoanalytic Writings on Classical Mythology and Religion: 1909–1960' *Classical World* 70, 225–48.

Glotz, G. 1877–1919a. 'Gorgones' in *DA* ii, 1615–29.

—— 1877–1919b. 'Perseus' in *DA* iv, 398–406.

—— 1904. *L'ordalie dans la Grèce primitive: Étude de droit et de la mythologie*. Paris.

—— 1906. *Études sur l'antiquité grecque*. Paris.

Goldman, B. 1961. 'The Asiatic Ancestry of the Greek Gorgon' *Berytus* 14, 1–22 and plates i–ix.

Goold, G.P. 1959. 'Perseus and Andromeda: A Myth from the Skies' *Proceedings of the African Classical Association* 2, 10–15.

Götter, Heroen, Herrscher in Lykien. 1990. Exhibition Catalogue. Vienna.

Gow, A.S.F., and Scholfield, A.F. 1953. *Nicander*. Cambridge.

Grainger, J.D. *The Cities of Seleukid Syria*. Oxford.

Halliday, W.R. 1933. *Indo-European Folk-Tales and Greek Legend*. Cambridge.

Halm-Tisserant, M. 1986. 'Le gorgoneion, emblème d'Athena: introduction du motif sur le bouclier et l'égide' *Revue archéologique*, 245–78.

Hammond, N.G.L., and Walbank, F.W. 1988. *History of Macedon* iii. Oxford.

Hampe, R. 1935–6. 'Korfugiebel und frühe Perseusbilder' *Mitteilungen des deutschen archäologischen Insituts: Athenische Abteilung* 60–1, 269–99 and plates 93–100.

Handley, E.W., and Rea, J. 1967. *The Telephus of Euripides*. London.

Hansen, W.F. 2002. *Ariadne's Thread: A Guide to International Folktales Found in Classical Literature*. Ithaca.

—— 2004. *Classical Mythology*. New York.

Hardie, P.R. 2002. *Ovid's Poetics of Illusion*. Cambridge.

Harris, J.R. 1916. *Picus who is also Zeus*. Cambridge.

Harrison, J. 1903. *Prolegomena to the Study of Greek Religion*. 2nd edn. Cambridge.

Harryhausen, R., and Dalton, T. 2003. *Ray Harryhausen: An Animated Life*. London.

Hartland, E.S. 1894–6. *The Legend of Perseus: A Study of Tradition in Story, Custom and Belief*. 3 vols., London.

Head, B.V. 1911. *Historia Numorum*. Oxford.

Heath, S. 1978. 'Difference' *Screen* 19, 51–111.

Heres, H., and Strauss, M. 1994. 'Telephos' in *LIMC* vii.1, 856–70.

Hermann, K.F. 1853. *Die Hadeskappe*. Göttingen.

Hertz, N. 1983. 'Medusa's Head: Male Hysteria under Political Pressure' *Representations* 4, 27–54.

Hetzner, U. 1963. *Andromeda und Tarpeia*. Meisenheim am Glan.

Heubeck, A., and Hoekstra, A. 1989. *A Commentary on Homer's* Odyssey. ii. *Books* ix–xvi. Oxford.

Hopkins, C. 1934. 'Assyrian Elements in the Perseus-Gorgon Story' *American Journal of Archaeology* 38, 341–58.

—— 1961. 'The Sunny Side of the Gorgon' *Berytus* 14, 25–35 and plates x–xvi.

Howe, T.P. [= T.P. Feldman] 1952. An Interpretation of the Perseus-Gorgon Myth in Greek Literature and Monuments through the Classical Period. Ph.D. Thesis, Columbia University. Available through UMI.

—— 1953. 'Illustrations to Aeschylus' Tetralogy on the Perseus Theme' *American Journal of Archaeology* 57, 269–75.

—— 1954. 'The Origin and Function of the Gorgon-Head' *American Journal of Archaeology* 58, 209–21.

Hughes, S.L., and Fernandez Bernades, J.A. 1981. 'Las Gorgonas: Guardianas de lo sagrado' *Argos* 5, 53–73.

Hulst, C.S. 1946. *Perseus and the Gorgon*. La Salle, IL.

Iconomopoulos [no initial given] 1889. 'Les jeux gymniques de Panopolis' *Revue des études grecques* 2, 164–8.

Imhoof-Blumer, F. and Gardner, P. 1888. *A Numismatic Commentary on Pausanias*. London.

Jacoby, F. 1923. *Die Fragmente der griechischen Historiker*. Multiple volumes and parts. Leiden.

Jameson, M.H. 1990. 'Perseus, the Hero of Mykenai' in *Celebrations of Death and Divinities in the Bronze Age Argolid*. Stockholm. 213–23.

Janko, R. 1994. *The Iliad: A Commentary*. iv. *Books 13–16*. Cambridge.

Joplin, P.K. 1991. 'The Voice of the Shuttle in Ours' in Higgins, L.A., and Silver, B.R. (eds.) *Rape and Representation*. New York. 35–64.

Kaiser Wilhelm II. 1936. *Studien zur Gorgo*. Berlin.

Kanellopoulou, C. 1988. 'Graiai' in *LIMC* iv.1, 362–4.

Kantor, H. 1962. 'A Bronze Plaque from Tell Tainat' *Journal of Near-Eastern Studies* 21, 93–117.

Karagiorga, T.G. 1970. *Γοργείη κεφαλή* Athens.

Kassel, R., and Austin, C. (eds.) 1983–. *Poetae Comici Graeci* (*K–A*). Berlin.

Kern, O. (ed.) 1922. *Orphicorum Fragmenta*. Berlin.

Kestner, J. 1984. 'Edward Burne-Jones and the Nineteenth-Century Fear of Women' *Biography* 7, 95–122.

Klimek-Winter, R. 1993. *Andromedatragöden*. Stuttgart.

Kofman, S. 1983. *L'énigme de la femme: La femme dans les textes de Freud*. Paris. Translated as *The Enigma of Woman: Woman in Freud's Writings*. Ithaca, 1985.

Krauskopf, I., and Dahlinger, S.-C. 1988. 'Gorgo, Gorgones' in *LIMC* iv.1, 285–330.

Kuhnert, E. 1897–1909. 'Perseus' in *ML* iii.2, 1986–2060.

Lambrinoudakis, B.K. 1971. Μηροτράφης. Μελέτη περὶ τῆς γονιμοποιοῦ τρώσεως ἢ δεσμεύσεως τοῦ ποδὸς ἐν τῇ ἀρχαίᾳ ἑλληνικῇ μυθολογίᾳ. Athens.

Lane Fox, R. 1973. *Alexander the Great*. London.

Langlotz, E. 1951. *Perseus*. Heidelberg.

—— 1960. *Der triumphierende Perseus*. Cologne.

Larson, J. 2001. *Greek Nymphs: Myth, Cult, Lore*. New York.

Lesky, A. 1967. 'Herakles und das Ketos' *AnzWien* 104, 1–6.

Lexicon Iconographicum Mythologiae Classicae (LIMC). 1981–99. 8 vols., Zurich.

Linforth, I.M. 1941. *The Arts of Orpheus*. Berkeley.

Liungman, W. 1961. *Die schwedischen Volksmärchen: Herkunft und Geschichte*. Berlin.

Llewellyn-Jones, L. 2007. 'Gods of the Silver Screen: Cinematic Representations of Myth and Divinity' in Ogden 2007, 423–38.

Lloyd, A.B. 1969. 'Perseus and Chemmis (Herodotus II.91)' *Journal of Hellenic Studies* 89, 79–86.

Lloyd-Jones, H.J. 1957. 'Appendix' in Smyth, H.W., trans. *Aeschylus* ii. Loeb Classical Library. 2nd edn. Cambridge, MA. 523–603.

Löcher, K. 1973. *Der Perseus-Zyklus von Edward Burne-Jones: Mit einem Résumé in englischer Sprache*. Stuttgart.

Lochin, C. 1994a. 'Pegasos' in *LIMC* vii.1, 214–30.

—— 1994b. 'Stheneboia' in *LIMC* vii.1, 810–11.

Lüthi, M. 1976. *Once upon a Time: On the Nature of Fairy-Tales*. Bloomington, IA.

Mack, R. 2002. 'Facing down Medusa: An Aetiology of the Gaze' *Art History* 25, 571–604.

Maffre, J.-J. 1981. 'Akrisios' in *LIMC* i, 449–52.

—— 1986. 'Danae' in *LIMC* iii, 325–30.

Marin, L. 1977. *Détruire la peinture*. Paris. Translated as *To Destroy Painting*. Chicago, 1995.

Marinatos, S. 1927/8. Γοργόνες καὶ Γοργόνεια' Ἐφημερὶς ᾽Αρχαιολογική, 7–41.

Martin, J. 1963. 'La mort d'Ariane et de Dionysos' *Revue des études grecques* 76, xx.

—— (ed.) 1974. *Scholia in Aratum vetera*. Stuttgart.

Mayor, A. 2000. *The First Fossil Hunters: Palaeontology in Greek and Roman Times*. Princeton.

Meiggs, R., and Lewis, D.M. 1989. *A Selection of Greek Historical Inscriptions to the End of the Fifth Century BC*. 2nd edn. Oxford.

Merkelbach, R., and West, M.L. 1967. *Fragmenta Hesiodea*. Oxford.

Meyer, P.M., *et al.* (eds.) 1911–98. *Griechische Papyrusurkunden der Hamburger Staats- und Universitätsbibliothek*. 4 vols., Leipzig (and elsewhere).

Milne, M. 1956. Review of Brommer 1955. *American Journal of Archaeology* 60, 300–2.

Morenz, S. 1962. 'Die orientalische Herkunft der Perseus-Andromeda-Sage' *Forschungen und Forschritte* 36, 307–9. Reprinted, Morenz 1975: 441–7.

—— 1975. *Religion und Geschichte des alten Ägypten*. Cologne.

Morris, W. 1868. *The Earthly Paradise*. London. Reprinted, Morris 1910–15: iii, 171–238.

—— 1910–15. *Collected Works*. 24 vols.

Müller, C. (ed.) 1878–85. *Fragmenta Historicorum Graecorum (FHG)*. 5 vols., Paris.

Müller, E. 1907. 'Die Andromeda des Euripides' *Philologus* 66, 48–66.

Munich, A.A. 1989. *Andromeda's Chains: Gender and Interpretation in Victorian Literature and Art*. New York.

Mylonas, G.E. 1957. *Ancient Mycenae: The Capital City of Agamemnon*. London.

Napier, A.D. 1986. *Masks, Transformation and Paradox*. Berkeley.

—— 1992. *Foreign Bodies: Performance, Art, and Symbolic Anthropology*. Berkeley.

Nilsson, M.P. 1932. *The Mycenaean Origin of Greek Mythology*. Berkeley.

Oakley, J.H. 1982. 'Danae and Perseus on Seriphos' *American Journal of Archaeology* 86, 111–15.

—— 1988. 'Perseus, the Graiai and Aeschylus' *Phorkides' American Journal of Archaeology* 92, 383–91.

—— 1997. 'Hesione' in *LIMC* viii.1, 623–9.

Obeyesekere, G. 1981. *Medusa's Hair: An Essay on Personal Religious Symbols and Religious Experience*. Chicago.

Ogden, D. 1997. *The Crooked Kings of Ancient Greece*. London.

—— 1999. *Polygamy, Prostitutes and Death: The Hellenistic Dynasties*. London.

—— (ed.) 2007. *A Companion to Greek Religion*. Oxford.

Owens, C. 1984. 'The Medusa Effect or the Specular Ruse' *Art in America* 72.1, 97–105.

Page, D.L. (ed.) 1962. *Poetae Melici Graeci*. Oxford.

Paoletti, O. 1988. 'Gorgones Romanae' in *LIMC* iv.1, 345–62.

Papadopoulos, J.K. and Ruscillo, D. 2002. 'A *Ketos* in Early Athens: An

Archaeology of Whales and Sea Monsters in the Greek World' *American Journal of Archaeology* 106, 187–227.

Pearson, A.C. 1917. *The Fragments of Sophocles*. 3 vols., Cambridge.

Petersen, E. 1915. *Die attische Tragödie als Bild- und Bühnenkunst*. Bonn.

Phillips, K.M., Jr. 1968. 'Perseus and Andromeda' *American Journal of Archaeology* 72, 1–23, with plates 1–20.

Phinney, E., Jr. 1971. 'Perseus' Battle with the Gorgons' *Transactions of the American Philological Association* 102, 445–63.

Potter, J. (ed.) 1715. *Clementis Alexandrini Opera*. Oxford.

Powell, J.U. (ed.) 1925. *Collectanea Alexandrina*. Oxford.

Radermacher, L. 1917. 'Danae und der goldene Regen' *Archiv für Religionswissenschaft* 25, 216–18.

Rathmann, W. 1938. 'Perseus (4) Sternbild' in *RE* 19.1, 992–6.

Rau, P. 1967. *Paratragodia: Untersuchung einer komischen Form des Aristophanes*. Munich.

—— 1975. 'Dar Tragödienspiel in den Thesmoporiazusen' in Newiger, H.-J. (ed.) *Aristophanes und die alte Komödie*. Darmstadt. 339–56.

Reid, J.D. 1993. *The Oxford Guide to Classical Mythology in the Arts, 1300–1990s*. 2 vols., New York.

Ribbeck, O. 1897. *Tragicorum Romanorum Fragmenta*. 3rd edn. Leipzig.

Riccioni, G. 1960. 'Origini e sviluppo del gorgoneion e del mito della Gorgone: Medusa nell' arte greca' *Rivista dell'Istituto Nazionale di Archeologia e Storia dell'Arte* 9, 127–206.

Robert, C. 1920. *Die griechische Heldensage* i. *Landschaftliche Sagen*. 4th edn. Berlin. = Preller, L., and Robert, C., *Die griechische Mythologie*. ii. 1 *Die Heroen*. Berlin.

Robertson, C.M. 1972. 'Monocrepis' *Greek, Roman and Byzantine Studies* 13, 39–48.

Roccos, L.J. 1994a. 'Perseus' in *LIMC* vii.1, 332–48.

—— 1994b, 'Polydektes' in *LIMC* vii.1, 427–8.

Roeger, J. 1924. *Aidos Kynee: Das Märchen von der Unsichtbarkeit in den homerischen Gedichten*. Graz.

Rohde, G. 1941. 'Picus' in *RE* xx.1, 1214–18.

Röhrich, L. 1981. 'Drache, Drachenkampf, Drachentöter' *Enzyklopädie des Märchens: Handwörterbuch zur historischen und vergleichenden Erzählforschung*. 5 vols., Berlin. iii, 787–819.

Roscher, W.H. 1884–90. 'Andromeda' in *ML* i.1, 345–7.

—— 1886–90. 'Gorgones' in *ML* i.2, 1695–1701.

—— 1879. *Die Gorgonen und Verwandtes*. Leipzig.

Ruffell, I. 2000. 'The World Turned Upside Down: Utopia and Utopianism in the Fragments of Old Comedy' in Harvey, D., and Wilkins, J. (eds.) *The Rivals of Aristophanes*. London. 473–506.

Ryan, R.J. 1993. trans. *Jacobus de Voragine: The Golden Legend. Readings on the Saints*. Princeton.

Sartre, J.-P. 1943. *L'être et le néant: Essai d'ontologie phénoménologique*. Paris. Trans. (H. E. Barnes) as *Being and Nothingness: A Phenomenological Essay on Ontology*. New York, 1956.

Schachter, A. 1981–94. *Cults of Boiotia: Bulletin of the Institute of Classical Studies*, Supplement 38. 4 vols., London.

Schauenburg, K. 1960. *Perseus in der Kunst des Altertums*. Bonn.

—— 1967. 'Die Bostoner Andromeda-Pelike und Sophokles' *Antike und Abendland* 13, 1–7.

—— 1981. 'Andromeda I' in *LIMC* i.1, 774–90.

—— 1992. 'Kepheus I' in *LIMC* vi.1, 6–10.

Schefold, K., and Jung, F. 1988. *Die Urkönige, Perseus, Bellerophon, Herakles und Theseus in der klassischen und hellenistischen Kunst*. Munich.

—— 1992. *Gods and Heroes in Late Archaic Greek Art* and *Myth and Legend in Early Greek Art*. Cambridge. Trans. of *Götter- und Heldensagen der Griechen in der spätarchaischen Kunst*. Munich, 1978.

Scherf, W. 1982. *Lexikon der Zaubermärchen*. Stuttgart.

Schmidt, H. 1907. *Jona: Eine Untersuchung zur vergleichenden Religionsgeschichte*. Göttingen.

Schmidt, L. 1958. 'Sichelheld und Drachenzunge' *Fabula* 1, 19–25. Reprinted in Schmidt, L. *Die Volkserzählung: Märchen, Sage, Legende, Schwank*. Berlin, 1963. 41–7.

Seaford, R.A.S. 2006. *Dionysus*. London.

Segal, R. (ed.) 1990. *In Quest of the Hero*. Princeton.

Shepard, K. 1940. *The Fish-Tailed Monster in Greek and Etruscan Art*. New York.

Simon, E. 1982. 'Satyr-Plays on Vases in the Time of Aeschylus' in Robertson, M., hon., Kurtz, D., and Sparkes, B. (eds.) *The Eye of Greece: Studies in the Art of Athens*. Cambridge. 123–48.

—— 1990. 'Hesperides' in *LIMC* v.1, 394–407.

Simpson, J. 1980. *British Dragons*. London.

Sissa, G. 1990. *Greek Virginity*. Cambridge, MA. Trans. of *Le corps virginal: La virginité féminine en Grèce ancienne*. Paris, 1987.

Slater, P.E. 1968. *The Glory of Hera: Greek Mythology and the Greek Family*. Boston.

Smith, C. 1884. 'Four Archaic Vases from Rhodes' *Journal of Hellenic Studies* 5, 220–40 and plates xl–xliii.

Smolenaars, J.J.L. 1994. *Statius* Thebaid *VII. A Commentary*. Leiden.

Snell, B., and Maehler, H. (eds.) 1987–9. *Pindari Carmina cum Fragmentis*. 2 vols., Leipzig.

Snell, B., Kannicht, R., and Radt, S., 1971–2004. *Tragicorum Graecorum Fragmenta*. 5 vols., Göttingen.

Sparkes, B. 1968. 'Black Perseus' *Antike Kunst* 11, 3–16.

Stern, K. van K. 1978. 'Heroes and Monsters in Greek Art' *Archaeological News* 7, 1–23.

Stewart, A.F. 1993. *Faces of Power: Alexander's Image and Hellenistic Politics*. Berkeley.

Stoll, H.W. 1884–6. 'Danae' in *ML* 1, 946–9.

Suhr, E.G. 1965. 'An Interpretation of the Medusa' *Folklore* 76, 90–103.

Tod, M.N., and Wace, A.J.B. 1906. *A Catalogue of the Sparta Museum*. Oxford. Republished Rome, 1968.

Ulansey, D. 1989. *The Origins of the Mithraic Mysteries: Cosmology and Salvation in the Ancient World*. New York.

Vermeule, E. 1979. *Aspects of Death in Early Greek Art and Poetry*. Berkeley.

Vernant, J.-P. 1981. 'L'autre de l'homme: La face de *Gorgô*' in Oleander, M. (ed.) *Le racisme: Mythes et sciences*. Brussels. 141–54.

—— 1989. 'Au miroir de Méduse' in Vernant, J.-P. (ed.) *L'individu, la mort l'amour: Soi-même et l'autre en Grèce ancienne*. Paris. 117–29.

—— 1991. *Mortals and Immortals*. Princeton. Incoporates revised and translated versions of Vernant 1981 and 1989.

Vernant, J.-P., and Ducroux, F. 1988. 'Features of the Mask in Ancient Greece' in Vernant, J.-P., and Vidal-Naquet, P., *Myth and Tragedy in Ancient Greece*. New York. 189–206.

Victor, U. 1997. *Lukian von Samosata: Alexandros oder der Lügenprophet*. Leiden.

Von Bubel, F. (ed.) 1991. *Euripides: Andromeda*. Palingenesia 34. Stuttgart.

Von Steuben, H. 1968. *Frühe Sagendarstellung in Korinth und Athen*. Berlin.

Warmington, E.H. 1935–40. *The Remains of Old Latin*. 4 vols., Cambridge, MA.

Warner, M. 1985. *Monuments and Maidens: The Allegory of the Female Form*. New York.

Watkins, C. 1995. *How to Kill a Dragon in Indo-European*. Oxford

Weicker, G. 1912. 'Hesione' in *RE* 8, 1240–2.

Wernicke, K. 1894. 'Andromeda' in *RE* i, 2154–9.

Werre-de Haas, M. 1961. *Aeschylus' Dictyulci: An Attempt at Reconstruction of a Satyric Drama*. Leiden.

West, M.L. 1966. *Hesiod: Theogony*. Oxford.

—— 1981. 'Simonides' Danae Fragment: A Metrical Analysis' *Bulletin of the Institute of Classical Studies* 28, 30–8.

—— 1985. *The Hesiodic Catalogue of Women*. Oxford.

—— 1989–92. *Iambi et elegi Graeci ante Alexandrum cantata*. 2nd edn. 2 vols., Oxford.

—— 1997. *The East Face of Helicon*. Oxford.

—— (ed.) 2003. *Greek Epic Fragments*. Loeb Classical Library. Cambridge, MA.

Wildman, S. and Christian, J. 1998. *Edward Burne-Jones, Victorian Artist-Dreamer*. Alexandria, VA.

Wilk, S.R. 2000. *Medusa: Solving the Mystery of the Gorgon*. New York.

Will, E. 1947. 'La décollation de Méduse' *Revue archéologique* 27 (sixth series) 60–76.

Woodward, J.M. 1937. *Perseus: A Study in Greek Art and Legend*. Cambridge.

Wright, M. 2005. *Euripides' Escape-Tragedies: A Study of Helen, Andromeda and Iphigenia among the Taurians. Oxford*.

Wüst, E. 1937a. 'Perses (2)' in *RE* xix.1, 973–4.

—— 1937b. 'Perses (3)' in *RE* xix.1, 974.

—— 1937c. 'Perses (4)' in *RE* xix.1, 974–5.

Yialouris, N. 1953. 'πτερόεντα πέδιλα' *BCH* 77, 3–17, 293–321.

Zorzetti, N., and Berlioz, J. (eds.) 1995. *Le premier mythographe du Vatican*. Paris.

INDEX